Linking Refugee Aid with Development

Development for Refugees, or Refugees for Development?

Yasuko Shimizu

Kwansei Gakuin University Press

About the author:
Yasuko Shimizu is a senior officer with the Office of the United Nations High Commissioner for Refugees. Her work with UNHCR has included assignments in Geneva, Uganda, Russia, Kosovo, Albania and Afghanistan. She has also served as a senior advisor at Japan International Cooperation Agency. She received her Ph.D. in Policy Studies from Kwansei Gakuin University in 2006.

Linking Refugee Aid with Development :
Development for Refugees, or Refugees for Development?

Copyright © 2008 by Yasuko Shimizu

First edition published 2006 as a Ph.D. Dissertation.
Revised edition published 2008.

All rights reserved.

No part of this book may be reproduced in any form or by any means without permission in writing from the author.

The views and opinions expressed in this book are those of the author and do not represent any official views of any aid agencies, governmental organisations, UNHCR or other UN agencies.

Kwansei Gakuin University Press
1-1-155 Uegahara, Nishinomiya, Hyogo, 662-0891, Japan
ISBN: 978-4-86283-032-6

Table of Contents

Acronyms and Abbreviations   5
Introduction   7

Chapter 1 Multidisciplinary Aspects of Refugee Studies   13
1.1 Research Questions and Methodology   13
1.2 Refugee Studies: From Legal Approach to Multidisciplinary Approach   20
1.3 Gap between Theories and Practices: Reality Counts   33
1.4 Summary   42

Chapter 2 International Protection of Refugees   45
2.1 International System of Refugee Protection   45
2.2 Refugee Assistance and International Communities   59
2.3 Refugees as a Threat?   69
2.4 Summary   80

Chapter 3 Refugee Aid and Development Doctrine   81
3.1 Initial Debates: Refugees for Development (the 1970s and the 1980s)   82
3.2 Recent Debates: Development for Refugees?   95
3.3 Criticism of the Doctrine   109
3.4 Summary   112

Chapter 4 Local Settlement   115
4.1 Local Settlement as Refugee Policy   116
4.2 Developmental Refugee Assistance in Place of Development Aid?   132
4.3 Summary   142

Chapter 5 Developmental Refugee Assistance in Local Settlement 145

5.1 Self-reliance and Integration:
    Developmental Objectives in Refugee Assistance? 146
5.2 Participation: Developmental Approach in Refugee Assistance? 162
5.3 Summary 182

Chapter 6 Case Study–Part I: Uganda's Local Settlement Refugee Programme 185

6.1 Model, Objectives and Methodologies 185
6.2 Uganda: General Background 192
6.3 Uganda: Political and Administrative Aspects of Local Settlement 199
6.4 Uganda: Legal Aspects of Local Settlement 210

Chapter 7 Case Study–Part II: Uganda's Local Settlement Refugee Programme 215

7.1 Participation Process 215
7.2 Integration: The Result of Local Settlement Process 220
7.3 Refugee Self-Reliance: Impact on Refugees 230
7.4 Discussion 242

Conclusion 247

Bibliography 253
Index 287

Acronyms and Abbreviations

4Rs	Repatriation, Reintegration, Rehabilitation, and Reconstruction
DAC	Development Assistance Committee
DAR	Development Assistance for Refugees
DDHS	District Directorate of Health Service (Uganda)
DED	German Development Agency
DLI	Development through Local Integration
ECHO	European Community Humanitarian Department
EU	European Union
EXCOM	Executive Committee (UNHCR)
FAO	Food and Agriculture Organisation
HDI	Human Development Indicator(s)
ICARA	International Conference on Assistance to Refugees in Africa
ICRC	International Committee of the Red Cross
IDPs	Internally Displaced Persons
IOM	International Organisation for Migration
JICA	Japan International Cooperation Agency
MoLG	Ministry of Local Government (Uganda)
NATO	North Atlantic Treaty Organisation
NIEO	New International Economic Order
ODA	Official Development Assistance

OECD	Organisation for Economic Cooperation and Development
OPM	Office of the Prime Minister (Uganda)
PRSP	Poverty Reduction Strategy Paper
QIPs	Quick Impact Projects
SPLA	Sudanese People's Liberation Army (Sudan)
SRS	Self-Reliance Strategy (Uganda)
TDA	Targeting Development Assistance for Refugee Solutions
UNCTAD	United Nations Conference on Trade and Development
UNDG	United Nations Development Group
UNDP	United Nations Development Programmes
UNHCR	United Nations High Commissioner for Refugees
UNICEF	United Nations Children's Funds
UNPROFOR	United Nations Protection Force
UNRWA	United Nations Relief and Works Agency for Palestine Refugees
WB	World Bank
WFP	World Food Programme
WNBF	West Nile Bank Front (Uganda)
the 1951 UN Convention (on Refugees)	Convention Relating to the Status of Refugees

Introduction

This study attempts to meet challenges from two parties who may stand in opposition to each other. One is a challenge from academia that traditionally requires meticulous literature reviews and searches for sophisticated theories. Academics demand that the "study" should be theoretically and academically sound. The other challenge comes from my colleagues who deal with every day complex problems in the field and who do not accept just any beautiful theory or useless "babble". They need more practical ideas and information that can be useful in improving policies and implementing aid programmes.

I, as an aid practitioner in the first place and also a Ph.D. candidate at the same time, face such demands from these opposing ends. Jacobsen and Landau (2003: 95) call it the "dual imperative." They state:

> ...as work becomes more academically sophisticated, many have the nagging suspicion that it becomes ever more irrelevant to practitioners and policy makers. The fear is that analysis may not address current crises, that the language and concepts used are too arcane or jargonistic, or that the questions asked (and purport to answer) are interesting only to other academics, not to those who work in the field, or to refugees and IDPs [Internally Displaced Persons] and war-affected people who live the situations studied. (p. 96)

Jacobsen and Landau are writing above from a researcher's standpoint. From my perspective, pressure from the dual imperative on me is no less than on researchers. I am primarily an aid practitioner and would be most unhappy if this study became "babble" which is totally useless to aid practitioners. At the same time, this study is also written for academic purposes and there is no question that it should meet academic standards.

The aim of this study is to examine the validity of the Refugee Aid and Development Doctrine and local settlement policy in refugee aid programme. Refugee Aid and Development is, in summary, one of the ideologies in the field of refugee aid which proposes that refugee assistance will become more useful to both refugees and host communities if it is linked with development programmes. Local settlement is a policy (and an aid programme) derived from the doctrine that promotes refugee self-reliance through agriculture-based activities

Like the theme of this study, i.e., the linkage between Refugee Aid and Development, linking the field practice of refugee assistance with academic research, thus far, does not seem to be easily achieved[1]. The study, as an outcome of academic activity by a refugee aid practitioner, is to accept both challenges, attempting to provide a theoretical analysis that should also help to improve the quality of refugee assistance.

Impetus to do the study stems from my own experience in refugee aid. I had worked for development programmes before joining a refugee aid agency in 1994. My first impression at a refugee aid agency some twelve years ago was that the public knew little about refugee assistance compared to development work: what it was aimed at, how it was actually organised and what needed to be

---

[1] Debates here are concerned about more "assistance" or "operational" part of refugee aid but exclude legal aspects such as status determination and interpretation of international instruments on refugee protection. The areas of the latter have a long history of interlocution between law scholars, UN and aid practitioners.

improved. Although general awareness on refugee work has greatly increased in the last ten years, there seems to remain a gap in understanding issues related to refugees and realities of refugee situations.

The same can be said about the theme of this study. Concerning the linkage between Refugee Aid and Development, there has been neither clear understanding about what it meant nor consensus on how it should be implemented among stakeholders and observers. Some people, including local populations, aid workers and evaluators, appear to believe that the idea is to make refugee assistance lead the development of a host community.

Local people who host refugees demand that a refugee agency should also consider taking up large scale infrastructure projects such as building roads or bridges. Refugee aid workers who subscribe to this school of thought seriously attempt to obtain skills and knowledge of such development work. Then, evaluators evaluate refugee projects according to the extent to which they contribute to development. Others may think, and may even feel threatened, that the refugee aid is going to replace development programmes. Colleagues from development organisations, for example, often asked me if our agency, which is a humanitarian refugee organisation, was going to encroach on the arena of their development work.

Therefore, this study is, first of all, to explain and analyse arguments surrounding Refugee Aid and Development. What is the Refugee Aid and Development Doctrine aimed at? Does it improve the quality of refugee assistance? This study first surveys the establishment of the Refugee Aid and Development Doctrine and its principles. What can local settlement refugee policy/programmes do? What are their achievements and limitations? What is "good" linkage of refugee assistance with development programmes? This study aims to answer these questions.

In order to examine these questions, the study takes a multi-disciplinary approach. The overall aid concept is based on one from social work called Person-in-Environment. The hierarchies of doctrine-policy and paradigm-theory are classified based on ones often used in political science. Analysis on debates surrounding Refugee Aid and Development are made, as law scholars often do, through review of international documents including relevant United Nations (UN) resolutions, reports of the United Nations High Commissioner for Refugees (UNHCR) to the UN General Assembly, documents issued by UN agencies, such as UNHCR EXCOM conclusions, UNHCR internal documents, and proceeding of relevant international conferences on Refugee Aid and Development[2].

Analysis of aid policies, approaches and techniques uses methods that policy/programme evaluators apply and that researchers on international aid use in their debates. Regarding the latter, there are more evaluations and research papers found in the arena of international development than humanitarian or refugee work. A case study is based on information obtained from project reports, previous research, documents from the concerned agencies and governments as well as my direct observations and communication with refugees and aid workers in the field.

The above methods of this study attempt to create a dynamic combination of different disciplines as well as a combination of theory and practice. Nevertheless, I am aware that these methods may give an impression of lacking focus or sophistication. Further, while attempting to obtain information from various sources to increase the validity of the study, I acknowledge the fact that my being an aid practitioner remains a bias in interpreting the data. I welcome advice for improvement and remain open to criticisms and alternative views on this subject.

---

[2] UN documents referred to in this study are ones available up to June 2005.

Chapter 1 provides an overview of refugee studies as an academic discipline, highlights a gap between research and practice, and presents the overall concept of the study. Chapter 2 explains the current environment surrounding refugee situations and the international system for refugee protection and assistance. Chapter 3 focuses its discussion on international debates on the Refugee Aid and Development Doctrine, policies and projects. From Chapter 4, the focus of the study moves from the international level to the national and project levels. Chapter 4 gives an overview of local settlement policy and its programmes. Chapter 5 examines key concepts and approaches that local settlement refugee aid programmes often use. These chapters concretise abstract concepts for practice and identify the usefulness and limitations of the "developmental" approach in refugee work. Based on the discussions of the previous chapters, Chapter 6 presents a model that shows the interrelation of factors affecting the local settlement process. Then, this chapter and the final chapter specifically study a case on Uganda's policy and aid programme for Sudanese refugees.

In conducting this study, I have attempted to be respectful and fair to people who dedicate themselves in refugee work: first of all, refugees themselves, host governments and communities, donors and aid workers. If the paper includes any description that may sound critical of refugees, governments, or aid workers, it is not at all intended to accuse any party but to make us acknowledge and respect the reality of refugee situations.

What I learnt from nearly fifteen years of experiences with refugees is that criticism does not produce positive results unless it is accompanied by efforts to understand the other party. We, namely people who deal with refugee affairs, can attain such understanding as long as we are ready to deal with realities that may not always be nice or beautiful. "Cool heads but warm hearts," said Alfred Marshall, a British economist. The words are also useful for humanitarian workers and scholars.

I would ask readers to note that views and opinions written in this paper are purely my own and do not represent any official views of any aid agency, governmental organisation or UN office.

The completion of this study was not possible without the help of many individuals. First, I would like to thank the refugees and my colleagues from government offices and aid agencies who were the inspiration for this study.

I am grateful to many scholars and colleagues who read earlier versions of the manuscript and provided me with insightful comments, especially, Professors Shun-ichi Murata, Koichi Koizumi, Akiko Sonoda and Tetsuo Kubota. Mr. Satoru Kurosawa provided helpful suggestions based on his broad experience with both development and humanitarian agencies.

My special thanks to Mr. Brian Baskerville for assisting me with English. Many other friends helped me edit the earlier versions.

Last but not least, my deepest gratitude goes to Mrs. Sadako Ogata, former UN High Commissioner for Refugees and President of JICA, for her warm encouragement that enabled me to complete this challenging work.

Chapter **1**

Multidisciplinary Aspects of Refugee Studies

This chapter will first give the objectives and methodology of this study, and provide a historical overview of refugee studies, presenting how refugee studies evolved as an academic area of study. This chapter, then, will discuss the reality of refugee work in the field and a gap between academic studies and the reality on the ground.

1.1 Research Questions and Methodology

Section 1.1 will provide an overview of this study, its objectives, research questions, and methodologies.

1.1.1 Background and Purpose of the Study

Every day, on TV news and in newspapers, we see people fleeing from wars. We hear stories about the individuals who became the victims of racial subjugation or political tyranny and had to seek asylum in another country. We also hear about people giving a hand to those who have fled and started life in new communities. The history of forced displacement of people may be just as old as human history itself. At the same time, there have been people all along who want to help the displaced persons.

The awareness of refugee issues among the international community as a whole, however, is rather a modern concept. Formal international response began in 1921 when the League of Nations, in reply to the appeal by the International Committee of the Red Cross (ICRC), appointed Fridtjof Nansen as the High Commissioner to deal with problems related to Russian refugees in Europe. He is known for "Nansen Passports" that allowed refugees, who had lost their national protection, to travel across borders and identify themselves.

Since then, the international system on legal protection and assistance for refugees has evolved in response to the world refugee situations. Today, the world map of refugees has changed considerably from that of the 1920s. Some of the characteristics of today's refugee situations include:
- The number of refugees increased to more than 20 million[3].
- Many (66%) of refugees, stay in developing countries[4].
- Many refugees stay for extended periods in countries of asylum without any foreseeable solution.
- The number of internally displaced persons (IDPs) has increased[5].

This study concerns situations relating to the first three points above. Presently, some 6.2 million refugees have stayed in countries of asylum over 5 years. Of them, the great majority are found in Africa, followed by regions of Central Asia, South West Asia and the Middle East. How to support host countries has therefore become

---

[3] According to UNHCR, as of 1 January 2004, there are over 17 million asylum seekers, refugees and others concern to UNHCR. In addition, Palestine refugees in the Middle East, under the mandate of United Nations Relief and Works Agency for Palestine Refugees (UNRWA), numbered over 4 million in 2002.

[4] The percentage is against the population of concern to UNHCR. This does not include Palestine refugees, but includes IDPs or asylum seekers that are of concern to UNHCR. The refugee statistics in this paper are based on UNHCR publications unless other sources are indicated.

[5] UNHCR extends its assistance to some 4 million IDPs as of January 2004.

an important issue in providing protection and assistance for refugees in economically underdeveloped communities.

In this connection, a school of thought since the 1970s maintains that refugee assistance should be more development oriented and linked with development programmes, so that the quality of assistance improves, and both refugees and local communities benefit from the assistance. The purpose of this study is to examine the validity of this aid doctrine.

1.1.2 Doctrine, Policy, Paradigm and Theory

"Doctrine" may not be a usual term when discussing refugee assistance. "Theory," "paradigm" or "policy" may be more frequently used in the literature on Refugee Aid and Development. It is appropriate at this juncture to closely examine these words.

The information presented in "theories" on Refugee Aid and Development often provides its historical background, rationale, objectives and principles. But this information does not determine the causality between phenomena in refugee situations or explain how refugee assistance affects such a causal direction. Could this be called a theory? In replying to this question, it may be appropriate to refer to Gorman's view which concluded that dialogue on Refugee Aid and Development has produced "a marginal and small body of theory" (1991a/1993: 148). Since then, much debate has taken place on Refugee Aid and Development; however, in terms of its theoretical development, little has changed compared with earlier days.

What constitutes a theory? The following are some of its definitions:

"Theories are general statements that describe and explain the causes or effects of classes of phenomena"(Van Evera, 1997: 7-8).

"A...theory is a reasoned and precise speculation about the answer to a research question... Theories usually imply several more specific descriptive or causal hypotheses" (King, Keohane & Verba,

1994: 19).

"[Theory can be defined] as a closely reasoned set of propositions, derived from and supported by established evidence and intended to serve as an explanation for a group of phenomenon" (Gorman, 1991a/1993: 148).

The definition of the term "doctrine" cannot be found in books on research methodology. The Concise Oxford English Dictionary defines "doctrine" as "a belief or set of beliefs held and taught by a church, a political party, etc." The Concise Oxford Thesaurus gives "creed," "credo," "dogma," "belief," "teaching," "ideology;" "tenet," "maxim," "canon," "principle," and "precept" as its synonyms.

According to the same references, "paradigm" is defined as "a world view underlying the theories and methodology of a scientific subject" and its synonyms include "standard", "prototype" and "archetype." Similarly, "policy" is "a course or principle of action adopted or proposed by an organization or individual." Its synonyms include "plans," "strategy" and "approach."

Reviewing these, it may be appropriate to say that paradigm is a way of viewing phenomena, the causality of which a theory should explain. Unlike a theory, a doctrine is not something that one can prove or disprove but it is a belief based on which one may act or policies may be established.

The statement earlier in this section, that is, "refugee assistance should be more development oriented and linked with development programmes so that the quality of assistance improve and both refugees and local communities benefit from the assistance," is not meant to be a hypothesis or theory to be proven but more like a "principle," "concept" or "precept". Thus, this statement can be regarded as a doctrine, rather than a theory.

Policies normally involve value judgement. For example, policies of some states may be based on a religion, while other states may have a policy not to reflect any religious practice in public services. Policies of private companies are normally based on the pursuit of profits while ones of public sectors may place more value on equality. A doctrine is, in other words, an underlying belief that supports the value of a particular policy. One may then pose a question as to whether this study is attempting to evaluate a belief that is subjective by nature.

The study does not judge whether the Refugee Aid and Development Doctrine, per se, is right or not, but examines whether it appropriately supports the ideas of refugee protection. Then, the study analyses if policies and aid programmes that are based on the doctrine can achieve, or have achieved, their initial objectives, and if not, the study goes on to explore how to improve the implementation of the policy. Based on a certain doctrine, policy makers propose policies on specific issues such as refugee affairs. Under the policy,

Doctrine: If refugee assistance is more linked with development programmes, it will benefit both refugees and host communities.

Countries of Asylum

Local Settlement Policy: Refugees should be integrated into the host communities and become more self-reliant.

Programme/project:
Local Settlement

Project activities:
Agriculture, infrastructure development, etc.

Countries of Origin

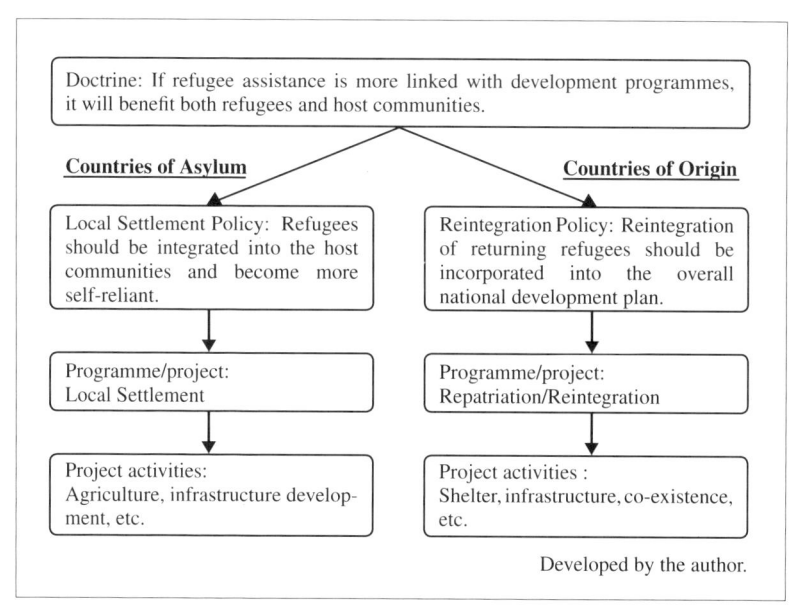

Reintegration Policy: Reintegration of returning refugees should be incorporated into the overall national development plan.

Programme/project:
Repatriation/Reintegration

Project activities:
Shelter, infrastructure, co-existence, etc.

Developed by the author.

Figure 1-1: Refugee Aid and Development: Doctrine, Policy and Project

more concrete projects will be planned and implemented. Figure 1-1 shows the relation of the Refugee Aid and Development Doctrine, its policy and programmes/projects.

1.1.3 Research Questions and Methodologies

This study examines situations on the left side of the above figure, that is, the cases of refugees in asylum countries, especially those of developing countries. On the one hand, the Refugee Aid and Development Doctrine has been attaining growing support among aid workers. UNHCR has supported projects that include infrastructure rehabilitation in hosting communities and productive activities for refugees. On the other hand, attempts to realise the doctrine are often considered a failure because of a lack of collaboration, failed projects or limited donor support.

Such discourse on the Refugee Aid and Development poses several questions. To begin with, is it appropriate for refugee assistance to be based on the doctrine? In answering this question, two points must be considered. One is whether the doctrine is in accordance with humanitarian principles of refugee protection. The other is whether the doctrine is actually useful to make assistance beneficial to refugees and hosting communities.

The second question derives from the evaluation of past attempts: Did the attempts really fail? There seems to be a consensus among researchers that the past attempts linking refugee aid with development have, in fact, failed. "Developmental" refugee projects such as small scale infrastructure construction were not sustainable in many situations, for example. However, it is important to point out that past debates overlooked the essential point of refugee assistance, that is, the impact of the assistance on refugees. It is important to note that the failure of the past discourse was due to its overemphasis on development of host communities with insufficient attention given to refugees' development.

This leads to the third question that concerns the operationalisation of the doctrine: How to realise the doctrine in refugee situations? The doctrine and its policies do not bring any outcome until they are transformed into concrete actions in the actual assistance programmes or public services. Even if the doctrine and its policies are proven to contain good values, nothing is brought to anyone unless projects are appropriately formulated, supported and carried out.

This study examines the issues of operationalisation at two levels: the international level and country/project level. If the past attempts were proven to be failures or ineffective, there must have been operational reasons for preventing smooth implementation of the doctrine. In terms of issues at the international level, previous studies mostly identified standoffs between donors and refugee-hosting African countries and the absence of development organisations in refugee-hosting areas.

These conclusions of previous studies, however, were not sufficient. If there was inadequate support from donors and development actors in the past, it is crucial to examine the factors that could prevent collaborated international efforts and find a wayforward. In this connection, this study will examine the roles of key international actors. The study will go on to the project/country level analysis. The study will identify interrelations among local actors of refugee assistance, and factors that affect refugees and local communities.

In examining these questions, this study applies a multidisciplinary approach with varied methodologies. International documents such as statements of international conventions, UN resolutions, documents issued by UNHCR, and its publications will be used as the primary tool to examine how the international system adopted the Refugee Aid and Development Doctrine. In addition, both academic papers and project reports are integral parts of the data that the study utilises to discuss issues relating to the operationalisation.

Furthermore, many data are brought from my own field experiences. These include reports obtained from field offices of UNHCR and aid agencies, direct communications with refugees, local people, local authorities, government officials and aid workers, as well as observations on different occasions such as food distribution, seminars and workshops, project monitoring and social and cultural events in refugee settlements.

1.2 Refugee Studies: From Legal Approach to Multidisciplinary Approach

This section will first explain how refugee studies evolved in recent years from a legal approach to a multidisciplinary approach. Then, this section will demonstrate how actual refugee work in the field is related to different academic disciplines. This section will then argue that issues related to refugees should be considered in relation to situations in which they are placed. In this connection, the section will finally present a refugee-in-environment model as a basis to view refugee situations.

1.2.1 Academia

Studies on refugee assistance are rather a new field of academic research. Traditional areas of refugee studies were mainly on status determination, international refugee protection, humanitarian principles, and national policies concerning refugees. It is law scholars and political scientists who have produced most of the analytical studies on refugee issues. It was not until the 1980s when studies on refugee issues drew broader attentions from various disciplines (Koizumi, 2001: 195). For example, the Refugee Studies Centre of Oxford University[6], a leading institution in its field, was founded in

1982. Later, Centre for Refugees at York University was founded in 1988.

While approaches from the law provide rich studies on the interpretation on the UN Convention on Refugees and analysis on national laws and policies, they may have little influence on what assistance should be provided for refugees and how to deliver it. Take food assistance for example: The legal approach may find the value of food assistance as a right to life from a human rights viewpoint. It thus provides rationale for food distribution in refugee assistance.

Legal discussion on food assistance, human rights, and protection of refugees, however, does not necessarily explain how to organise food assistance effectively. Should the distribution be on an individual basis, or a household basis, or a group/community basis? Should the distribution be done by aid workers or together with refugees? To discuss the delivery of assistance, it is necessary to add other elements.

In this connection, researchers started paying attention to the effectiveness and/or the approaches of refugee assistance in countries of asylum, especially those in developing countries. Harrell-Bond's *Imposing Aid* (1986) is a classic analysis of the (in-) effectiveness of refugee assistance. Her research, applying anthropological methods, examined the (in-)effectiveness of refugee assistance to Ugandan refugees in Southern Sudan, arguing that the ineffectiveness was largely due to the negligence of aid workers to refugees' real needs and their potentials (Harrell-Bond, 1986). She was one of the first few advocates who urged aid workers to bring out refugees' internal strengths through assistance programmes.

Studies on refugee assistance brought multidisciplinary research-

[6] Oxford publishes several journals on refugees including *Journal of Refugee Studies, International Journal of Refugee Laws, Refugee Survey Quarterly* and others on forced migration.

ers to refugee studies. Take, for example, *African Refugees: Development Aid and Repatriation* (Adelman & Sorenson, 1994). This book is a compilation of research papers published in the 1980s. Out of 16 contributors, three researchers are from political science or international relations, two each from environment studies, geography and "refugee studies," one each from the fields of law, economics, mental health, rural development, and hydrogeology. In addition, two are not strictly academics but policy makers/aid practitioners. Mixed contributors from a broad range of academic disciplines and practitioners are similarly found in another book, *Refugee Aid and Development: Theory and Practice* (Gorman, 1993).

What characterises these studies on refugee assistance is the blurring of lines between various disciplines. They are linked through the central theme: refugees. This is the very characteristic that makes "refugee studies" an independent academic field. It can be explained better in comparison with mental health studies on refugees.

The studies on refugee mental health were mainly undertaken in the countries of resettlement. From the 1980s to the early 1990s, a number of researchers in North America did research on the adaptation of resettled refugees to their new countries. Berry (1989, 1990) and Westermeyer (1983, 1988), among others, made important contributions to the studies on mental health of Asian refugees who resettled in North American countries. The participation of mental health professionals in studies on refugees contributed to broadening academic (and public) attention to issues related to refugees.

Nevertheless, studies of Berry and Westermeyer remain within the field of mental health studies (rather than refugee studies in a strict sense). Adaptation, stress, and coping are traditional areas of mental health studies. Research on the same themes can be carried out with any population, not only refugees. In the studies of Berry,

Westermeyer and others in this group, refugees are the test subjects and refugee adaptation is the theme of their mental health study. Naturally, their analyses are clearly based on either psychological or psychiatric perspectives[7].

On the other hand, readers of research papers on refugee assistance may not easily surmise the academic background of each researcher until they look at his/her personal history. For example, Harrell-Bond's research (1986) was described above as having applied an anthropological approach. This could be determined from attached questionnaires on refugees' demographics, cultural and religious information, and a statement by one of her assistants that she was an anthropologist. It must be her insight on people and culture, as an anthropologist, that led her to the main argument that aid workers should not impose (certain types of) aid on refugees but the latter should be encouraged to participate in aid programmes. However, it is important to note that anthropological discussion is not at all the focus of her study. The theme of her study is about refugee assistance and an appropriate approach, but not about any traditional anthropological theme such as, say, relations between Ugandan ethnic Kakwa refugees and Sudanese ethnic Kakwas in a host community.

Similar examples can be found in other studies on refugee assistance. When examining international debates on refugee policy, researchers often combine different methods including reviews on UN resolutions and documents on international conferences, inter-

---

[7] Another example of this kind was Marx, social anthropologist, who applied a sociological method to "understand the sociology of refugees" (Marx, 1990 : 189). Similar to Berry and Westermeyer, Marx attempted to establish a concept of a specific academic discipline, i.e., sociology, in understanding refugees. In this sense, his work (as well as Berry's and Westermeyer's) still remains within sociological studies and this presents a clear contrast with studies of Harrell-Bonds and others that were discussed in subsequent paragraphs.

views with aid workers and/or policy makers, and analysis on international relations or politics. For example, Macrae's research in 1999 followed more or less this formula, but she also studied specifically a health sector (Macrae, 1997, 1999, 2001)[8].

When conducting research at the project level, the approaches of the researchers may not be identified as any traditional academic disciplines such as economics, anthropology or the law. Mostly, their approach is a combination of interviews with refugees and aid workers/policy makers, qualitative analyses of data obtained from the interviews, and reviews of policy documents and project reports. Their research may not be centred on a single academic discipline and not necessarily one that the researchers originally studied. In other words, the researchers on refugee policy and assistance formed an independent area of study as "refugee studies," rather than framing it within one of the traditional academic disciplines. Among the researchers in this category are Kibreab (1987, 1989), Armstrong (1988, 1991), Callamard (1991, 1994) and Jacobsen (2001).

However, the other side of such a multidisciplinary approach is the lack of clarity in methods of analysis. In addition, another recent trend in studies on international aid further blurs the definition of "study." In recent studies on international aid or policy studies in general, there has been a cross-over between practitioners' evaluation on policies/projects and academic researches on them. The former is normally based on what is called a logical framework that identifies causality between input (e.g., quantity of relief items or number of aid workers) and output (e.g., number of clinics built) and analysis of impact (e.g., overall health condition of beneficiaries of

---

[8] Macrae (and her colleagues) recently studies donor behaviours and aid coordination (Macrae, 1999, 2001, 2002; Macrae & Leader, 2000; Macrae et al., 2002). This is another new subject of refugee studies from the late 1990s. As opposed to earlier analysis on the UN and states, studies in this category include donors and NGOs in their research.

the service)[9]. The use of such an analytical tool, however, is no longer limited to practitioners. With academics beginning to include more practical components recently, such tools that practitioners use are often introduced in university textbooks now.

The present situation, on the one hand, contributes to bridging academia and field work but, on the other hand, again, poses certain levels of ambiguity in defining what constitutes an academic study. This study on refugee policy is not free from such risk while attempting to apply a multi-disciplinary approach and link practice with academics. The application of social work's Person-in-Environment model through this study is an attempt to reduce the risk. The Person-in-Environment model, showing the interrelation between a client (person) and systems (environment), can offer a useful tool to understand refugee situations.

Social work, which is a helping profession and a field of study that deals with social issues, policy and skills to approach identified problems, shares common concepts with those of refugee situations. The difference is that social work often deals with domestic issues, while refugee issues are international by definition, even though refugees are supported and regulated by the system in a country of asylum. Therefore, discussions of policies on refugee issues and assistance programmes must consider two layers (i.e., international and national) of the refugees' environment.

The model in this study has evolved as the discussion has developed. But one core idea in this study is that refugee issues should be examined in the context of interrelations of refugees (persons) with the actors of assistance, stakeholders and resources available (environment). Therefore, to understand "Refugees in

---

[9] The definitions of input, output, impact and other terminology used in project evaluation may differ among agencies and organisations. This study does not discuss the details of logical framework.

Environment," it is logical that this study should attempt to apply a multi-disciplinary approach; legal perspectives to examine the rationale for the doctrine, social work perspectives to view the refugee situation, international development studies for analysis on aid approaches, and anthropological as well as psychological viewpoints to understand problems that refugees face.

Before going on to consider refugee assistance in the field, the rest of this sub-section will give a brief overview of Japanese academic research on refugee studies. In Japan, major studies on refugee issues remain within the fields of law and political science.

Homma is one of the pioneers on refugee law. He supervised the compilation of the Japanese translation of international human right laws including the Convention Relating to the Status of Refugees, which was published by UNHCR Tokyo in 1987. His book, titled *Nanmin Mondai Towa Nanika* [What is the Refugee Problem?] (1990), was the first Japanese textbook on the international system on refugee protection and a history of refugee issues in Japan. He also published important work on human rights and refugees (2000, 2001).

Obi, another law scholar and an experienced practitioner in the area of refugee protection, studies from perspectives of international refugee law. Her recent research is on UNHCR's approaches to refugee issues in Asia (Obi, 2004). She has served, among other functions, as senior legal and protection officer both at UNHCR Headquarters and field offices in Asia and Africa.

Other Japanese researches mainly surround international and domestic refugee laws or policies by political scientists and law scholars (for example, Aragaki, 2001; Matsusumi, 1999; Shimada, 2002; Takeda, 1991).

Refugee studies from other disciplines, however, are very much limited in Japan. Koizumi, specialised in forced migration, is one of few Japanese researchers who promotes interdisciplinary studies on refugee issues (1998, 2001, 2005). His book, titled *Nanmin Towa Nanika* [What Are Refugees?] (1998), is a good introduction to refugee studies. Compared with Homma's book (1990) that is more centred on the history of international system of refugee protection, Koizumi takes up a broader range of issues arisen from human displacement such as the impact of massive refugee influx on developing host countries. Koizumi is also a pioneer of Japanese research on Refugee Aid and Development (Koizumi, 1994, 1995).

Lastly, Ogata (1995, 2002, 2005) is the most internationally distinguished Japanese figure in relation to refugee work. She is a scholar of international politics and served as UN High Commissioner for Refugees from 1990 to 2000. She has been a strenuous advocate of Refugee Aid and Development. However, her perspectives on refugee issues may exceed beyond the bounds of the refugee studies that this section explains. While her position as High Commissioner for Refugees inevitably focused her actions on displaced populations, she did not limit her arguments to refugee assistance. Her overall message has been on the need for a coordinated world approach, or the integration of humanitarian assistance, development and security, which could better respond to, or even prevent, complex political emergencies.

1.2.3 Field

In the field, refugee aid workers are not usually conscious of the link between their work and academic disciplines. Nevertheless, their attempts for improving the quality of assistance are indeed based on knowledge that various disciplines provide. Table 1-1 shows some examples of multidisciplinary aspects in the practice of refugee work.

The concept of international protection provides rationale for giving refugees assistance. Refugees are people whose safety is not protected in their own country and who thus flee from home. They may be travelling without any legal documents such as passport or other documents for identification. Therefore, the first concern is to ensure international protection that grants the status, stay and rights of refugees in countries of asylum. Once the legal status of refugees is secured, their next challenge is daily survival. Without a place to stay or food to eat, their basic right to life cannot be ensured. Achieving the concept of protection, therefore, goes beyond legal protection, requiring concrete assistance such as delivery of food, shelter and health services.

In organising assistance, an anthropological approach has been found to be essential. When conducting needs assessments, aid workers should ask not only what refugees need but also about their traditional values, culture and human dynamics in the family and community. For example, who are the decision makers in the refugee community and families? What is considered to be most important or hated in the community? What is the traditional thinking on gender?

Table 1-1: Multidisciplinary Aspects of Refugee Work

Area of Refugee Work	Related Academic Discipline
Refugee protection	The Law
Concept of assistance	Social Work, International Development
Needs assessment	Cultural Anthropology
Project implementation	Cultural Anthropology, Sociology
Self-reliance of refugees	Economics, Psychology, International Development
Aid coordination	International Relations, Political Science

Developed by the author.

If aid workers organise a project for female-headed households, for example, the expressed needs may be for additional food and household items. But delivering the items may not be the best way to deal with the problem. Aid workers should first learn if there is any traditional self-help system to support vulnerable persons in the refugee community. If there is, does it still function? If not, why not? The indigenous system may be destroyed because, for example, able-bodied men died during the war, or children were separated from their family during flight. Or, on another level, many adults may have lost their dignity after losing their profession and property.

When a refugee community has experienced such a tremendous loss, the project should be organised as to replace what they lost and enhance their own strengths. Instead of simply delivering the relief items, it may be necessary to create an opportunity to encourage women to express their feeling to each other and to find a way by themselves to provide mutual moral support.

The other important influence on refugee assistance comes from international development aid. Participation (of refugees and local stakeholders), environment, gender and sustainability are among the contemporary issues brought from international aid to refugee assistance. Environment and gender, for example, became policy priorities in refugee work in the 1990s just as they had been in international development. The UNHCR Executive Committee adopted in1990 the framework of the policy on refugee women[10], and, in 1994, on the environment[11]. Nevertheless, if I may add from my own experiences, awareness among refugee aid workers on these two subjects, especially gender, was rather low until the mid-1990s.

---

[10] *UNHCR Policy on Refugee Women*, EXCOM, 41st session, A/AC.96/839, 20 August 1990.
[11] *Report of the Fourty-Fifth Session of the Executive Committee of the High Commissioner's Programme (Geneva, 3-7 October 1994)*, A/AC/96/839, 11 October 1994, para.25.

Some did not believe that "women's" issues are something that refugee assistance should handle.

With influence from donor states, notions on environment and women gradually have come into the mainstream of refugee protection and assistance since the late 1990s. Compared with international development that had already taken up Women in Development and Gender and Development concepts in the 1980s, reactions from the refugee aid workers were rather slow. Similarly, Refugee Aid and Development debates were heavily influenced by international development. This will be discussed in subsequent chapters.

Contributions from social work theories may not have gained fair recognition in refugee work. However, as explained earlier, the overall concept of refugee assistance very much coincides with social work's Person-in-Environment aid model. As previously noted, it is a useful model to understand a situation where individual refugees are placed, and to analyse relations among refugees, their community, host community, government and other actors.

The strength perspective, another social work's aid approach, also shares much in common with refugee assistance. The strength approach urges social workers to pay more attention to the strength of the clients rather than their deficit or weakness (Saleebey, 1997). This perspective fits the value that Refugee Aid and Development Doctrine inherits: Refugees are not passive poor recipients of services but individuals with potentials to grow and contribute to their community.

In this sub-section, I have explained the link between refugee work and several academic disciplines such as the law, international relations, psychology, anthropology, social work and international development. As such, dealing with refugee issues necessarily interfaces with various academic fields.

1.2.3 Refugee-in-Environment

Figure 1-2 shows the Refugee-in-Environment conceptualisation, based on Person-in-Environment from the field of social work. Unlike the original model, individual refugees are placed in a three-tiered environment.

First, refugees live in relation to their own refugee community. In asylum, refugees retain links with other individuals, friends, relatives or leaders of the refugee community. In most of the refugee situations, however, their community may be weakened after their flight. Their formal social services and education systems are destroyed. Informal self-help systems and families are also impaired. Some of the family members may have been lost during their flight and people may not be able to afford to take care of others while they are preoccupied with their own survival.

The second environment that surrounds refugees is the host community. Individual refugees and the refugee community interact with systems of a host country and host community. The host country/community has its own political and legal systems, public services, economic system, religious norms and cultural practices. These systems of the host country/community and refugees mutually affect each other.

Outside the refugee and host communities is the international aid community, the third environment. One way of assisting refugees is that the international community can directly assist the first circle, i.e., the refugee community, to enhance individual strength of refugees and capacity of their community. If traditional mechanisms of community-based self-help are destroyed, this assistance should help refugees rebuild it.

The other way for the international community to assist refugees is for the assistance to develop the capacity of host countries. In terms of the legal system, for example, UNHCR approaches states for the latter to accede to the UN Convention relating to the Status of

32   *Linking Refugee Aid with Development*

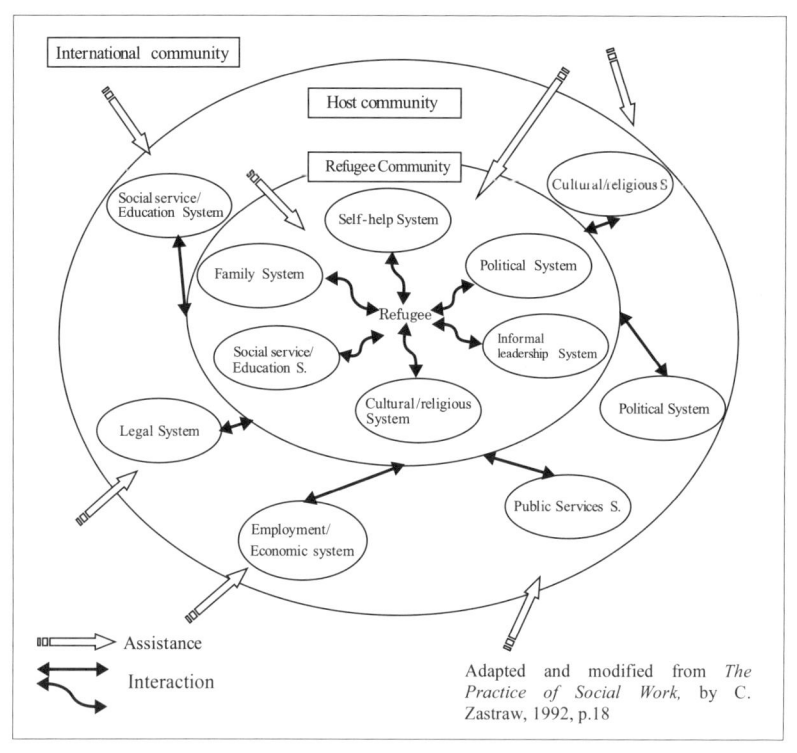

Figure 1-2: Refugee-in-Environment

Refugees (1951) and its Protocol (1967). They also work with state governments to establish or improve national refugee laws in their respective countries.

Likewise, international assistance to strengthen national/local systems of public services, social services, education and the economy can improve the national system to respond to the needs of refugees.

The model (see Figure 1-2) suggests that a refugee or refugee community is not an isolated entity but rather their lives are interrelated with all the elements of the surrounding host environment and are further linked with the international community. Therefore, issues relating to refugees and assistance for them should be analysed with consideration to the dynamic relations among refugees, host communities, governments and international communities. For this reason, this study analyses issues at both the international level and national/project level.

1.3 Gap between Theories and Practices: Reality Counts

The previous section illustrated the multidisciplinary aspects of refugee studies and emphasised a need to look at a refugee situation in relation to the surrounding environments. This section will examine the realities of refugee protection/assistance in the field.

1.3.1 Gaps
After receiving researchers in the field, aid workers often feel that the resulting research papers do not provide any practical solutions to problems in the field. Such feelings may be based on two shortcomings of research on refugees: (1) Research papers do not include any new findings for practitioners; and (2) Research papers may be right in theory but their assumptions do not match the realities of the field.

Studies with the first shortcoming above may still have value to academics who do not have direct knowledge of a refugee situation even if they have no merit for practitioners. As for the second type of criticism, research papers that are long on theory and short on reality, may also be found in any other social science field. However, it may be reasonable to say that the gap between the theory and the practice is more salient in refugee work than in some other field of study.

To examine the gap between theory and practice, the remainder of this chapter will be largely devoted to explaning three realities that are often missed in theories and research on refugees.

1.3.2 Activist's Approach, Academic Approach and Protection Approach

The first reality is related to differences in approaches among three professions, namely protection workers, human rights activists, and academic researchers. The following will serve to illustrate this point.

> **Hypothetical Case 1:** A number of refugees fled from ethnic cleansing in their country and reached the border to a neighbouring Country A. The government of Country A closed the border, rejecting the admission of refugees. Refugees including elderly persons, women and children are stuck at the border. There are no accommodation or sanitation facilities. All the refugees have been weakened by a long journey and some became ill. A week later, two children die and many others are suffering from infectious diseases. An immigration officer working on the spot feels sorry for them but is not allowed by his head office to grant entry to the refugees. At night, he secretly lets an elderly couple into the country because they were trying to reach their relatives.

In such a situation, human rights agencies and activists may report to the world on the inhumane response of Country A to the human crisis. For example, they may make a press release similar to the following: "The Government of Country A has been coldly rejecting refugees who are the victims of ethnic cleansing in their country. No international aid has reached the refugees so far and they have been suffering from hunger for more than a week. The elderly persons are weakened and many children are suffering from potentially fatal infections. Yesterday, two infants died of hunger. We demand that Country A accept the refugees and allow aid workers to provide assistance for them."

This can be called an advocator's approach. It makes the public aware of what is happening, raises their interest in human rights, and increases international political pressure for Country A to take a more humane response to the refugees on their border. Eventually, the government of Country A may change their position and allow refugees to enter their territory.

Law scholars analyse the situation based on human rights laws. They may develop their argument quoting the Convention Relating to the Status of Refugees and other international human rights laws. They assert right to asylum and refer to the *non-refoulement* principle as an international customary law[12]. They may also study situations to which exceptions of the *non-refoulement* principle can be applied. Such analysis by jurists helps to establish an international standard concerning states' responsibility to protect the rights of refugees. The type of academic approach may eventually press states to take more appropriate measures in face of a human crisis.

Refugee aid workers for protection, however, may not take either of the two approaches above. The most pressing issue in this case is to have Country A permit the admission of the refugees as soon as possible. Advocacies, public protest, or academic analysis may not yield an immediate positive result. Rather, field actions to respond to pressing needs for refugee protection should take into

---

[12] *Convention Relating to the Status of Refugees*, 1951. Article 33(1). Non-refoulement is the principle that prohibits states from forcibly returning refugees to a territory where they face danger. The non-refoulement principle is considered to be at customary status (Kim, Serita & Fujita, 1998; Lauterpacht & Hethlehem, 2001; Obi, 2004). In addition, UNHCR Executive Committee concluded in 1977 that the non-refoulement principle should be applied at the border as well as within the territory of a state. This will be discussed in Chapter 2.

consideration political, cultural, religious and even psychological aspects that may affect the government policy on refugees. Aid workers, then, have to choose the most result-oriented options under all the given circumstances.

No doubt, a government has considerable concerns over the impact of refugee influx on its nation, including ones relating to national security, the economy and politics. In such situations, publicly accusing the government of their "inhumane" acts is least likely to succeed because the government may not want to be seen by its people giving into external pressure. Similarly, it might only sound offensive if an aid worker refers to international conventions when negotiating with a local immigration officer in the field.

Instead, refugee protection in the field may require a more discreet approach. Aid workers have to find the most pragmatic ways of communicating with the government officials to persuade them to take more appropriate measures. Field workers may simply have to continue patient and persistent dialogue with government officials. Or, they might approach religious leaders and others who can positively influence the government.

Another way is more covert. For example, in Case 1, an immigration officer at the border sympathises with refugees and considers admitting them secretly into the country. In such a case, a field worker might choose to cautiously approach such an officer individually and seek out any possible arrangement to "exceptionally" allow the most vulnerable refugees to enter the country.

Illustrating possible actions taken by three different professions in this hypothetical case highlights that in the actual practice of refugee protection, academic analysis, which certainly sets the standards of refugee protection in the long run, cannot always solve a particular problem on the spot. Although academic knowledge is important in order for the field practitioners to set principles in their work, academic knowledge itself does not materialise the protection concept, nor provide an action plan in field practice.

The difference in approach among academics, human rights agencies and those of protection may arise from their respective relations with the host government. The scholars take a situation as a case for study and government's reactions for analysis. Human rights agencies may see the government as an opponent. The government, however unreasonable it might be, is the primary actor in refugee protection, and, thus, a partner with UNHCR and any other aid agencies/practitioners working for refugees.

A pragmatic approach may be chosen in actual practice of refugee protection. Actions that can create hostility should be avoided as much as possible. Even though the two parties stand in opposition to each other, refugee aid practitioners first have to understand the sensitivity of the situation in which a host government is placed. They, therefore, have to tactfully choose the most suitable approach to any unresolved problem[13]. As such, in analysing refugee protection and assistance, it is important to avoid theory-centrism and look also at the realities in the field.

1.3.3 Donor-Recipient vs. Partnership

The second point that academic research often miss is the difference between international assistance given to states for the purpose of refugee protection and other general international aid such as development assistance. Observers of refugee assistance frequently base their argument on an improper assumption concerning the relationship between governments of countries that host refugees and aid agencies giving assistance to the governments of

---

[13] This type of approach, i.e., taking a discreet and diplomatic approach to states or individuals that may be infringing on the principle of refugee protection, also faces criticism when some actions by the protection agency is seen as inappropriate concession to the government or individuals concerned. Chapter 2 will discuss such debates.

host countries for refugee protection.

Observers often regard the above as a donor-recipient relationship as is the case in bilateral development aid. Development "donors" bring in funds, human resources and equipment for the sake of the development of a "recipient" country. On the surface, the case of refugee protection may appear to be very similar: Vehicles are loaned to government offices, clinics are rehabilitated, and schools are built. Contrary to outward appearance, however, the relationship between the state and UNHCR is and should be quite different from that of a donor-recipient.

Above all, the host government is the one that provides safe asylum for refugees. Their primary role is, so to speak, a "giver" or a "helper" instead of an "aid recipient." However, if a state does not have adequate financial or human resources to assume their responsibility to protect refugees, international "aid" comes in to support the government's efforts[14]. Such assistance normally takes the form of funds, equipment and infrastructure rehabilitation. In this context, the relationship between a state and UNHCR should be called a "partnership," which is more equal than the relationship between a donor and a recipient country.

Such a partnership may pose a challenge if a state has little political will for refugee protection, if its financial accountability is low, or if it is in a condition of so-called "quasi-statehood[15]." Another example of refugee protection can be illustrated by a dictatorship with corrupted leaders.

---

[14] Statute of the Office of the United Nations High Commissioner for Refugees states in its Chapter 1.1 that "The United Nations High Commissioner for refugees, ... shall assume the function of providing international protection, ... *by assisting Governments* [italics added]..."

[15] The concept of quasi-statehood was presented by Jackson (1990) as an independent state in a juridical sense while they "...do not disclose the empirical con-

> **Hypothetical Case 2**: Government of Country B does not have any desire to protect refugees. Rather, it regards them as a threat to its national security. An illegal tax is reportedly often imposed on refugees. The government office responsible for refugees receives funds, vehicles, computers and other equipment from external aid agencies to register refugees and manage a refugee camp. However, unaccountable expenditure of funds and inappropriate use of vehicles are often observed.

Should the assistance for the government of Country B be stopped because of their human rights violations and alleged misuse of funds? Answering this question is not simple. The purpose of assistance for the government of Country B is to protect the rights of refugees, or improve their protection capacity. Punishing the government may not automatically improve the situation. The same principle as in the earlier Case 1 can be applied to this case.

Hard-stick-approach may fail. While maintaining respect for and diplomacy with the primary provider of refugee protection, that is the state, aid workers should still find ways to have the state correct their malfeasance. The challenge is, however, that with such a difficult partner, a diplomatic approach may not succeed in making effective changes. The important point of this example is that without understanding the dual roles of a state, that is, a helper in refugee protection and a recipient of international aid, analysis of refugee assistance may miss a pertinent point.

---

stituents by which *real* states are ordinarily recognized (Jackson, 1990: 519-549)" and they are often deficient in protecting human rights or provide socio-economic welfare (Jackson, 1990: 31). Though there are criticism of his analysis (Macrae, 1999; Aalberts, 2004), the term is still useful, as Macrae stated (1999: 12) in the sense that he distinguished the "empirical" from juridical components of the sovereignty.

1.3.4 Complexity in Refugee Community

The third reality that researchers often miss concerns complexity of refugee communities. Refugees are often characterised as people who have problems and need help. Indeed, refugees are people who had to flee their country because of fear of prosecution or armed conflicts and then have to stay in a country other than their own. By definition, refugees need assistance in order to protect their rights.

To look at refugees solely as those who need assistance, however, is to miss part of the bigger picture. A refugee community is more diversified than a single group of mere victims. Diversity is not only about language or ethnicity, but also about personal interests and political orientation. Some refugees simply seek survival, some educational or professional opportunities, and others political achievements. The presence of the last group is often ignored in public debates or the literature in spite of the fact that it actually poses serious problems in refugee situations.

Politically active individuals exist in many refugee situations and they may become a threat to the protection of other refugees. Chapter 2 will illustrate the case of Rwandan refugees in the Democratic Republic of Congo (former Zaire): Rwandan Hutu soldiers performed military exercise in refugee camps, practically holding the majority of refugees hostage. It was an extreme case that everyone took up for debate. Behind such an obviously problematic situation, there are many other cases that are not so evident.

Take an example of refugees and food. In many refugee camps, food rations are given per household and the amount is set according to the number of family members. There are often some refugee families who try to gain additional rations by registering inflated family size or obtaining an extra ration card. As long as they do such manipulation purely for survival, most people may feel sympathetic to them, even if their action is illegal.

A problem arises when a group of politically motivated individuals organise their community to obtain extra food rations, collect them and send them to soldiers who are back in their country, fighting against their central government. No one could consider this to be a survival strategy and all would agree that such abuse of the assistance should be stopped.

The difficulty lies in the fact that realities are somewhere in the continuum from the obviously politicised case to the innocent coping strategy. Most of the time, situations and answers are not clearcut. In some situations, refugees do cheat the system but not for political objectives. In other situations, the line between the innocent and the politicised is blurred. Suppose a soldier fighting in his country visits his family in a refugee camp and takes some food from them when returning to a battle. Did he carry a gun with him or leave it in his country? Did his mother share her own food ration with him or is his name already registered in the camp even though he spends most of his time fighting back in his country?

Where can one draw the line in the continuum to distinguish the bad from the innocent? Even if one can draw a line "theoretically," how is it possible in a practical sense to "investigate" whether each refugee actually stays within the boundary of innocence? It is important to note in this example that working with refugees in the field means, unlike a scientific experiment in the laboratory, dealing with a highly variable community that a researcher cannot control. It is this uncontrollability that makes the theory-centric debates less convincing.

Moreover, it is necessary to point out that "controlling" refugee situations contradicts the spirit of refugee protection. Controlling a refugee situation requires severe restriction of their basic human rights such as freedom of movement or the right to work. In addition, open and careless debates on refugees' "improper behaviour" may mislead the public into the stigmatising false impression that all the refugees abuse the assistance system. Consequently, not only do academics pay little attention to these realities, but also practitioners are unable to address them sufficiently.

The purpose of narrating rather a long story has been to reiterate the importance of seeing refugees as an ordinary human group that consists of people with diverse interests, problems, strengths and desires. Just as in a community of Japanese, American or Chinese people, a refugee community has vulnerable persons, powerful ones, talented youths, innocent children and a handful of ill-motivated individuals. Taking a refugee community as a single group of poor persons thus distorts the reality[16].

This sub-section illustrated realities that researchers often ignore when considering refugee situations. Some of the realities may not be comfortable to look at or to accept. As a practitioner, personally, I also find it is difficult to point out the shortcomings of asylum countries or some refugees' behaviours. Nevertheless, it is vital to note that to discuss policies and projects means talk of the real world as it is not controlled science laboratories.

1.4 Summary

This chapter first presented the purpose of this study and research questions. The study aims to examine the validity of Refugee Aid and Development as a refugee aid doctrine. Then, an overview was given on the multidisciplinary aspect of refugee work and refugee studies. Refugee-in-Environment, based on social work's Person-in-Environment model, was presented to understand refugee situations and relationships among refugees, other actors

---

[16] Stedman & Tanner's work (2003b), a collection of studies on refugee manipulation and the involvement of asylum governments, is a valuable study on such reality.

and the system of refugee assistance. The chapter concluded with a discussion of the gap between realities in refugee assistance and academic studies, stressing the importance to recognise the reality in analysing refugee situations.

Chapter 2

International Protection of Refugees

Chapter 1 provided an overview of how refugee studies developed as an academic field of study and discussed a linkage between research and practice. The last section of that chapter presented a refugee-in-environment model on which this study is based on. Chapter 2 will discuss why international communities should provide protection and assistance for refugees and urge the need for policies to promote the coexistence of refugees and local communities. The first sections of the chapter will provide basic information on international system on refugee protection. The chapter will then attempt to refute the view that refugees are threats and argue that they are not only burden to host communities but can become useful asset.

2.1 International System of Refugee Protection

Before discussing policies on refugee assistance, this section will provide an overview of the international system of refugee protection. The section will first provide a history on how international communities responded to refugee problems and then discuss issues related to the humanitarian principles of refugee work.

2.1.1 Establishment of UNHCR
International approaches to refugee relief started after World

War I when the war and subsequent political strives displaced a large number of people in Europe. Granted, since ancient times, people have been forced to flee because of armed conflict or fear of persecution. Until the post World War I era, however, there had been no consolidated response as an international community. In 1921, the League of Nations decided to start dealing with refugee problems as an international issue in response to an appeal by ICRC. This is generally regarded as the beginning of the international approach to refugee problems[17].

In the same year, Fridtjof Nansen of Norway was appointed to be the first High Commissioner for refugees[18] in order to support over 1 million refugees from Russia (see Table 2-1). Nansen particularly attended to the legal protection of refugees, establishing travel and identity documents that are even today called Nansen passports. He also supported the employment of 600,000 refugees in host countries in collaboration with the International Labour Organisation (ILO). Nansen further dealt with resettlement to third countries and repatriation. When negotiations about repatriation to the Soviet Union failed, Nansen worked to arrange measures to provide a legal status for Russian refugees in their host countries. It is generally agreed that Nansen's work in the early days formed the basis of today's focus of UNHCR, that is, provision of legal protection, assistance in host countries, and arrangement of durable solutions.

In 1933, James McDonald was appointed as independent High

---

[17] The history of the establishment of international system on refugee protection is based on information from UNHCR, State of the World's Refugees, 2000, and Homma, 1990.
[18] Nansen's official title was High Commissioner on behalf of the League in connection with the problems of Russian refugees in Europe. In addition to Russian refugees, his responsibility was later extended further to Greeks, Bulgarians, Armenians and certain other groups.

Table 2-1: International Approaches to Refugee Issues

	International responses to refugee issues	Mandate	Major issues and activities
1921	Appointment of the High Commissioner on behalf of the League in connection with the problems of Russian refugees in Europe	Arrange durable solutions for Russian refugees	Russian refugees, Voluntary repatriation, Employment in countries of residence, Resettlement to third countries, Assisted more than one million people
1933	Appointment of the High Commissioner for refugees from Germany	Relief of refugees from Germany	Resettlement of 80,000 refugees in Palestine and other countries.
November 1943	Establishment of the United Nations Relief and Rehabilitation Administration (UNRRA)	Assist in the relief and rehabilitation of war devastated areas	Assistance in repatriation of some 7 million refugees
July 1947	Establishment of International Refugee Organisation (IRO)	Assist European refugees in arranging durable solutions, identification, registration care and assistance, and protection	Resettlement of over 1 million of east European refugees, Jewish refugees to the US, Australia, Israel, Canada and Latin American countries. Repatriation of 73,000 refugees
February 1952	Closure of IRO		Some 400,000 refugees remained in Europe.
May 1950	Establishment of the United Nations Relief and Works Agency for Palestine Refugees (UNRWA)	Deliver assistance for Palestine refugees in the Near East	Provide assistance for Palestine refugees defined as people whose normal place of residence was Palestine for a minimum of two years preceding the 1948 conflict and who, as result of this conflict, lost both their home and means of livelihood and took refuge in 1948 in the areas where UNRWA operates.
January 1951	Establishment of the United Nations High Commissioner for Refugees (UNHCR)	Provide international protection of refugees and seek permanent solutions for them.	
July 1951	Adoption of the UN Convention relating to the Status of Refugees by the UN General Assembly		

Developed by the author based on information from *The State of the World's Refugees*, by UNHCR, 2000, and

Commissioner for refugees from Germany[19]. Although McDonald managed to establish two treaties concerning the protection of refugees from Germany, his work faced continual challenges from Nazi Germany. The limit of McDonald's achievements was due to the reluctance of the international community to become involved in the problem. The League of Nations continued to regard it as Germany's domestic issue and governments of other countries were reluctant to accept Jews into their countries. They expected the problem to be solved when the Jews would all migrate to Palestine (Homma, 1990: 63). A great number of Jews, however, continued leaving Germany as Nazis had hardened persecution.

The Cold War continued creating refugee flow from the eastern block through the 1940s. In response, the UN General Assembly decided in 1949 to establish the Office of the United Nations High Commissioner for Refugees (UNHCR) initially for three years from January 1951 to deal with refugees from East European countries[20]. All through the initial period of international responses, the international community regarded refugee issues as primarily an issue within Europe and expected it to be resolved sooner or later[21].

Contrary to the initial expectations, new refugee situations occurred one after another. The Hungarian Crisis in 1956 forced some 200,000 people to flee to Austria and other neighbouring countries in that year. In the 1960s and 1970s, the centre of refugee problems moved from Europe to Africa and Asia. Accordingly, UNHCR expanded its responsibilities to outside Europe. In this process, the Protocol Relating to the Status of Refugees, adopted in

---

[19] High Commissioner for refugees (Jewish and others) coming from Germany.
[20] UN General Assembly Resolution 319 (IV), 3 December 1949.
[21] The system to assist Palestine refugees was separately established in 1950 as the creation of the United Nations Relief and Works Agency for Palestine Refugees (UNRWA), based on UN General Assembly resolution 302 (IV) of December 1949.

1967, removed the time limitation of "events occurring before 1 January 1951" that was included in the 1951 UN Convention's definition of a refugee.

The Statute of the Office of the United Nations High Commissioner for Refugees that was adopted by the UN Generally Assembly in December 1950[22] defined the mandate of UNHCR in Chapter II, Articles 8 and 9. In summary, UNHCR's responsibility is to provide protection of refugees by:
1. Promoting the conclusion and ratification of international conventions for the protection of refugees;
2. Promoting through agreements with governments (of asylum countries) measures to improve the situation of refugees;
3. Assisting governmental and private efforts to promote voluntary repatriation or assimilation within new national communities.

The first role concerns the promotion of international refugee laws, the second deals with the assistance and protection in countries of asylum, and the third is related to the promotion of durable solutions. In 1951, Convention Relating to the Status of Refugees was adopted by the UN General Assembly, defining a refugee as a person who:

> ...owing to well-founded fear of being persecuted for reasons of race, religion, nationality, membership of a particular social group or political opinion, is outside the country of his nationality and is unable or, owing to such fear, is unwilling to avail himself of the protection of that country; or who, not having a nationality and being outside the country of his former habitual residence as a result of such events, is unable or owing to such

---

[22] UN General Assembly Resolution 248 (V), 14 December 1950.

fear, is unwilling to return to it[23].

Concerning the characteristics of UNHCR work, Article 2 of the statute specifies "The work of the High Commissioner shall be of an entirely non-political character; it shall be humanitarian and social...." The article, defining the essence of UNHCR's work as non-political and humanitarian, is crucial for UNHCR in providing protection for refugees without being affected by politically opposing groups or nations.

2.1.2 International Protection

One of the most important principles in refugee protection is the *non-refoulement* principle. It is a concept which prohibits states from forcibly returning refugees to territories where they face danger. Though one may ask whether a state may be free to reject asylum seekers at the border before their entry without being criticised for refoulement (Homma, 1990), it is fairly generally agreed that the

---

[23] *Convention Relating to the Status of Refugees*, 1951. Chapter 1, Article 1. A. (2). Researchers (Homma, 1986; Kurino, 1986; ICIHI, 1986; Weiner 1995; Koizumi, 1998; Mandal, 2005) as well as UNHCR seem to agree that the present definition of refugees does not cover all the people who are in need of international protection. The most typical case that may not fall in the scope of the current definition is people who are forced to flee their country because of armed conflict or war. However, the definition by the African Union includes such populations in refugees (see *OAU Convention Governing the Specific Aspects of Refugee Problems in Africa*, 1969, Article 1, para.2.). In practice, the definition has been applied with flexibility and UNHCR includes under their responsibility those who are displaced from their home countries by conflict. Following the practice, this study includes in the category of refugees people who have been displaced from their countries of origin because of conflict. It, however, does not consider immigrants or people displaced by natural disasters as refugees. For further reading on UNHCR's discussions on the definition of refugees, see EXCOM Conclusion No. 22, XXXII,1981;c and UNHCR *Notes on Interpreting the Refugee Definition and on Complementary Forms of Protection*, Inter-Office Memorandum No. 38/2001, para. 11.

principle of *non-refoulement* includes a right to asylum, i.e., asylum seekers at the border should not be denied for entry.

The 1951 UN Convention does not explicitly grant a right to asylum, but there is a view that the term "refoulement" in French and Belgian laws commonly covers rejection at the border (Lautepacht & Bethlehem, 2001: 28-29). UNHCR's Executive Committee (EXCOM) reaffirmed in 1977 that the principle of *non-refoulement* is applicable to the situation at the border (and within a state)[24]. In 1979, EXCOM further supported this position in its Conclusion No. 15[25].

Apart from the *non-refoulement* principle, the 1951 UN Convention contains provisions on rights to employment, education and free movement[26]. Though analysis on the provisions of the 1951 UN Convention is outside of the scope of this study, it is useful to highlight the point that the 1951 UN Convention provides basic principles on the rights and obligations of refugees and the responsibilities of states.

Durable solutions: UNHCR considers three durable solutions: Voluntary repatriation, local integration (local settlement)[27] and resettlement. Though UNHCR's definitions of each durable solution are not strictly consistent, especially for local integration (settlement)[28], general ideas of the three durable solutions can be sum-

---

[24] UNHCR EXCOM Conclusion No. 6 (XXVIII), 1977, para. (c).
[25] Ibid, No. 15 (XXX), 1979, para (c).
[26] *Convention Relating to the Status of Refugees*, Articles 17, 22 and 26.
[27] UNHCR uses two terms, local integration and local settlement in its documents. Most of its protection-related documents use the term "local integration" while the programme documents use "local settlement." See for example, UNHCR's *Protection Training Module*, 2005 and *Programme Manual - Chapter 4*, 1995. In this study, the term "local integration" will be used as one of durable solutions while "local settlement" refers to a programme promoting settlement activities in countries of asylum and thus promoting opportunities for local integration.
[28] UNHCR's *Protection Training Module* of 2005 defines local integration as a

marised as follows:
- **Voluntary repatriation** is to allow refugees to resume a normal life in their home countries. This is considered the most preferred solution.
- **Local integration**[29] is, when voluntary repatriation is not possible, to provide opportunities for refugees to become more self-sufficient and become integrated into the economic and social life of a country of asylum.
- **Resettlement to a third country** is applied only if the first two options are not feasible for ethnic, political or economic reasons.

Voluntary repatriation is, understandably, considered as the most favourable solution. Resettlement used to be the main option for Eastern European refugees in the 1950s and for Indochinese refugees since the late 1970s. In the case of the former, countries of the western block welcomed refugees not only as a source of labour but also to create politically positive images of their own countries as opposed to refugee-producing socialist states. With regard to Indochinese refugees, over 1.3 million people were resettled to more than 15 countries from 1975 to 1995 (see Table 2-2). On the other hand, the number of refugees who were voluntarily repatriated was small: Some 109,000 returned to Vietnam and 24,000 to Laos, for example[30].

---

solution when "refugees settle permanently in the country of asylum, " while its *Framework for Durable Solutions* issued in 2003 includes a situation where a state opts to "gradually" integrate refugees.

[29] Whether or not local integration can be one of the durable solutions poses some questions. This will be discussed in subsequent chapters.

[30] Solutions for Indochinese refugees were based on the conclusions of the two international conferences held in Geneva in 1979 and 1989. In May 1979, in order to avoid risky illegal departure from Vietnam, the Orderly Departure Programme

Table 2-2: Resettlement of Indochinese Refugees, 1975-1995

Countries of resettlement	Cambodian	Lao	Vietnamese	Total
Australia	16,308	10,239	110,996	137,543
Belgian	745	989	2,051	3,785
Canada	16,818	18,274	103,053	138,145
Denmark	31	12	4,682	4,725
Finland	37	6	1,859	1,902
France	34,364	34,236	27,071	95,671
Germany	874	1,706	16,848	19,428
Japan	1,061	1,273	6,469	8,803
Holland	465	33	7,565	8,063
New Zealand	4,421	1,286	4,921	10,628
Norway	128	2	6,064	6,194
Sweden	19	26	6,009	6,054
Switzerland	1,638	593	6,239	8,470
Britain	273	346	19,355	19,974
the USA	150,240	248,147	424,590	822,977
Other countries	8,063	4,688	7,070	19,821
Total	235,485	321,856	754,842	1,312,183

Source: *The State of the World's Refugees*, UNHCR, 2000, p. 9

(ODP) was established. Under the programme, the Vietnamese authorities allowed the exit of those wishing to leave the country for family reunion and other humanitarian reasons. The resettlement figures in Table 2-2 include those who departed under ODP.

To other refugees, however, resettlement opportunities were limited compared with the number of refugees that was ever growing from the late 1970s. (For total number of refugees, see Figure 2-1 below.) Camp-based relief assistance, called a Care and Maintenance programme, was provided for those refugees in countries of asylum. However, continuing assistance for a large number of refugees without foreseeable solutions posed challenges from all angles: For refugees, relief-oriented assistance did not give them any dignified life. For governments of countries of asylum, hosting refugees for a long duration became a serious burden. And for donors, providing funds for an indefinite period was impossible.

Local settlement, therefore, began to attract attention as a more solution-oriented project that could provide opportunities for refugees to become self-reliant and thereby alleviate the burden on host countries (For the changing nature of world's refugee issues, see Table 2-3.).

Developed by the author based on information from
The State of the World's Refugees, UNHCR, 2000, p. 310.

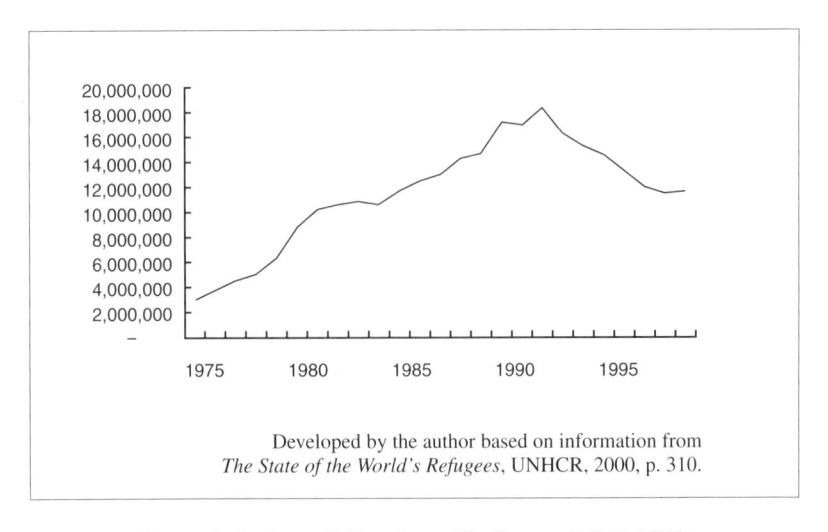

Figure 2-1: Overall Number of Refugees (1975-1999)

International Protection of Refugees

Table 2 -3: Major World's Refugee Problems (1950s–1990s)

Main characteristics of refugee issues	International incidents	Refugees fled from:	Refugees fled to: (number of refugees, if known)	Durable solutions
1950s: Refugee problems in Europe	Hungary crisis	Hungary	Austria, former Yugoslavia	-Most of the refugees opted for resettlement -9% of the refugees repatriated
Late 1950s to 1960s: - Refugee problems in Africa	UNHCR did not intervene into Chinese refugees' problem in Hong Kong until 1957.			
	Algerian war of independence (1954-1962)	Algeria	Tunisia (151,903 people), Morocco (11,0245 people)	-Repatriation, -Resettlement to France
	Biafran war (1967-1970)	Nigeria	Equatorial Guinea, Gabon, Côte d'Ivoire	Repatriation
	Coup d'etat in Rwanda	Rwanda	By 1994, some 150,000 Tutsi Rwandans fled to Congo, Uganda, Burundi and Tanzania.	Not solved until the 1990s
	Independence of other African countries and subsequent civil wars	Congo, Rwanda, Burundi, Angola, Mozambique, Guninea-Bissau, etc.	Republic of Congo, Zambia, Botswana, Senegal, Tanzania	Not all solved in the 1960s
1970s: - Refugee problems in Africa prolonged - Number of refugees growing in Africa and Asia	Civil war in Mozambique	Mozambique	Some 1.7 million refugees fled to Malawi, South Africa, Swaziland, Tanzania, Zambia, and Zimbabwe.	To be aggravated in the 1980s
	- Civil war in Pakistan - War between India and Pakistan (1971)	Pakistan (East, The area became the independent state of Bangladesh)	India (10 million refugees)	Repatriation to Bangladesh
	Communist's victories in Indochina	Viet Nam, Laos, Cambodia	The Philippines,Thailand, Malaysia, Singapore, Indonesia, Hong Kong	Resettlement, Not completely solved in the 1970s.
1980s: Proxy wars in Africa, Asia and Central America caused large-scale displacement.	Wars in Horn of Africa	Ethiopia (and Eritrea)	Sudan, Somalia, Kenya, Djibut	Not solved until the 1990s.
	Civil war in Sudan	Sudan	Ethiopia, Uganda, Kenya, Congo	Not solved until the mid 2000s
	Soviet invasion of Afghanistan (1979) and subsequent civil wars	Afghanistan	Pakistan (3,250,000 from 1979–1990) Iran (3,060,000 from 1979–1990)	
	Civil wars in Nicaragua, El Salvador and Guatemala	Nicaragua, El Salvador and Guatemala	The US (refugees from Nicaragua) Mexico, Costa Rica, Honduras	

Main characteristics of refugee issues	International incidents	Refugees fled from:	Refugees fled to: (number of refugees, if known)	Durable solutions
1990s: -End of Cold War -End of Proxy Wars - New inter-ethnic conflicts and Civil Wars	Withdrawal of Soviet troops from Afghanistan (1989)	Repatriation (not completed)		
	End of wars in Latin America	Repatriation		
	Peace accords in Cambodia (1991)	Repatriation (over 360,000 people)		
	General Peace Agreement for Mozambique (1992)	Repatriation (1,700,000people)		
	Inter-ethnic conflicts in former Soviet Union : Armenia-Azerbaijan conflict, civil wars in Tajikistan and Georgia, war in Chechnya	Some 9 million people displaced in the region in the 1990s.		Repatriation
	Gulf War (1991)	Iraq (Kurdish)	Turkey, Iran	Repatriation
	Wars in the Balkans (1991–95)	Some 2,500,000 people were displaced within the region or fled to Western Europe.		Repatriation
	Genocide in Rwanda (1994)	Rwandans (Hutu)	Zaire (1,200,000), Tanzania (580,000), Burundi, (270,000), Uganda (100,000)	Repatriation
	Wars in West Africa	Liberia, Sierra Leone,	Guinea, Cote d'Ivoire, Ghana	Repatriation
	Kosovo Crisis (1998–99)	Kosovo (ethnic Albanian)	Macedonia (228,000) Albania (426,000) Montenegro (45,000)	Repatriation
	Independence of East Timor (1999)	East Timor	Indonesia	Repatriation

Developed by the author based on *The State of the World's Refugees*, UNHCR, 2000, and *Nanminmondai towa Nanika*, H.Homma 1993.

Humanitarianism: The other importance attached to UNHCR's work is its non-political and humanitarian nature as defined in its statute. While UNHCR deals with refugee affairs that are the consequences of political struggles, placing its work outside the political arena allows the organisation to minimise the influence from politically opposing parties.

If UNHCR were involved in the political process, refugees might see UNHCR as supporters of a government that caused them to flee. Or, the government might regard UNHCR as its opponents. In either case, the organisation would not be able to effectively advocate for refugees (see Box 2-1).

Box 2-1: Humanitarian principles

Humanity: Human suffering should be relieved wherever it is found. The inherent dignity and other human rights of individuals and groups must be respected and protected.

Impartiality: Humanitarian assistance should be provided without discrimination. Relief must address the needs of all individuals and groups who are suffering, without regard to nationality, political or ideological beliefs, race, religion, sex or ethnicity. Needs assessments and relief activities should be geared toward priority for the most urgent cases.

Neutrality: Humanitarian relief should be provided without bias toward and against one or more of the parties to the political, military, religious, ideological or ethnic controversy which has given rise to the suffering. Humanitarian actors must not allow themselves to become allied with a party to a conflict.

Source: *Handbook for the Military on Humanitarian Operations,*
UNHCR, 1995, 3.1.

However, drawing a line between humanitarian actions and political activities is not always clear to all parties. For example, in a situation where armed groups frequently attack refugee camps, UNHCR officials may have to negotiate with them to ensure the safety of the camps. In such negotiations, the line between humanitarian concerns and political issues may become blurred.

Repatriation may be another example. In discussions on voluntary repatriation with countries of asylum and origin for a tri-partite agreement, each party may have political motives. The government of a country of asylum may fear of losing international attention after the departure of refugees. Or on the contrary, it may want refugees to leave the country as fast as possible even if the return is against their will. Once refugees return home and face discrimination or oppression, such events can hardly be separated from political issues. UNHCR's work may even touch upon the issue of sovereignty.

As such, separating humanitarian issues from political concerns is not always clear-cut. Some observers point out that the blurred definition on humanitarian actions caused continuous debates on this subject[31]. In this case, however, searching for precise definitions on the two and obliging UNHCR to pursue the defined humanitarian actions would not necessarily be helpful.

The Hutu Rwandan refugee camps in eastern Zaire serve as a good example. These camps became the main military base for armed Hutu groups. The latter, with the support of Zairian government, continued military activities in the camps. Ordinary refugees including women and children became their political hostages. UNHCR, delivering services in the camps, were accused of supporting the militarisation of the refugee camps. The then High Commissioner, Sadako Ogata, emphasised the fact that more than

---

[31] UNHCR, *The State of the World's Refugees*, 2000, pp. 19-22. It is not clear whether this particular statement represents UNHCR's official position or not.

half of the camp populations were women and children and that the discontinuation of the assistance would have the greatest impact on the survival of these most vulnerable refugees (Ogata, 2005: 201). At the same time, UNHCR requested, through the UN Secretary General, that states deploy their military or police forces to assist in removing armed elements from the camps. These attempts, however, were unsuccessful.

This case shows the difficulty in clearly separating humanitarian actions from political issues. The fact that UNHCR continued delivering assistance in camps with armed elements in them already raises a question about whether UNHCR retained the required neutrality. But if UNHCR had stopped the services, the organisation would have ignored the pressing needs of the most vulnerable. Therefore, UNHCR requested through the UN Secretary General states to assist in separating armed groups from civilian refugees. This request, primarily based on humanitarian concern, went through the political wing of the UN. Whichever option the organisation took, it is ambiguous whether UNHCR's actions were strictly non-political.

The above example shows that defining "humanitarian" may not always provide clear answer as to what UNHCR should do in any given situation. The issue may be a matter of choice in approach between expressing a strong objection against a group infringing on human rights of others by stopping aid, or responding to the urgent human needs of the most vulnerable at the risk of equally benefiting armed groups.

2.2 Refugee Assistance and International Communities

The previous section reviewed the international system of refugee protection, durable solutions and the humanitarian principle of refugee work. This section will provide an overview of the actors in refugee assistance and their roles.

2.2.1 Actors and Stakeholders

States: States bear the primary responsibility of refugee protection. The UN General Assembly Resolution 428 (V) Article 2, adopted in December 1950, requires that states should cooperate with UNHCR by:
1. Becoming parties to international conventions on refugees;
2. Admitting refugees to their territories;
3. Making agreements with UNHCR to improve the situation of refugees;
4. Promoting the assimilation of refugees;
5. Providing refugees with travel and other documents.

Apart from establishing status determination procedures and registration of refugees, governments of countries of asylum normally offer land for refugee camps/settlements in case of a mass refugee influx. It is also possible that a government deploy national police, military, or both, to secure the safety of refugee camps.

UNHCR: As seen in the previous section, UNHCR is responsible for assisting governments in providing protection and assistance for refugees. How far UNHCR assists a government often depends on the capacity and will of the government concerned. In a country where the government has not acceded the 1951 UN Convention on Refugees and its 1967 Protocol, UNHCR might focus its efforts on promoting the ratification of the international conventions. In a country whose economic performance is poor, UNHCR may financially support its government offices and non-governmental organisations in providing protection and assistance. Generally, UNHCR's work can be summarised as:
1. Promoting international conventions on refugee protection

and supervising its implementation;
2. Advising states on establishing national laws and policies on refugee protection;
3. Assessing refugee situations and coordinating with the government, NGOs and other UN and international agencies on activities for refugee protection and assistance;
4. Assisting government and non-government organisations in providing protection and assistance.

Refugees: Refugees are primarily the beneficiaries of assistance and the subject of protection. It should, however, be recognised that they are important actors in refugee protection and assistance as well. In many situations, refugees establish their own committees. Leaders participate in needs assessment and delivery of services. They work on a voluntary basis as distributors of food and relief items, community workers, and members of assessment missions. Some of the refugees find employment at UNHCR or other aid agencies.

In some situations, refugees mobilise themselves for their own protection, for example, by patrolling around refugee camps. Some refugee committees have their own conflict resolution mechanism to intervene into disputes within their community. Though levels of refugee participation may vary depending on the situations, generally, refugees are not only the recipients of aid but also active participants in the aid system. At the same time, refugee participation poses several issues for consideration. In the Hutu Rwandan refugee camps that were discussed in the previous section, for example, leaders, namely Hutu soldiers, did not at all represent ordinary refugees. This topic relating to participation will be discussed in detail in Chapter 5.

Implementing agencies: Organisations and agencies that actually deliver services such as health care or food assistance to refugees are called implementing agencies. Most of the implementing agencies are national or international non-governmental organisations (NGOs) along with some governmental offices of donor countries. In some countries, government offices of a country of asylum implement assistance programmes.

Many of the implementing agencies arrange agreements with UNHCR (or tripartite agreements with UNHCR and the government of a country of asylum) and receive funds for the implementation of agreed activities. Some other agencies work with their own funds.

Other UN and international agencies: Among UN and international agencies other than UNHCR, the World Food Programme (WFP) is the most closely engaged in refugee work. WFP is responsible for providing food in refugee situations. In addition, WFP is active in supporting School Feeding Programmes and what is called Food-For-Work[32] that may be extended to refugees or refugee-hosting areas.

The United Nations Development Programme (UNDP), United Nations Children's Funds (UNICEF), and Food and Agriculture Organisation (FAO) are often active in refugee reintegration situations in the areas of development, governance, potable water, health, education and agriculture.

The work of the ICRC is also crucial in refugee situations. Their family reunion programme traces family members who were separated from each other during their flight. The International Organisation for Migration (IOM) is engaged in the logistics for refugee resettlement and repatriation in many situations.

Donors: Corresponding with the world's trend of decreasing

---

[32] Food-For-Work is a community-development programme in which food is provided for a community in exchange for their work to build community infrastructure.

Official Development Aid (ODA) in the 1990s[33], UNHCR suffered from a continuing shortage of funds (see Figure 2-2). For other UN agencies, the funding situation was no better. In particular, funds for programmes to link between relief and development work may often fall into a gap between emergency funds and funds for development activities. Denmark noted in its report in 2002[34] that both UNICEF and WFP received adequate funds for their relief and development projects but little donor response to their rehabilitation projects.

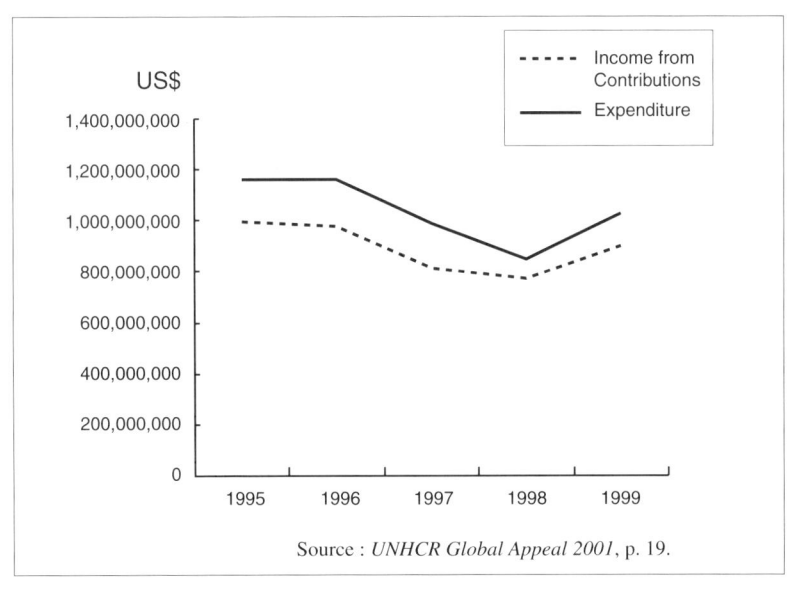

Source : *UNHCR Global Appeal 2001*, p. 19.

Figure 2-2 : UNHCR Incomes vs Expenditure (1995-1999)

---

[33] United Nations Conference on Trade and Development, *The Least Developed Countries 2000 Report*.
[34] Danish Ministry of Foreign Affairs, *The Multilateral aid Response to Violent Conflict: More than Linking Relief and Development*, Draft Report, Centre for Development Research, 2000.

64   *Linking Refugee Aid with Development*

Other actors and stakeholders: Apart from the above, local elders, authorities and administration may actively participate in the process of refugee assistance. Militaries began to appear on the humanitarian scene in the 1990s. In addition to peacekeeping forces that are to enable aid workers to carry out their work (e.g., UNPROFOR in Bosnia), even militaries party to a conflict (e.g., NATO during the Kosovo Crisis, or the US military in Afghanistan since September 2001) organise "humanitarian[35]" activities in recent human crises.

2.2.2 Coordination:

This section will give a brief overview of the coordination among three actors: the government of a host country, UNHCR and implementing agencies. The government of a country of asylum, often jointly with UNHCR, establishes overall policies on refugee assistance. Implementing agencies under an agreement with UNHCR, normally work on the assistance within the set framework. However, the details of each activity should be coordinated among the government, UNHCR, implementing agencies and other stakeholders.

To illustrate the above, following is a hypothetical example, which supposes that a government decided to offer a local settlement programme to refugees. The government first identifies land for the settlement and requests UNHCR to establish a refugee settlement there. In this case, UNHCR may draw up an overall settlement plan which they want an implementing agency to use in building the settlement. Alternatively, the implementing agency may want to propose their own plan. Once the work starts, problems may occur: No water

---

[35] Whether activities supported by a group party to a conflict can be called humanitarian assistance remains a question. Therefore, the term "humanitarian" is used with quotations in this sentence.

vein is found; a road leading to the site becomes impassable during the rainy season; or refugees do not like the place, etc. In such cases, the government and UNHCR together with the implementing agency intervene.

As such, the relations between the government, UNHCR and implementing agencies are unique in the sense that the relationship is neither contractor-employer nor donor-recipient. In the former, a contractor should strictly follow what the employer specifies in a contract. In the latter, a recipient agency has freedom to implement its own programme that a donor has agreed to fund. Under an agreement with UNHCR and implementing agencies (and with a government), the implementation of activities is a collaborative process based on partnership.

Coordination among actors has become increasingly crucial in recent refugee assistance. There are more stakeholders and actors involved in refugee assistance. They also have become more active in voicing their opinions on refugee assistance (see Figure 2-3).

It is often pointed out that the roles of donors have been changing since the late 1990s. Prior to that, donors used to allow UN agencies to decide on the usage of funds once they contributed to humanitarian assistance programmes including ones for refugees. This was because they generally understood that humanitarian assistance commonly requires fast responses without making detailed plans in advance. Since the late 1990s, however, donors became more demanding in the usage of their funds. As a result, more funds are directly transferred to NGOs of donor countries or are earmarked for specific activities. For example, UNHCR reported that 80% of its total budget was earmarked in 1999[36].

Bilateralism has increased. Surhke, Barutcske, Sandison and Garlock (2000) report that UNHCR received only 3.5% of aid that

---

[36] UNHCR, *Global Report 1999*.

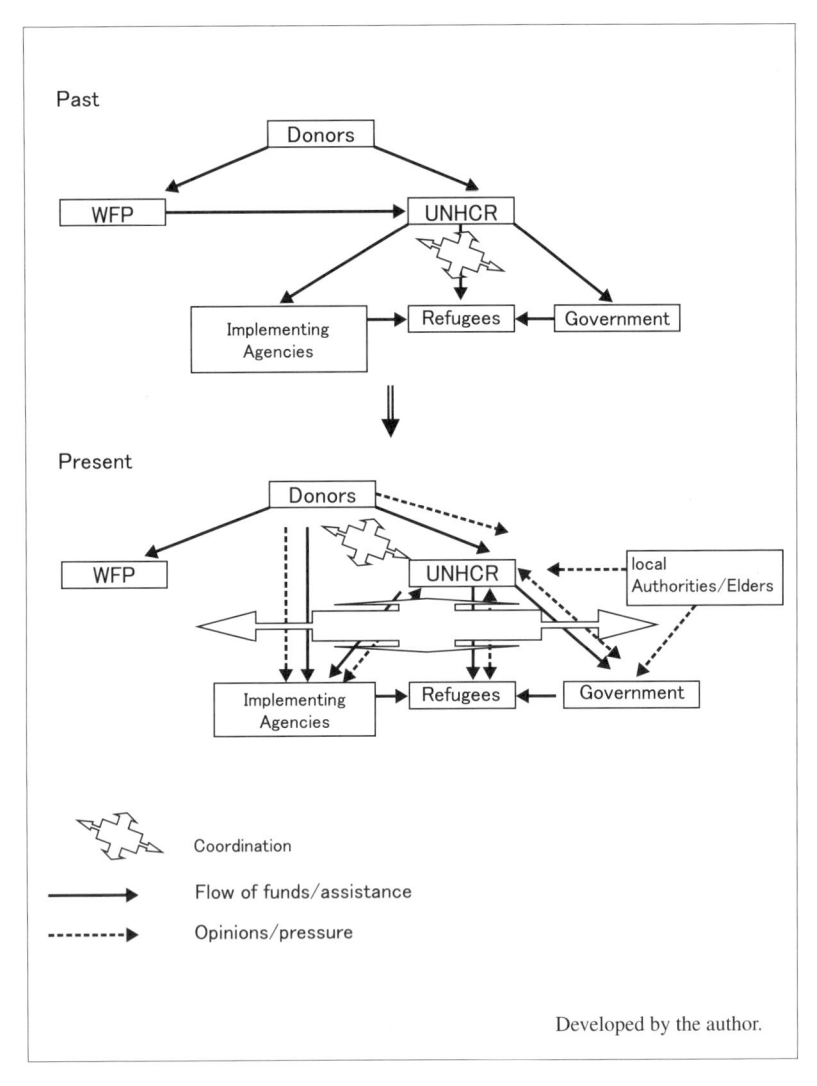

Figure 2-3: Coordination in Refugee Situations - Past and Present

the European Union (EU) provided in the Kosovo Crisis. UNCTAD also reported that 70% of the total aid of members of Development Assistance Committee (DAC) had been in the form of bilateral assistance[37]. A study by Macrae et al. (2002: 17) also found the same trends among European and North American donors. According to the study, bilaterally managed expenditure[38] on humanitarian assistance of these donors increased by 150% from 1996 to 1999 while those to multilateral agencies (e.g., UN agencies) increased by only 32%. The trend was particularly obvious in the assistance of the European Community Humanitarian Department (ECHO) which increased its bilaterally managed expenditure by 475% during the same period (Macrae et al., 2002: 17).

It is generally believed that one of the reasons for the trend is that donors began questioning the effectiveness of UN agencies and their humanitarian assistance and wanted to use humanitarian aid as their own diplomatic strategy (Suhrke et al., 2000; Macrae et al., 2002). For example, the evaluation of UNHCR's response to Kosovo Crisis by Suhrke et al. (2000: xi) points out that the government of the USA, rather than UNHCR, took initiatives to solve the problem when the Macedonian government refused to acccept Kosovo refugees.

Many aid organisations, observers, and donors themselves also expressed criticisms of the donor trends. A common concern was that the donors' intention to reflect their political interests on humanitarian assistance resulted in the imbalanced allocation of resources: Emergency operations raised significant levels of funds

---

[37] United Nations Conference and Development, *The Least Developed Countries 2000 Report.*
[38] Bilaterally managed expenditure includes earmarked contributions to UN agencies, direct contracting to NGOs, and donors' own operations (Macrae et al., 2002: 17).

while protracted refugee situations like those in Africa did not receive adequate support (Suhrke, 1994; UNHCR's evaluation, 1994; UNDP Rwanda report, 1998; Fukada, 1998; Danish Ministry of Foreign Affair's report, 2000).

The Kosovo Crisis, where bilateral aid predominated, was a typical case. As Suhrke et al. emphasised (2000), bilateralism, coupled with weak coordination capacity of UNHCR, contributed to inefficient resource allocation in this crisis. During the Kosovo Crisis in 1999, Albania received a flow of NGOs, the total of which reached some 180 at the peak of the emergency (Suhrke et al., 2000: 6). Most of the NGOs funded by their respective governments did not seem to pay much attention to coordination or resource allocation[39]. Instead, many decided to operate in large regional towns or areas with easy access from the capital. Refugee camps directly supported by donor governments enjoyed high standards of assistance while there were other areas with no assistance at all. This was a typical case of neutrality and impartiality being affected because of heavy influence from donors' political interests.

Cooley & Ron (2002) studied relations between NGOs and donors/UN agencies from the point of power-relations. Their argument was that because NGOs are afraid of possible conflicts between donors/UN agencies and themselves, they would not express their views, thus eventually hindering the improvement of assistance. In addition, Cooley and Ron claimed that NGOs would not share information even among themselves because of competition. Consequently, this would create duplication and gaps of assistance. Although there are some merits in their argument on power-relation, it is not very certain from this author's experiences how absolute such a power-relation is. NGOs, though not having much power in policy making,

---

[39] Based on this author's own observation in the country at the time from January to May 1999.

still have influence in designing project activities and raising protection concerns. Rather, there may be more relevance in another point of theirs, namely that assistance in emergency operations may not ensure quality because of its hastened work (Cooley & Ron, 2002: 29). It seems more likely that time constraints are more crucial challenges in coordination with broad ranges of actors.

Though participation of local actors and refugees will be discussed in Chapter 5, it is appropriate to mention now that local actors and refugees have increasingly been participating in planning on refugee assistance in recent refugee situations. Because of broader ranges of actors and stakeholders with different interests and opinions, coordination in refugee assistance today is becoming more complex.

2.3 Refugees as a Threat?

The previous sections provided basic guides on international system on refugee protection/assitance and actors and stake holders who are involved in the system. This section will examine world phenomena that appear to be against refugees and refute the view that support anti-refugee campaigns. The section, then, argues that assisting refugees is an inevitable need from a humanitarian view point. It further argues that refugees are not only burden but can become asset to host communities.

2.3.1 Refugees-as-Threats

Are refugees dangerous threats to nations receiving them and their nationals? Judging from world incidents surrounding refugees and asylum seekers, it appears that refugees are perceived as threats. In 1996, thousands of Rwandan refugees were killed when they were returned by force from their camps in Zaire (the present Democratic

Republic of Congo). More recently in August 2001, the Australian government rejected a boat that carried some 400 Afghan asylum seekers. In the same year, the Pakistani government officially closed its border against Afghans who fled from deteriorating security situations at home[40]. The government of Japan accepted only 305 refugees from 1981, when it had acceded the UN Convention Relating to the Status of Refugees, to 2002[41]. Even including some 10,000 Indochinese refugees whom Japan has accepted since 1978, the number remained low compared with other industrialised countries[42].

Reviewing previous controversies (for example, ICIHI, 1986; UNHCR's Status of the World's Refugees 1995; Weiner, 1995; Koizumi, 1998), there are three main reasons why refugees are not welcomed:
1. Refugees are seen as political and/or diplomatic threats.
2. Refugees are seen as social and/or cultural threats.
3. Refugees are seen as economic threats.

Refugees as political threats: The first issue concerns state security. Refugees are the victims of political struggles, but some people may think that refugees will bring problems to the national security of asylum countries. A government may fear that refugees might collude with anti-government groups or guerrillas once they enter the country. An example is the Macedonian case during the Kosovo crisis in 1999. Ethnic Albanian Kosovars fled from Serb atrocities that escalated after the initiation of NATO's air strike on

---

[40] It is, however, worth noting that Pakistan assisted people who "illegally entered" the country and later accepted them as "humanitarian cases."
[41] Japan's Ministry of Foreign Affairs' HP.
[42] According to UNHCR's statistics, the US and Australia, for example, accepted 13,200 and 1,900 refugees respectively in 1999 alone.

24 March 1999. The Macedonian government, a country also consisting of minority Albanians and Slavs, refused the admission of Kosovo Albanians because of concern over possible destabilisation of its state security (Suhrke et al., 2000: 10).

In another case, accepting refugees may cause a diplomatic problem with the country of origin as the acceptance (by the country of asylum) of refugees can be seen as a criticism of the authority of the country of origin. Weiner (1995/1999: 265) presents the case of the US that accepted the Iranian Shah (i.e., king) for the purpose of medical treatment after the Iranian Revolution. Furious Iranian revolutionists accused the US government of giving the Shah "protection" (as a refugee). According to Weiner (1995/1999: 263), the US's admission of the Shah was the cause of the later incident in which Iranians took American citizens hostage in Iran.

Refugees as social threats: The typical example of the second case is xenophobia, or the phenomenon that people develop irrational dislike and strong feelings against people from other countries such as immigrants and refugees. Until the early 1970s, Western countries, enjoying growing economies, vigorously accepted refugees and immigrants as labour forces. After the late 1970s, the political mood became reactionary when western economies slowed down.

With recession and unemployment becoming serious in the 1980s, conservative parties and rightist politicians targeted their policy debates on the control of aliens (ICIHI, 1986; Thranhardt, 1992; Weiner, 1995; Koizumi, 1998). In Switzerland, an attempt was made to limit the ratio of foreigners against the number of Swiss nationals; Britain restricted the issuance of visas to Sri Lankans; Germany started a programme to return guest workers to their home; In France, the ultra-rightist political party began a campaign against foreigners. Under these circumstances, the British government rejected the admission of Tamils from Sri Lanka, who should have been regarded as asylum seekers. The refugee status determination process in industrialised countries is often linked with their immigration policies. The case of the Tamils was a typical situation in which asylum seekers (who could have been granted refugee status) became victims of xenophobia.

Japan is not immune to xenophobia. In Western countries, xenophobia is aroused in relation to their deepening economic problems. In contrast, what underlies Japanese xenophobia is people's desire for a homogeneous society. Kim (2003) states that Japanese xenophobia is derived from the ideology of racial superiority and the notion that aliens are potential criminals. Similarly, Weiner (1995/1999: 123) also points out that Japan, compared with European countries, is an exclusive society that values the importance of "Japaneseness".

Refugees as economic threats: The third reason concerns the cost of receiving refugees. Xenophobia in Europe after the late 1970s has already been mentioned. During the same period, the cost to manage status determination systems and welfare schemes for asylum seekers dramatically increased. According to UNHCR[43], such cost increased from US$500 million in 1983 to US$7 billion in 1990 in the 13 major industrialised countries.

The economic burden is even more serious in developing countries. Countries of asylum should provide basic services, including land, shelter, food and health care, for refugees. This is a serious and heavy burden for governments of refugee-hosting developing countries that are not able to deliver adequate services even for their own people. Nationals, understandably, feel that the budget for refugees should be diverted to services that would benefit themselves. What often makes the situation worse is the environmental impact of refugee presence. A massive influx of refugees often causes the destruction of woods to establish camps and the heavy usag of trees for

---

[43] UNHCR, *The State of the World's Refugees*, 1995.

daily fuel use by refugees.

Hardin, known for the theory of the commons (1968) and lifeboat ethics (1974), views these problems from the point of resource allocation. The theory of the commons claims that commons (or the land/resources affecting the whole community), once they becomes open for public use, will be overused exceeding their capacity and such unrestricted use of the commons will result in environmental degradation.

Applying this theory to immigrant issues, he explores in his article titled "Living on a Lifeboat" (1974) the question of whether or not limited resources can be allocated to immigrants and refugees who are not the citizens of a concerned country. Hardin asserts, "Unrestricted immigration ... speed[s] up the destruction of the Environment in rich countries" (1974: 9), criticising an open-door policy as disregarding the interests of descendants (1974: 10). He states that an exception can be given to refugees because they are forced to flee from their countries for political reasons. Even in this case, however, he claims that refugees should accept restricted birth rights in order to control the total population of the country (Hardin, 1974: 12).

As such, these arguments form the basis for the "refugee-as-threat" view. Considering all of the above, it can be reasonably said that the views of local populations on refugees as political threats or economic burdens have certain reasonable grounds, at least from their point of view. However, from the viewpoint of refugees, does such a negative perspective sound fair? Do they actually exist only as threats or burdens in a host society?

2.3.2 Refugees-as-Assets

Definition of refugees: To answer the first question, it is useful to examine the definition of refugees in comparison with that of immigrants. The 1951 UN Convention provides the definition of refugees as presented in the first section of this chapter.

A migrant worker is defined as "a person who is to be engaged, is engaged or has been engaged in a remunerated activity in a State of which he or she is not a national."[44]

Derived from the definition is the characteristic of refugees as opposed to immigrants, that is, its aspect of forced movement. Refugees are forcibly displaced due to undemocratic political system, dictatorships, conflicts, or other unfavourable political situations. Certainly, poverty and economic recession in a home country do create a situation where people have to move to another country as migrant workers. Nevertheless, the fundamental difference is that refugees are not guaranteed their physical safety by their home government while immigrants enjoy such protection.

Difficulties lie in the fact that distinction between refugees and (illegal) immigrants is not always clear in the screening process (Kurino, 1986; Weiner, 1995; Koizumi, 1998). The screening of refugees from immigrants is difficult mainly because proving "well-founded fear" is not an easy task for asylum seekers. Although the phrase was added in the definition originally to include people who can present adequate reasons for fear of persecution in addition to those who have already been the victims of persecution (Aragaki, 2001), it also requires applicants to present "objective elements" as well as "subjective" fear to prove "well-founded" fear. However, such proof is often elusive.

Regarding the burden of proof, Aragaki (2001) warns that decision makers' assessments of an application for asylum may not be adequate because of the difficulty in obtaining information on countries of origin, especially with regards to human rights. Many researchers and observers claim that in such an inadequate status

---

[44] *International Convention on the Protection of the Rights of All Migrant Workers and Members of Their Families*, 1990, Part I, Article 2.1.

determination process, asylum seekers from developing countries have often been wrongly treated as economic immigrants (ICIHI, 1986; Santel, 1992; Aragaki, 2001). To make matters worse, some people who attempt to abuse the refugee status determination system for their entry make it even more difficult to distinguish refugee cases from immigrants (ICIHI, 1986; Homma, 1986).

Taking all of the above into consideration, it is not reasonable from the refugees' perspectives if governments deny their entry even if those governments may have some reasonable concerns over the impact of the refugees. Those who support refugee-as-threat view do not seem to consider the very point that distinguishes refugees from (illegal) immigrants but misunderstand as if refugees have a place to return to when rejected by countries other than their own.

Then, consider the second question: Are refugees only a burden or threat to host countries? Earlier in this chapter a situation was presented in which refugees' presence might pose a threat to national security. It should be equally recognised, however, that in other situations, governments of countries of asylum might actively utilise refugee presence for their political purposes. When the government of a country of asylum shares common political interests with those of refugees, the former may use the latter for its own diplomatic motives (Stedman & Tanner, 2003a).

The cases of Rwandan refugees in Zaire and Afghan refugees in Pakistan are examples known to people who have dealt with these situations. Under the protection of the Zairian government, Hutu Rwandan refugees[45] were conducting military training in refugee

---

[45] Refugees should be civilian. Therefore, strictly speaking, they cannot be called refugees, but rather "Hutu soldiers" or "armed elements" in refugee camps. Concerning the civilian nature of refugee camps, see UNHCR, EXCOM Conclusion No. 26 (XXXIII): *Note on the Protection of Refugees in Armed Conflict Situations*, EC/SCP/25; EXCOM Standing Committee, 14th Meeting, EC/49/SC/INF.2; General Assembly Resolution 60/128, A/RES/60/128, para. 13.

camps. Pakistan used Afghan refugees, who had fled from the Soviet invasion in 1979, for its anti-Soviet campaign (Grare, 2003). Governments' condoning, permitting or encouraging the presence of soldiers in refugee camps would place other ordinary refugees in danger. In Zaire, opposing factions attacked refugee camps because of the presence of soldiers in them. Although such an obvious case as Zaire may be extreme, there are more subtle but similar situations in many refugee places.

The militarisation of refugee camps, is clearly to be avoided. The important point here, however, is that "refugees-as-security threat" tells only one side of the overall refugee situation. They do not consider the fact that many governments of countries of asylum do not admit the fact that they utilise refugee presence for their political advantage while emphasising the burden of hosting refugees[46].

Similarly, it is also appropriate to revisit the "refugees-as-economic threat" view: While the supporters of this view regard refugees (and immigrants) as competitors in the labour market, they do not examine how refugee labour, especially low-paid labour, contributes to economic growth. A study done by the Sustainable Development Policy Institute (SDPI, 2003) showed the positive impact of Afghan refugees on Pakistan's GDP. The researchers found that refugees contributed to the economic growth of Pakistan by their engagement in local business, their low-paid employment in production, and their increased demand for relief items by virtue of their presence. Similarly, UNHCR reported on Mozambican refugees who had been settled in Zambia in the late1980s. With agricultural land given by a host government, most of the Mozambican refugees became self-sufficient by 1992

---

[46] Stedman & Tanner (2003b) is one of few studies on the political use of refugees by the governments of asylum countries.

and even introduced rice farming and vegetable growing that were new to local farmers, who soon copied them[47]. Although the research lack adequate quantitative data, it is a valuable study that highlights the positive impacts of refugees on host communities.

Some may argue that refugees enjoy better life than local people in developing host countries. Others, based on case studies such as Tanzania or Pakistan, assert that refugees have fewer assets, weaker purchasing power, a smaller social network, and restricted access to the labour market and social services and they suffer from more restricted rights and exploitation compared with local populations (Armstrong, 1988; Jacobson, 2001; SPDI, 2003). The claim that refugees have more access to relief services than locals appears to contain some truth. Local people in a refugee-hosting area, which is often on the periphery of a host developing country, have usually very limited possessions and limited access to services. It is understandable if a relief system that brings refugees food, water and health services provokes envy among locals.

The claim that refugees are better-off than locals, however, does not ring particularly true. It overlooks the fact that refugees do not have such coping mechanisms as ones that locals probably have, especially at the beginning of their stay in a country of asylum. Similar to the studies mentioned above, this author also observed, in her field experiences, that refugees had lost not only their assets and professions but families and social networks upon which they had relied. They had limited access to employment or business opportunities. They were forced to restart their life literally from scratch in a foreign country where the laws, culture and systems might not support them as well as in their own country. Without free assistance, their survival may not be possible.

So far, various viewpoints on refugees have been presented. To

---

[47] UNHCR, *The State of the World's Refugees*, 1995, p. 168.

summarise, although there are some legitimate reasons for raising concern over the presence of refugees, some of the refugees-as-threat views fail to consider the special circumstances in which refugees are placed. They also fail to take into account the positive impacts that refugees can have on host communities. What can be drawn from this analysis is the inter-relation between refugees and a host country. The refugees' presence does affect the host communities/country either positively or negatively, while how the host communities/country treat refugees also affects the way that refugees live (or behave) in the country. If a host country takes an exclusive refugee policy and its society dislikes foreigners, refugees will have no chance to become good members of that society. Kato (1994) says:

> By making efforts to create conditions for coexistence with others ... we can bring about a generous society where we can foster a matured awareness and regard refugees not as the costly subjects of protection but as people with whom to live together. Furthermore, such a society that integrates refugees as compatriots offers the prospect of re-vitalising itself through developing latent talent of refugees and creating opportunities to exchange various ethnics and colourful cultures (p. 18)[48].

This study supports Kato's view and makes the assumption that refugees can become an asset to a host community/country, instead of being a burden, through efforts to promote coexistence of the two communities. Such a position as Kato's and this study's to promote coexistence is more based on social values and human rights while the "refugee-as-threat" position is more focused on the survival of a country (of asylum) and its people. The latter might sound convincing in today's world where many individuals struggle against uncer-

---

[48] The original is in Japanese, translated by the author.

tainty due to poverty, recession or continued conflict. However, since it is realistically and ethically impossible to maintain such "problematic populations" in a single place in the world, it is inevitable to consider how to achieve the coexistence of refugees and nationals of a host country.

The stand-off of the two positions appears to be similar to controversies on economic growth and the environment in the 1970s. At that time, the question was a choice between "economic growth with environmental destruction" or "environmental protection with slow economic growth" (Meadows et al., 1972; Barkley & Seckler, 1975). Today, however, the environment has become an element that must be taken into consideration in development programmes without question. Similar to environmental issues, the existence of refugees is one of the facts that the present world cannot ignore but must learn to manage as long as wars, dictatorships and oppression continue to exist in the world.

So far, the views on refugees as threats and as assets have been mentioned as two opposing positions. However, the world indeed has responded to refugee situations with the two positions mixed. For example, many countries, both developing and industrialised, have provided protection or granted temporary asylum even when xenophobic reactions existed in the countries. Japan also improved the procedure for refugee status determination.

This brings us to the point that policies and assistance programmes should promote "fostering a matured awareness," living together with refugees and "developing their latent talent". Local settlement, which this study will examine, is one of those policies that promote the coexistence of the two communities.

2.4 Summary

This chapter refuted the refugee-as-threat view and argued that assisting and protecting refugee is a humanitarian need to which international communities should inevitably respond. Although there are reasonable reasons for state governments and their people to view refugees as threats and burden, refugees are, by definition, people who cannot enjoy national protection in their own country and that because of that, international communities should find ways to assist them.

Furthermore, refugees, who are often seen as economic burden to host communities, were found to create positive impacts on host communities in the past. Whether refugees are burden or can become assets to host communities do not solely rely on refugees, but how host communities treat refugees makes impacts on them. Therefore, this study urges the need for policies to develop refugees' potentials, make them useful to host societies, and promote coexistence of refugees and host communities.

This chapter also provided basic information on the international system of refugee protection, its humanitarian principle, and actors/stakeholders involved in the system. The discussion emphasised the requirement for UNHCR's work to remain non-political while acknowledging that the actual situations may often blur the distinction between humanitarian and political concerns. The chapter illustrated the changing nature of coordination, which is becoming increasingly more complex with more actors with various interests involved in recent refugee situations.

Chapter **3**

Refugee Aid and Development Doctrine

Chapter 2 first reviewed the international system of refugee protection and discussed its principle and reality, its humanitarian and non-political aspects. Chapter 2 then went on to survey the pervasive perception that refugees are a threat and burden to host governments and communities. The analysis of the last chapter, however, concluded that refugees may become assets to the host community depending on how the host government and communities receive them. The last chapter, therefore, urged the need for policies to benefit both refugees and local communities and promote the coexistence of the two.

This chapter will examine the appropriateness of the Refugee Aid and Development Doctrine as a basis for policies on refugee protection and assistance. For this purpose, sections 3.1 and 3.2 will first review the international process and the evolution of the Refugee Aid and Development debates. These sections will highlight how refugee situations changed as world politics changed from the 1950s to the 1990s and will also explain how such changes in refugee situations impacted the Refugee Aid and Development debates. The sections will further examine how the international community, mainly UNHCR, formalised the Refugee Aid and Development Doctrine in the international system of refugee protection. Finally, section 3.3 will examine the criticisms of the doctrine.

3.1 Initial Debates: Refugees for Development (the 1970s and the 1980s)

This section will explain that debates on Refugee Aid and Development emerged as a new approach to the development of African countries. For this purpose, the section will first explain that changing world political and economic environment increased refugee population in developing countries after the 1970s and highlight that the changes in refugee situations in these decades necessitated to link refugee assistance with development activities. The section will also discuss another political trend, i.e., NIEO movement, which oriented the initial debates on Refugee Aid and Development to the development of African countries rather than development of refugees. The section will then examine the initial process of Refugee Aid and Development discourse, i.e., the ICARA process.

3.1.1 Changing Refugee Situations

Behind the emergence of the Refugee Aid and Development Doctrine were three new dimensions of the refugee situations after the late 1960s: (1) refugee movements scaled up after the 1970s, (2) they occurred mostly in developing countries unlike in the previous decades when refugee issues were concentrated mainly in Europe[49], and (3) no solution to the new refugee situations in developing countries, especially in Africa, was foreseen in the immediate future.

In the late 1970s, refugee population drastically increased in

---

[49] In 1494-50, there were people fleeing from China to Hong Kong for political reasons. UNHCR survey indicated that of Hong Kong's population (some 2.25 million at that time), 30% of them could have been classified as "refugees" In the 1950. This was the first case of UNHCR's involvement, albeit limited, in a refugee situation outside Europe. UNHCR, *The State of the World's Refugees*, 2000.

African countries (see Figure 3-1). The refugee population increased in Africa from some 1.6 million in 1975 to 4.8 million in 1979. Despite some fluctuation in the 1980s, the overall upward trends led to 5.8 million refugees in Africa by 1990s (i.e., 362% increase within 15 years). With the Cold War heightened during these decades, a number of proxy wars that erupted in Africa, Central America and Afghanistan dramatically increased the world refugee population. Until the 1960s, the total refugee population did not exceed 2.5 million people[50]. However, it increased to 2.8 million in 1975, 5 million in 1978, 8.4 million in 1980 and nearly 15 million by the end of 1989.

Such a scale of refugee presence created unprecedentedly complex problems. Refugee situations in the previous decades had been more manageable. In 1954, refugees who were not yet able to find their solution or "who [did] not wish to be repatriated and who [had] not been completely assimilated" in the countries of residence numbered only 350,000[51]. For many of those 350,000 refugees whose solutions had not been established, UNHCR recommended resettlement to a third country or "economic integration" of many of such refugees in the countries of residence. The proposed budget amounted only to US$2,450,000 covering housing schemes, vocational training, economic assistance and other services that were to facilitate the integration of refugees in the countries of residence[52].

Similarly, in the case of some 200,000 Hungarian refugees in Austria and Yugoslavia in the first half of 1957, more than 170,000 had already been resettled in over thirty countries and some 27,000

---

[50] The refugee statistics of the 1960s are based on UNHCR, *The 1951 Refugee Convention: Questions & Answer*, 2003, p. 12. The rest of the statistics are from UNHCR, *The State of the World's Refugees*, 2000, Annex 3.
[51] *UNHCR Report to the UN General Assembly*, A/2648, 1954, para. 232.
[52] Ibid.

84   *Linking Refugee Aid with Development*

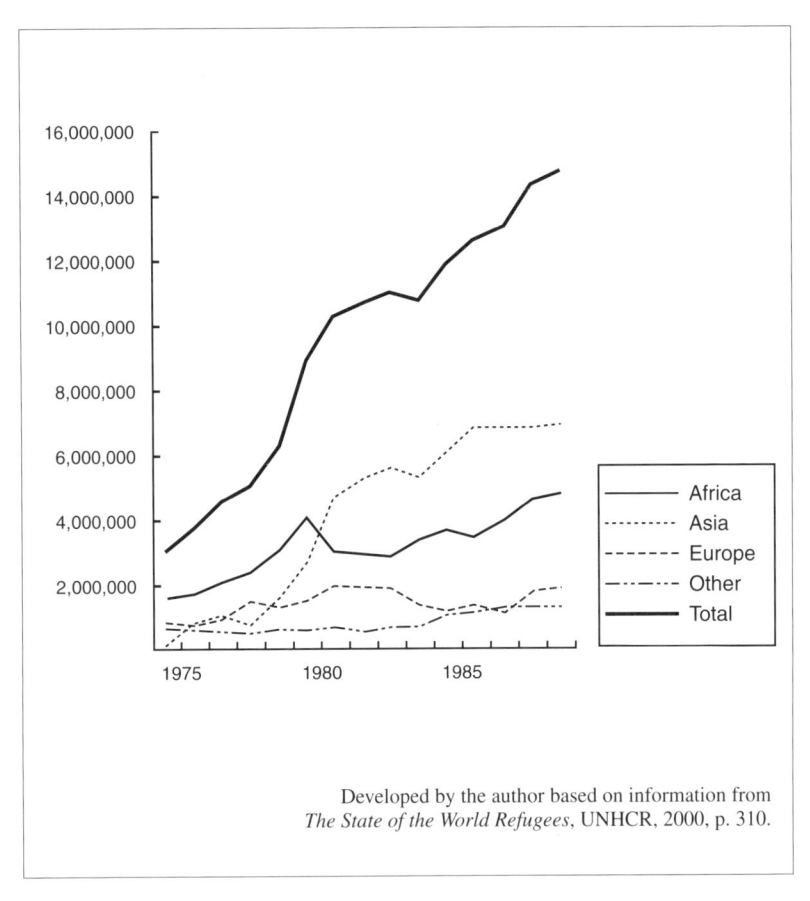

Developed by the author based on information from
The State of the World Refugees, UNHCR, 2000, p. 310.

Figure 3-1: Refugee Population in the 1970s and 1980s

voluntarily returned to Hungary by the end of the year[53]. To sum up, refugee problems in the 1950s found their permanent solutions in a relatively short time and without much resource required.

Rapid progress in European refugee situations until the mid-1960s was the results of the political and economic situations in which European and North American countries were placed. Those countries, first of all, enjoyed economic growth and needed more labourers. They, linking refugee policies with those on immigrants, were thus able to absorb refugees as permanent immigrants in their countries. More precisely, receiving refugees as immigrant labourers matched their economic interests.

The other contributor to rapid improvement in refugee situations until the early-1960s was the Cold War. Western countries' receiving refugees from the Eastern block had obvious political implications, creating positive images of the West. These political and economic situations made it possible to bring solutions to the refugee problems through resettlement to western countries.

Situations after the mid-1960s, however, were different. First, the wars in Africa and Latin America did not have any foreseeable end, offering no option for voluntary repatriation. Complicating the matter were changes in economic situations of European and North American countries that used to receive refugees from Eastern Europe. Western economies were no longer at their peak but had slowed down after the late 1960s. Refugees as a potential labour force were not attractive any longer. Hence, resettlement as a durable solution rapidly declined in scale[54].

On the one hand, prolonged wars blocked any voluntary repa-

---

[53] *UNHCR Report to the UN General Assembly*, A/3828, Rev.1, 1958, para. 2, 4, 22, and 23.
[54] The exception was Indochinese refugees (see Chapter 2). For 20 years from 1975, some 1,312,000 Indochinese refugees were resettled in third countries.

triation while on the other hand, resettlement opportunities were not open to many. Consequently, the majority of refugee situations, which were mostly in developing countries, could not be resolved, with a number of refugees having to remain in countries of asylum for prolonged periods[55].

The large scale presence of refugees brought serious challenges to host countries where their infrastructure was already fragile. While the host governments could not provide adequate infrastructure even for their own people, sheltering, feeding and providing health and other basic services for refugees became an additional burden. Environment degradation also raised serious concern, for example, when trees were cut down for daily fuel in refugee camps. Under such circumstances, African countries started appealing to the international community with regard to the negative impact of refugees on the development of their nations and the burdens that were imposed on them. This was the beginning of the debates on Refugee Aid and Development.

3.1.2 Pre-ICARA Process

The initial debates on Refugee Aid and Development led by African countries thus focused mainly on the development issues of host countries and the international responsibilities for burden-sharing. Consequently, debates on Refugee Aid and Development in the early days did not pay adequate attention to the quality of refugee life nor responsibilities of host countries.

It is generally considered that two International Conferences on Assistance to Refugees in Africa (ICARA I and II), which were held in Geneva in 1981 and 1984, were the first milestones of international debates on refugee aid and development. This is generally accepted,

---

[55] Such refugees who stay in countries of asylum for a prolonged period are called "protracted refugee" caseloads.

but, the initial arguments of African countries cannot be isolated from an atmosphere pervading Africa and the world in the 1960s and 1970s when African countries began vigorously appearing on the international scene with their ideology on development. Although the previous studies ignored it, it is important to understand the influence of the North-South relations on the initial debates on Refugee Aid and Development. Behind the evolution of the Refugee Aid and Development debates in the early days was a movement called the New International Economic Order (NIEO).

NIEO was a movement in the 1970s with the aim of establishing fair economic relation between developing and developed countries. Developing countries saw themselves as "subordinate" (Amin, 1990) to developed countries in the old economic order. NIEO aimed to replace it with an equal relationship in which rights and demands of the developing countries would be respected. In May 1974, the UN General Assembly adopted the "Declaration and Program of Action of the New International Economic Order" [56] and later in the same year approved the "Charter of Economic Rights and Duties of States" [57].

The Declaration and Program of Action of the New International Economic Order stated in its preamble the objective of NIEO was to "correct inequalities and redress existing injustice... eliminate the widening gap between the developed and the developing countries" [58]. The principles of the declaration highlighted rights and sovereignty of the developing countries over their own territory and resources, responsibilities of developed countries for assisting developing countries, and respect for development based on indigenous cultures and systems.

---

[56] UN General Assembly Resolution, A/RES/3201(S-VI), 1974.
[57] UN General Assembly Resolution, A/RES/3281 (XXIX), 1974.
[58] UN General Assembly Resolution, A/RES/3201(S-VI), 1974.

In the Charter of Economic Rights and Duties of States, statements on the rights and interests of developing countries became more explicit. The objectives can be summarised as follows[59]:
1. Promotion of the economic growth of developing countries ;
2. Achievement of more rational and equitable relations between developing and developed countries;
3. Strengthening of economic independence of developing countries; and
4. Promotion of effective international cooperation for development[60].

Bringing NIEO to the UN was the result of many years of preparation by developing countries to respond to their unequal relations with developing countries. The creation of the United Nations Conference on Trade and Development (UNCTAD) in 1964 was a precedent to NIEO. Then in 1973, the Fourth Conference of Heads of States or Governments of Non-Aligned Countries at Algiers adopted the formal proposal of NIEO, which was eventually brought to the UN in 1974. Although losing its momentum in the 1980s, the movement of NIEO eventually led to the adoption of Rights to Development in 1986[61].

As such, the third-world led NIEO movement in the 1970s is often considered as a great triumph of developing countries (Amin, 1990; Caspersz, 2004; Sato, 2004), through which African countries gained power to voice their claims to the international community.

It is worth noting that the Refugee Aid and Development debates emerged in this political trend of the decade. Although not many previous studies pointed out the linkage between the NIEO

---

[59] UN General Assembly Resolution, A/RES/3281 (XXIX), 1974, Preamble.
[60] UN General Assembly Resolution, A/RES/3281 (XXIX), 1974.
[61] UN General Assembly Resolution, A/RES/41/128, 1986.

movement and Refugee Aid and Development[62], Callamard (1990/1993) implicitly mentioned their connection:

> The call for RAD [Refugee Aid and Development] is representative of the broader attempt by African governments to re-establish their legitimacy as the focal point of development planning, in the face of international criticisms, structural adjustment programs imposed by external organizations, and national crisis. RAD seeks to reverse the circumstantial and fragmented concept of refugee assistance by attributing to the political agency, that is the state, a leading role in the design and implementation of refugee programs. (p. 142)

Considering the international trends surrounding the development of African countries in the 1970s, it is only natural that the initial debates on Refugee Aid and Development centred on the development of African countries rather than true linkage of refugee assistance with development. Consequently, development of refugees was placed in a secondary position.

3.1.3 ICARA Process

Table 3-1 shows main international conferences, sessions of the UN General Assembly and UNHCR Executive Committees that took up the issues on refugees in Africa. Already in the 1960s and 1970s, African countries had ideas to incorporate refugee pro-

---

[62] During the ICARA process, the linkage between Refugee Aid and Development and NIEO as well as the right to development was debated among researchers. For example, in 1985, a year after ICARA II, a seminar on "Refugee and Development in Africa" took place in Sweden. At this seminar, researchers such as Nobel (1987a: 47) and Dieng (1987:55) presented papers on rights issues relating to development. Although in the seminar, Kibreab (1987: 63) and Bulcha (1987: 73) presented cases of refugee situations in Sudan, seminar discussion centred on development of African nations (Nobel, 1987: 61, 91).

grammes into larger development schemes called "zonal development" (Betts, 1984/1993; Gorman, 1986). It is, however, ICARA I and ICARA II that drew international attention to refugee problems in Africa and the need for "new approaches"[63] that link refugee assistance with development programmes.

The achievement of ICARA I was the attainment of international recognition on the sacrifice of refugee-hosting countries in Africa and consensus for the needs of additional infrastructure in refugee-hosting areas. The UN General Assembly's resolution 35/42 in 1980, in which the convening of ICARA I was decided, recognised "social and economic burden placed on African countries of asylum as a result of the increased influx of refugees and subsequent impact on their development ...and their] heavy sacrifice"[64] and appealed to "the international community to provide all necessary assistance to the countries of asylum"[65].

ICARA II brought forth a concept in approaching the problems and concrete proposals for development projects needed in refugee-hosting countries. Its Declaration and Programme of Action started with the global responsibility for refugee problems in Africa and "the need for equitable burden-sharing by all ... members [of the conference]" [66]. The president of the conference also stated that the conference was supposed to be "the translation into reality of the new concept which consisted in linking Refugee Aid and Development aid....and [this new approach would be] a new form of co-operation for development [italics added][67]".

A total of 128 projects of US$362 million were proposed, in addition to US$160 million that had already been incorporated in the

---

[63] *Report of the Secretary-General, Addendum*, A/39/402/Add.1, 1984.
[64] UN General Assembly Resolution, A/RES/35/42, 1980, Preamble.
[65] Ibid., para. 8.
[66] *Report of the Secretary-General*, A/39/40, 1984, Annex, para. 2.
[67] Ibid., para. 35

Refugee Aid and Development Doctrine 91

UNHCR's 1984 budget[68]. The number of refugees in Africa in 1984, according to UNHCR, was some 3.4 million persons. The proposed projects included ones on agriculture (e.g., hydro-agricultural development, irrigation schemes), education (e.g., construction of schools, skills development), health (e.g., construction and rehabilitation of hospitals), water (e.g., construction and rehabilitation of wells and other water supply infrastructure) and other infrastructure construction (e.g., road building)[69]. These figures show that the scale of the refugee problems and assistance became tremendous level compared with the budget of some US$2.45 million for 350,000 European refugees in the 1950s. The budget per capita increased from US$7 to US$153 in thirty years.

Because of the inclusion of this large amount of projects, ICARA II is often considered as a pledging conference (Koizumi, 1998). Although such a judgement on ICARA II is indeed correct, it is also worth recognising the importance that the conference formed the conceptual foundation of the Refugee Aid and Development as an aid doctrine. Apart from the emphasis on the burden-sharing and infrastructure projects in refugee-hosting communities, ICARA II also urged solution-oriented and development-oriented refugee assistance, and further provided an implementation framework to achieve such objectives.

The Declaration and Programme of Action of ICARA II highlighted local settlement as desired approach in the countries of asylum "where voluntary repatriation is not immediately feasible"[70]. Voluntary repatriation, no doubt, was regarded as the most ideal situation. If it was not possible, settlement programmes were recommended as a more favourable option than care and maintenance.

---

[68] Ibid., para. 6.
[69] *Report of the Secretary-General, Addendum*, A/39/402/Add.1, 1984, para. 35.
[70] *Report of The Secretary-General*, A/39/402, 1984, Annex, II, para. 3.

92 Linking Refugee Aid with Development

Table 3-1: Main International Conferences and Discussions on Refugee/Returnee Aid and Development

Year	International Conference, Meetings (Ones in italic are concerned about returnee aid and development.)	Key Points
1967	Conference on the Legal, Economic, and Social Aspects of African Refugee Problems	(1) Recommend zonal integration and development schemes to benefit both refugees and the local population.
1979	the Pan-African Conference on the Situation of Refugees in Africa	(2) To incorporate refugee programmes into larger development schemes
1980	UN GA, 25 November 1980 (A/RES/35/42)	UN General Assembly Resolution 35/42 (1) Recognition on the "heavy sacrifices that the countries of asylum are making" for assisting refugees (2) Urging international community to support refugee-hosting countries (burden-sharing)
1981	First International Conference on Assistance to Refugees in Africa (ICARA I), Geneva, 10 April, 1981 (A/RES/35/42, A/RES/36/124)	UN General Assembly Resolutions 35/42 and 36/124 (1) The burden of the host countries was recognised. (2) International financial support was sought.
1984	Second International Conference on Assistance to Refugees in Africa (ICARA II), Geneva, 9-11 July 1984 (A/39/402, A/39/402/Add.1)	Declaration and Programme of Action (1) Solution-oriented programmes such as voluntary repatriation and local settlement should be promoted. (2) UNDP is the main actor for developmental activities. (3) UNHCR is the focal position for all refugee affairs.
1984	UNHCR EXOM, 28 August 1984 (A/AC.96/645)	Conclusion (1) Adoption of Principles of Action in Developing Countries
1984	UN GA, Thirty-ninth session, 22 August 1984	UN General Assembly Resolution 39/139 (1) Endorses the declaration and programme of Action of ICARA II. (2) Local integration to be promoted when voluntary repatriation is not feasible.
1991	UN GA, Seventy-eighth session, 19 December 1991	Resolution 46/182 (1) Ensure "a smooth transition from relief to rehabilitation and development.
1994	*UNHCR, EXCOM, 11 October 1994 (A/AC.96/839)*	Conclusion on the Continuum from Relief to Rehabilitation and Development (1) Enhance the capacity of UNHCR to "support voluntary repatriation and a sustainable reintegration of the returnees in their countries."
1996	*UNHCR, EXCOM Standing Committee, 2nd Meeting, 18 March 1996 (EC/46/SC/CRP)*	UNHCR Assistance Activities in Countries of Origin (1) Strengthen cooperation with other international agencies (UNDP, WFP, UNICEF) to ensure a sustainable and durable solution in countries of origin.

1997	UNHCR, EXCOM Standing Committee, 6th meeting, 6 January 1997 (EC/47/SC/CRP.7)	Social and Economic Impact of Large Refugee Populations on Host Developing Countries Conclusions: (1) "The heavy price" of providing asylum recognised. (2) Donors' support to mitigate the negative impact not adequate. (3) "International solidarity" and "burden-sharing" emphasised.
2001	UNHCR Africa bureau, 1 January 2001 (Prepared for the panel discussion of 3 October 2002 during EXCOM 52nd session)	Discussion Paper on Protracted Refugee Situations in the African Region (1) Linking refugee assistance to national development (2) Refugee "participation" in the planning, design, implementation, monitoring and evaluation (3) The promotion of empowerment and "self-reliance" of refugees is core concerns" of UNHCR under its mandate to achieve durable solutions. (4) Refugees as active and productive members of society and "agents of development" if given the opportunity...
2001	UNHCR Informal Consultations, 14 December 2001	New Approaches and Partnerships for Protection and Solutions in Africa: Addressing Protracted Refugee Situations in Africa (1) Need for a new strategy to shift the focus from provision of care and maintenance assistance to empowerment of refugees to attain self-reliance
2002	Global Consultations on International Protection, 4th Meeting, 25 April 2002 (EC/GC/02/6)	Local Integration (1) A comprehensive strategy will need to recognise the proper place of local integration and self-reliance in the pursuit of durable solutions.
2002	UNHCR EXCOM, 53rd session, 30 September - 4 October 2002 (A/AC.96/973)	Conclusion (1) Endorse the Agenda for Protection contained in document A/AC.96.965/Add.1 Decisions (1) Reaffirming the importance of international solidarity and burden and responsibility-sharing as a fundamental princip (2) HC's Closing Statement (3) Self-reliance and empowerment of refugees is important.
2003	UNHCR, EXCOM, Standing Committee, 28th meeting, 16 September 2003 (EC/53/SC/INF.3)	Framework for Durable Solutions for Refugees and Persons of Concern (1) Development Assistance for Refugees (DAR) (2) Repatriation, Reintegration, Rehabilitation and Reconstruction (4Rs) (3) Development through Local Integration (DLI)
2004	UNHCR, EXCOM, Standing Committee, 30th meeting, 10 June 2004 (EC/54/SC/CRP.14)	Protracted Refugee Situations (1) Being a refugee involves all the three dimension of poverty: lack of income and assets, voicelessness and powerlessness. (2) Refugee self-reliance is the key element in any strategy dealing with the effects of prolonged and stagnant exile.

Developed by the author based on information obtained from documents listed in the table, OAU documents and *Refugee Aid and Development* by R. F. Gorman, Appendix 1, 1993.

The idea of local settlement was to provide opportunities for refugees to settle in local communities, become self-sufficient, and participate in the development process of host countries. Hence, ICARA II, on the one hand, urged infrastructure-building projects in refugee-hosting communities and, on the other hand, promoted refugees' self-sufficiency.

Concerning the implementation of local settlement projects, the conference encouraged the close coordination between refugee services and development services. The declaration of ICARA II required UNDP to provide technical and capital assistance to strengthen the social and economic infrastructures of host countries while UNHCR remained to support overall refugee matters including the settlement of refugees.

Following ICARA II, UNHCR's Executive Committee (EXCOM) in 1984 adopted the Principles for Action in Developing Countries, which reads, in part:

> Where voluntary return is not immediately feasible, conditions should be created in the country of asylum for temporary settlement of the refugees and their participation in the social and economic life of the community, so they can contribute to its development. For these refugees it is essential to free themselves from dependence on relief, and reach a situation where they can take care of themselves, as soon as possible[71].

With this EXCOM action, the promotion of local settlement officially became one of the UNHCR policy matters. As seen in this section, the ICARA process consolidated the foundation of the Refugee Aid and Development Doctrine.

Pursuing these international debates and agreements, develop-

---

[71] *Refugee Aid and Development, Principles for Action in Developing Countries*, EXCOM, the thirty-fifth session, A/AC.96/645, 1984, para. (d).

ment-oriented refugee programmes (local settlement) started in various countries of asylum including Malawi, Somalia, Tanzania, Uganda, and Pakistan. Land-abundant nations including Zambia, Uganda and Tanzania chose agriculture-based rural settlement projects. Countries that were not able to provide land for refugees, such as Pakistan and Malawi, still provided opportunities for them to be engaged in small-scale business and employment[72].

3.2 Recent Debates: Development for Refugees?

This section will examine debates on Refugee Aid and Development in the 1990s and after. The debates of the 1990s first judged that attempts to link refugee aid with development in the previous decade had mostly failed. Then, the world attentions moved away from refugee situations to returnee situations. In the 2000s, the Refugee Aid and Development was put forward by UNHCR.

3.2.1 Failure in the ICARA Process

Both researchers and aid practitioners seemed to agree that most of the attempts in the 1980s to link refugee aid and development met with failure. For example, UNHCR's review in 1994 concluded that "the efforts made to date in the area of refugee aid and development had limited results..."[73]. NIEO already lost its momentum in the 1980s with countries in the northern sphere starting to criticise it. Similarly, surrounding the efforts to link refugee aid with development were critical donors' responses, reluctant development actors, and inadequate initiatives from host governments. All these contributed to the end of the ICARA process.

---

[72] UNHCR, *The State of the World's Refugees*, 2000.
[73] UNHCR, *Returnee Aid and Development*, 1994.

In later attempts, experiences in the 1980s were not put to use but forgotten. The same problems were indeed repeated again later in the 1990s in attempts to link refugee repatriation with development programmes in their war-torn home countries. Further in the 2000s, renewed efforts for Development Assistance for Refugees (DAR) need to be based on the lessons learnt from the 1970 to 1980s. Therefore, it is worth revisiting the attempts in the ICARA process and identifying lessons useful to today's refugee aid operations.

What became evident in the ICARA process were conflicts of interest among actors surrounding Refugee Aid and Development. UNHCR[74] and researchers[75] on refugee assistance generally agreed that stand-offs between donors and refugee-hosting countries had led to the insufficient funding for projects. They also agreed that gaps in administration and programme management resulted in limited responses from development agencies.

Refugee-hosting countries were interested in gaining compensation for damages caused by refugee influx. They hoped additional resources would be secured for this purpose (Gorman, 1990/1993: 64; Koizumi, 1998: 150). They were, however, less keen to grant refugees economic and social rights that were prerequisite for engaging refugees in productive activities (Gorman, 1990/1993: 70; Callamard, 1991/1993: 142; Crisp, 2001:4). They were also not keen to incorporate refugee-related issues into national development plans (Gorman, 1990/1993: 77).

The main interest of the donor states, on the other hand, was the overall decrease in world refugee populations. Indeed, the total

---

[74] Ibid. See also UNHCR, *The State of the World's Refugees*, 1995 and 2000.
[75] Among the reviews that commonly pointed out the stand-offs between donors and African countries, Gorman's study (1990/1993) presents its unique analysis on actors with quantitative data and qualitative analysis on actors' behaviours.

refugee population continued to increase from the 1980s to the early 1990s, reaching over 27 million people in 1995. Africa alone hosted over 11 million refugees in 1995 as opposed to some 5 million in 1989[76]. The donor states suspected that African countries were using the Refugee Aid and Development debates to obtain additional funds for their development rather than solving refugee problems (Crisp, 2004: 4). Donor support quickly shrunk after ICARA II.

From 1985 to 1991, only some US$12 million were contributed to UNDP's Trust Fund for Refugee-Related Development Activities in Africa (Gorman, 1990/1993: 71). Though additional unreported amounts were channelled through bilateral assistance directly from donors to refugee-hosting countries, the amount given to the Trust Fund was meagre compared with over US$300 million projects called for at ICARA II. Donors, while assigning UNDP to be responsible for development projects in refugee-hosting communities, did not give the tools (i.e., funds) for the agency to assume its responsibility.

On the other hand, host governments, too, did not play assertive roles to attract donor funds. Most of the projects that the governments presented were unfeasible (Gorman, 1990/1993: 73; Koizumi, 1998: 147). Neither did they take assertive actions to mainstream issues of the refugee-hosting areas into their national development plan. Callamard (1990/1993: 137) criticised such trends as focusing on infrastructure construction in refugee-hosting communities as "an alternative development using refugee assistance," rather than linking refugee assistance with development that the Refugee Aid and Development Doctrine is supposed to promote. Similarly, Koizumi (1998: 145) viewed the same phenomena as development

---

[76] These numbers include other persons of of concern to UNHCR such as returnees and internally displaced persons, the number of which significantly increased from the 1990s.

assistance for African countries with little attention given to refugees. Though not many research and reports provide evaluation on the host governments, the views of Callamard and Koizumi seem to be appropriate[77].

On the side of the UN, UNDP, though having been active in technical assessment for ICARA II, was rather reluctant to ensure infrastructure projects in refugee affected areas (Betts, 2004; Gorman, 1990/1993; Koizumi, 1998). One of the problems often observed was that a short-cycle of refugee-related projects did not match the traditional multiple-year project management systems of the development agency. Gorman (1990/1993: 78) stated that UNDP did not make adequate efforts to reconcile the differences. This situation inevitably made UNHCR embark on small-scale infrastructure projects and introduce more developmental activities in their projects. However, as seen in subsequent chapters, development-oriented activities by UNHCR cannot make much impact on the development of host communities.

All in all, the ICARA process, though presenting reasonable grounds for its argument, had no aggressive central promoter for its implementation. Consequently, when international politics changed in the 1990s and voluntary repatriation became feasible in various situations in the world, Refugee Aid and Development was forgotten in the international community. In this context, researchers and practitioners concluded that attempts in Refugee Aid and Development in the 1980s failed. Such a conclusion seems to be appropriate in a sense that commitment of actors to the Refugee Aid and Development had never been adequate and that the issues of protracted refugee situations became neglected in the 1990s.

Previous evaluations, however, overlooked an important point,

---

[77] Based on this author's experiences with local stake holders of refugee assistance.

that is, impacts on refugees. They were all based on the viewpoints of development of host communities but without considering the aspects of refugees' development. Nor did they evaluate the impacts on relationships between refugees and locals. Did any developmental activities such as agriculture or business have any positive impacts on refugees? Did infrastructure projects contribute to the improvement of relation between refugees and locals? These questions, which were important from the viewpoint of refugee protection, were not adequately examined. The ICARA process was a failure. Lack of donor support, and the like, however, formed only part of its failure; in fact, the important failure was that the process did not pay sufficient attention to refugees.

3.2.2 Refugees Forgotten (the 1990s)

After the end of the Cold War, the proxy wars began ending in many countries, which enabled refugees to return to their homes. The world, thus, turned its attention from refugee-hosting countries to post-conflict countries to which refugees were returning. Similarly, Refugee Aid and Development shifted its focus from host countries to refugee repatriation and reintegration in countries of origin.

The issues of refugee repatriation, and returnee reintegration in relation to the reconstruction of war-torn home countries were more appealing to the international community than those concerning the development of refugee-hosting countries. As A. Betts (2004: 4) stated, many donor states have their economic and political interests in the reconstruction of countries in post-conflict situations. UNHCR began aggressively approaching development actors such as the World Bank and Japan International Cooperation Agency (JICA) to make arrangements for the latter to enable early intervention in post-conflict countries.

The international system of refugee protection of the 1990s

was thus mostly focused on refugee repatriation and reintegration of returnees with little attention given to protracted refugee caseload. Loescher (2003) criticised this repatriation-only approach as follows:

> Because UNHCR focused almost entirely on repatriation during the past decade, it also virtually ignored other possible solutions, often to the detriment of refugees. With less donor funding for operations other than repatriation and emergency relief, a range of traditional solutions-local integration projects, educational programs, income-generating projects, and the promotion of refugee participation-disappeared from the Office's [UNHCR's] possible options for long-staying refugee populations. (p. 10)

The positive side of the 1990s, however, was that the need to link humanitarian assistance with development gained consensus in the international community. In this decade, problems similar to ones identified in the ICARA process were taken up as "gap" issues (Crisp, 2001); Funding gap, relief-development gap and gaps related to programme management were discussed. Frequently debated was how to fill the gap between humanitarian (or returnee) aid and development: The need for the early intervention of development actors was seriously sought.

In 1999, UNHCR initiated what was called the Brookings Process with development actors and concerned governments to improve cooperation and funding mechanism. The World Bank and other international development agencies began seriously adjusting their traditional development approach to a more flexible one. Equally advocated was a "Do-no-Harm" approach that urged humanitarian workers not to isolate their activities but to make them contribute to the peace and development process (Anderson, 1999; Anderson & Woodrow, 1988).

In sum, the debates in the 1990s overshadowed the protracted refugee situations though raising overall awareness for the need to link relief with development. Whether such an increased awareness on the link between relief and development will finally lead to a better collaboration between refugee assistance and development programmes in countries of asylum is an interesting question when observing the ongoing efforts for Refugee Aid and Development (RAD) and Development through Local Integration (DLI) in the 2000s. The author acknowledge an improved *approach* in the early 2000s but still reserve an answer to the question whether such a new approach has yielded or will yield visible *outcomes*.

3.2.3 Development for Refugees? (the 2000s)

In the 2000s, the Refugee Aid and Development Doctrine, with UNHCR leading the process of concept building, advanced to a policy directly connected with refugee protection. Based on experiences in the 1990s, UNHCR attempted to improve the implementation of linking refugee aid and development under the Convention Plus Initiative. However, the on-going process also appears to repeat the same problems as in the 1980s.

After the focus on returnee aid and development in the 1990s, the turning point came in 2001 when UNHCR Africa Bureau prepared a discussion paper for EXCOM. The document tabled Refugee Aid and Development once again for policy discussions, warning the situation of protracted refugee situations and addressing the quality of asylum life[78]. UNHCR stated in the document that the

---

[78] A protracted refugee situation refers to "one where, over time, there have been considerable changes in refugees' needs, which neither UNHCR nor the host country have been able to address in a meaningful manner, thus leaving refugees in a state of material dependency and often without adequate access to basic rights (e.g., employment, freedom of movement and education) even after a substantial number of years spent in the host country." UNHCR, *Protracted Refugee Situations in the African Region: Discussion Paper*, 2001.

concept of "minimum standards" might fail to ensure refugees' meaningful and dignified life in exile especially when refugees had to stay in exile for prolonged period and further urged adopting the concept of "essential needs" that include civil, social, and economic rights to attain economic self-sufficiency and self-reliance[79].

Subsequently, UNHCR's Informal Consultation in 2001 and Global Consultation in 2002 discussed the issues of refugee self-reliance and local integration in protracted refugee situations[80]. In 2002, UNHCR EXCOM endorsed the Agenda for Protection that included local integration as part of a comprehensive strategy for durable solutions[81].

Discussions at UNHCR's Standing Committee of EXCOM stated that refugees in camp situations for prolonged periods are deprived of such right as freedom of movement, employment, access to land, and education[82]. The synthesis of these became UNHCR's Development Assistance for Refugees (DAR) approach under the Framework for Durable Solutions[83] and Convention Plus Initiative.

---

[79] UNHCR, *Protracted Refugee Situations in the African Region: Discussion Paper*, 2001, para. 4.

[80] UNHCR, *New Approaches and Partnership for Protection and Solutions in Africa: Addressing Protracted Refugee Situations in Africa*. UNHCR informal consultation, December 2001.

[81] UN General Assembly, *Report of the Fifty-Third Session of the Executive Committee of the High Commissioner's Programme*, A/AC.96/973, 8 October 2002.

[82] *Framework for Durable Solutions for Refugees and Persons of Concern*, EXCOM Standing Committee, 28th Meeting, EC/53/SC/INF.3, 16 September 2003; *Convention Plus: Targeting Development Assistance to Achieve Durable Solutions for Refugees*, Discussion paper prepared by Denmark and Japan, High Commissioners forum, 2004.

[83] *Framework for Durable Solutions for Refugees and Persons of Concern*, EXCOM Standing Committee, 28th Meeting, EC/53/SC/INF.3, 16 September 2003.

The Convention Plus Initiative officially launched in 2003 with the overall aim of "addressing all the pressing issues pertaining to refugee protection in today's changing world" [84] that the 1951 UN Convention on Refugees and its 1967 Protocol did not effectively deal with. "Targeting Development Assistance for Refugee Solutions (TDA)" is aimed at one of its objectives, which is to improve "burden and responsibility sharing" through having "North and South [work] together to find solutions for refugees [85]".

TDA is a combined concept of Refugee Aid and Development and Returnee Aid and Development consisting of:
1. Development Assistance for Refugees (DAR)/Development through Local Integration (DLI) for refugee situations.
2. Repatriation, Reintegration, Rehabilitation and Reconstruction (4Rs) for post-conflict countries or countries of origin.

In the Convention Plus Initiative, UNHCR urges donor states to accept burden-sharing, as in the ICARA process. What may be more explicit in this initiative than in the ICARA process are:
1. Emphasis on the development and right of refugees;
2. Incorporation of Refugee Aid and Development concept into refugee protection and durable solutions;
3. Responsibilities for host countries to integrate refugees into their society;
4. Involvement of donor states in the concept building pro-

---

[84] UNHCR, *Lubbers Launches Forum on Convention Plus Initiative*, 27 June 2003.
[85] UNHCR, *Framework for Durable Solutions for Refugees and Persons of Concern*, Core Groups on Durable Solutions, 2003, p. 8. There are three elements in the Convention Plus Initiative. TDA is one of three elements of the Convention Plus Initiative. The other two are strategic resettlement and irregular secondary movement.

cess;
5. UNHCR's participation in development forums to place refugee issues on development agendas.

Concerning points 1 and 2, UNHCR's Informal Consultations in 2001 stated, "...there is a need to shift the focus ... to empowerment of refugees to attain self-reliance"[86]. UNHCR's EXCOM Standing Committee in 2004 further stated, "Refugees' self-reliance is the key element in any strategy dealing with the effects of prolonged and stagnant exile"[87].

The Convention Plus Initiative process is still less assertive about the responsibilities related to host governments (Points 3) than the first two points. Nevertheless, the Framework for Durable Solutions for Refugees and Persons of Concern mentions such points as "the political will of the host government"[88] with regard to Development Assistance for Refugees and "its progressive assurance on refugees' rights and entitlements as those enjoyed by local citizens including freedom of movement, access to education and the labour market, access to public services and assistance"[89].

Another new attempt in this process is the involvement of donor states in the concept-building of Convention Plus (Point 4). Denmark and Japan have become the focal countries of TDA. They have drafted discussion papers on development assistance for refugee

---

[86] UNHCR, *New Approaches and Partnership for Protection and Solutions in Africa*: Addressing Protracted Refugee Situations in Africa,UNHCR informal consultation, December 2001.

[87] UNHCR, *Convention Plus: Targeting Development Assistance to Achieve Durable Solutions for Refugees*, Discussion Paper Prepared by Denmark and Japan, High Commissioner's forum, 2004.

[88] *Framework for Durable Solutions for Refugees and Persons of Concern*, EXCOM Standing Committee, 28th Meeting, EC/53/SC/INF.3, 16 September 2003, p. 10.

[89] Ibid., p. 25.

solutions, presenting their respective priorities in TDA[90]. While donors were basically passive in the ICARA process, the engagement of focal countries in the initiative appears to be intended to oblige their commitment to supporting refugee-hosting communities/countries.

UNHCR, under the initiative, began to participate more actively in development forums (Point 5). The agency became a member of the UN Development Group (UNDG) in 2003. In the same year, the agency took the initiative of joining the OECD/DAC Network on Conflict, Peace and Development Co-operation. They further attempted to include displacement issues in Poverty Reduction Strategy Papers (PRSPs)[91].

The Convention Plus Initiative does not present any dramatically new ideas but it is rather the repackaging of previous debates and attempts from the 1970s to 1990s. It can be said, however, that Convention Plus Initiative attempted, for the first time, to synthesise issues on the development of host countries and those of refugees into the agency's protection mandate, at least at the concept level.

Whether the improvement in the concept will lead to the visible results on the ground will depends on, as seen in the failure in the ICARA process, the commitment of the actors, notably donors, host governments, UNHCR and development agencies, refugees and local stakeholders. However, whether UNHCR is to succeed in making them commit is rather sceptical. Since this chapter deals with the international level, the following discussions will consider host governments, donors and development agencies.

---

[90] UNHCR, *Convention Plus: Targeting Development Assistance to Achieve Durable Solutions for Refugees*, Discussion paper prepared by Denmark and Japan, High Commissioner's forum, 2004.
[91] UNHCR, *Poverty Reduction Strategy Paper: A Displacement Perspective*, October 2004; World Bank, *Toward a Conflict-Sensitive Poverty Reduction Strategy: Lessons From a Retrospective Analysis*, Report N. 32587, 2005.

As discussed in the previous sub-section, the ICARA process did not present adequate incentive for actors to commit themselves to refugee aid and development. Donor states expected the decrease in refugee population, not adequately supporting local settlement programmes. Development actors were not keen enough to overcome their administrative or operational obstacles in supporting refugee-hosing areas. Governments of refugee-hosting countries claimed additional funds, but did not mainstream refugee-related development activities in their development plans. UNHCR failed to serve as an effective coordinator or an advocator for the Refugee Aid and Development Doctrine, but expanded its activities to developmental projects in refugee-hosting areas[92].

Lacking commitment of actors to their respective roles but allowing them to act out of their own interests, refugee aid and development did not succeed in the ICARA process. Similarly, without the firm commitment of actors, the Convention Plus Initiative may not succeed, either. Can the Convention Plus Initiative overcome the problems of the 1980s?

Earlier, this chapter pointed out that UNHCR is less vocal about the responsibilities of actors. UNHCR's lack of assertiveness is particularly shown on documents related to DAR and DLI. The Framework for Durable Solutions lists advantages of the Development Assistance for Refugees (DAR) for actors, which is reflected on the left column of Table 3-2, but little is mentioned about their responsibilities[93]. DAR, however, includes challenges and responsibilities

---

[92] UNHCR's projects on infrastructure for host communities and agriculture and other productive activities for refugees do not include such a comprehensive dimension as usual development projects should have. For this reason, this study uses the term "developmental" or "development-oriented" projects for "developmental" activities of humanitarian agencies to distinguish them from full-scale development programmes organised by development agencies.

[93] *Framework for Durable Solutions for Refugees and Persons of Concern,*

that each actor should take up (see the right column of Table 3-2).

UNHCR's modest appeal to donors and host governments may be the result of the agency's efforts to strike a balance among different interests of various actors. Nevertheless, silence about the responsibilities of the actors may result in the repeat of the failure of the ICARA process. Although assigning two donor countries to be the focal countries of DAR and studying the PRSP process seem to be part of the attempts to gain support from donors and development agencies, such efforts would not produce visible results unless they were sustained for an adequate period.

Furthermore, it is important to continue bilateral discussions with host governments, donors and development agencies. In doing so, UNHCR may need to repack the idea of the Refugee Aid and Development Doctrine in a concept that development actors usually use. DAR and DLI, which are UNHCR specific, are foreign languages to development actors and donors. However, it is important for humanitarians or UNHCR to use "common language" with development actors if they seriously wish to link humanitarian actions with development. Until recently, UNHCR and refugee aid practitioners did not pay much attention to the concepts and mode of operation of development organisations. However, it is primarily humanitarians that have been longing for development actors to come closer to their operation but not the contrary. Instead of insisting on their own way of thinking or work style, it is time that humanitarians approach development actors.

After the failure of macroeconomic centrism, more human-centric concepts are found in the international development arena. Among them are a rights-based approach, human security and human development. All of these, better known to development and donor

---

EXCOM Standing Committee, 28th Meeting, EC/53/SC/INF.3, 16 September 2003, pp. 14-15.

Table 3-2: Refugee Aid and Development: Opportunities and Responsibilities

	Opportunities	Responsibilities
Refugees	- Human development - Enhanced well-being	- Commitment to self-reliance - Appropriate leadership
Host Government/Community	- Development opportunities - Contribution by refugees to development process - Avenues for additional funding - Disparities between refugees and local people to decrease	- Granting refugees rights equal to those enjoyed by nationals - Inclusion of issues related to refugees and refugee-hosting areas into national development plan
Donors/Development Actors	- Opportunities to meet MDGs - Focus of their resources on development-oriented activities rather than long-term refugee care and maintenance - The incentive to secondary movement of refugees to reduce	- Ensuring funds/aid to refugee-hosting communities/countries
UNHCR	- Shared international responsibilities for refugee protection and assistance - Foundations for sustainable programme leading to durable solutions - Diminished psycho-social problems in refugee camps - Refugees' gaining skills that can contribute to the development of their own country once voluntary repatriation becomes feasible	- Longer-term commitment to development-oriented projects - Advocate for the concept of Refugee Aid Development to donors, host countries and development agencies - More effective coordination with other actors

Opportunity boxes were adapted from *Framework for Durable Solutions for Refugees and Persons of Concern,* EC/53/SC/INF, 2003. Responsibility boxes were developed by the author.

communities, embrace both humanitarian and development concerns. Applying such concepts in advocating Refugee Aid and Development Doctrine may help gain interests of development actors, host governments and donors.

3.3 Criticism of the Doctrine

As seen in the previous discussions, the Refugee Aid and Development Doctrine is two-fold: development for refugee-hosting communities (and countries), and development for refugees. The first point is relevant for refugee policy in a sense that assisting/protecting refugees can be attained through fair burden-sharing and broader cooperation within the international community. The second point is even more important from the point of refugee protection. The second point presented the view that refugees have right to live dignified lives and that refugee assistance should enhance their potentials to grow and contribute to their own lives and the development of host communities. By addressing the development needs of both refugees and host communities, the doctrine has a value as a basis for refugee assistance policy.

Before closing this chapter, it is appropriate to discuss criticisms of Refugee Aid and Development. Since the purpose of this chapter is to review the validity of the doctrine, this brief section will take up criticisms that are derived from the principles of humanitarian assistance and refugee protection, but will not deal with operational issues such as implementation process or project cycles. (These issues will be discussed in Chapters 4 and 5.)

3.3.1 Humanitarian Principles

Some researchers question the validity of the Refugee Aid and Development Doctrine in accordance with international humanitarian laws. Mackintosh (2000: 8), for example, argued that a developmental approach in humanitarian assistance contravenes the humanitarian principle of neutrality. She explained that the concept of neutrality has two dimensions. One is about the ideological neutrality of humanitarian actions. The other is about economical neutrality. Mackintosh (2000: 9) stated, "...assistance which is intended to support the local economy runs contrary to the strictures of international humanitarian law."

Mackintosh's argument, however, seemed to have gone too far. The basis for her argument is Paragraph c), Article 23 of Geneva Convention IV, which is to prevent relief items from benefiting any party to a conflict. Paragraph c) provides that a party to the conflict is obliged to allow free passage of relief goods in their territory, intended for the civilians of another party to the conflict when there are no serious reasons for fearing "that a definite advantage may accrue to the military efforts or the economy of the enemy through the substitution of ... goods...".

The starting point of Refugee Aid and Development is the notion that local resources such as health facilities, water supplies and even forests are damaged or over burdened by refugee influx and thus, developmental assistance is meant to ameliorate such situations[94]. First of all, therefore, infrastructure projects under the Refugee Aid and Development has no relation with a war economy that paragraph c) concerns.

Second, constructing small-scale infrastructure cannot anyway make such significant impact as the scale of a "definite advantage". Such significant changes may occur only when development actors organise comprehensive development programmes in refugee-hosting communities. Humanitarian agencies with some small-scale infrastructure projects or developmental activities, however, do not produce such a great impact (as discussed in subsequent chapters).

---

[94] It may become a concern, though, in countries of origin when refugees return home. In post-conflict situations, frequently, war-lords may still control certain geographical areas, and developmental assistance in such places requires appropriate caution to prevent aid from favouring any war-economy and thus hampering the peace process.

3.3.2 Right and Entitlement

More frequently expressed is a criticism from a right and entitlement perspective. Local settlement policy engages refugees in productive activity such as agriculture. As their production increases, free food ration is reduced gradually and eventually eliminated completely. Similarly, some other free services such as water, health and education may not remain free forever. Refugees will be asked to contribute to school fees, health fees and maintenance of wells.

Many, including refugees, researchers and aid workers, criticise such reduction of free services as cuts in entitlement (for example, Macrae & Bradbury, 1998; Bradbury, 1998). This criticism does not have much relevance at the concept level because the notion of self-reliance, a principle of the Refugee Aid and Development, came out of the experiences that free aid services did not meet refugees' right to development, or they even create negative psychosocial impacts. This is, therefore, not a question on concept or principle.

Rather, the argument that the reduction of free services is the denial of refugees' entitlement may become pertinent in the reality of refugee situations. Once a poor assessment decided to reduce services excessively, it might result in deprivation of minimum entitlement for refugees. The Refugee Aid and Development Doctrine contains key principles of self-reliance and integration that should lead to a more dignified refugee life in asylum. The self-reliance principle, at the same time, is accompanied by a risk of undermining refugees' entitlement to assistance if it is not properly implemented.

An explanation may be found in what Armstrong (1998) called "the wave-like 'development trajectory.'" Armstrong pointed out the difficulty of refugees who are obliged to adjust themselves to continuous transitions from crisis at home, to flight, to emergency assistance with access to free services, and to development-oriented assistance with fewer free services (Armstrong, 1998:65). Refugees who may not have recovered from shock, anger, or mourning the loss of their families, and other traumatic events may not be psychologically prepared to restart their life, cultivate land, produce crops or become independent from food aid. If aid workers promote self-reliance too fast, it may overburden vulnerable refugees instead of stimulating their potentialities.

To strike a balance between the welfare of vulnerable refugees and the promotion of self-reliance, a mechanism is needed to assess the socio-economic status of individual refugees in the context of social, economic and legal conditions of a given host country. However, such assessments on the level of self-reliance and the situations of vulnerable refugees are not at all easy.

In short, the issue primarily concerns the implementation of the Refugee Aid and Development Doctrine and local settlement policy. Difficulties in its implementation do not negate the conceptual value in the doctrine. Now, the issue of operationalisation of the doctrine comes in. Even a meaningful doctrine may fail if its concepts are not interpreted into operational terms.

3.4 Summary

This chapter examined the validity of the Refugee Aid and Development Doctrine by reviewing the evolution of the debates on the doctrine. The analysis of this chapter concluded that the Refugee Aid and Development is useful as a doctrine for refugee protection and assistance. The doctrine includes two pillars: development for refugee-hosting communities and development for refugees. Addressing the need for development in refugee-hosting areas is relevant because providing international protection and assistance for a large number of refugees cannot be attained through a government of host country, especially if the country is economically poor.

It can be achieved through the international cooperation and fair sharing of the burden and responsibilities.

The essential importance of the doctrine, however, lies in the second point, i.e., development of refugees. This is to recognise the need and the right of refugees to dignified asylum life, urging to make refugee assistance enhance refugees' capacities, encourage their participation in the delivery of assistance and promote their self-reliance.

The analysis on the ICARA process, however, suggested that the implementation of the doctrine cannot be attained without the commitment of all the actors. To address this problem, this chapter proposed that the Refugee Aid and Development be repacked in one of concepts better known to development actors and donors (e.g., human security). The analysis of the ICARA process also suggested that there were operational issues that hindered the process. Similarly, review of the criticisms of the Refugee Aid and Development Doctrine suggested that the doctrine and local settlement policy might fail unless operational aspects of the doctrine were examined.

Chapter 4
Local Settlement

Chapter 3 examined the evolution of the Refugee Aid and Development Doctrine within the international system of refugee protection. It also provided an overview of the concept of the doctrine itself and local settlement as a refugee policy drawn from the doctrine. The chapter concluded that the doctrine is meaningful because of its attention to the human development of refugees and their rights beyond mere survival. Chapter 3 pointed out that the failures in past attempts to link development with refugee aid were partly due to the lack of commitment of international actors to implementation. Chapter 3 also pointed out that the inadequate operationalisation of the Refugee Aid and Development Doctrine equally contributed to the failure in implementing the doctrine.

This chapter (and subsequent chapters) will, therefore, deal with operational issues at the country and programme/project level, and examine local settlement as a refugee policy and a refugee programme. The chapter will identify effective developmental refugee assistance and its value. This chapter will further argue that developmental refugee assistance, nonetheless, cannot replace development programmes and that the latter is indispensable to achieve the objectives of local settlement.

For this purpose, Section 4.1 will outline UNHCR's local settlement programmes with an overview of its world trends and major activities, and identify developmental activities that refugee assistance programmes of local settlement can effectively organise.

Section 4.2 will highlight the differences between development and humanitarian (refugee) assistance and the limitation of the latter in the development of refugee-hosting countries. This section will argue that developmental refugee assistance should focus its objectives on the well-being of refugees and the harmonious coexistence of refugees and locals. This section will further suggest future actions that should be considered for improving the linkage of refugee aid and development.

4.1 Local Settlement as Refugee Policy

This section will first review the principles of the Refugee Aid and Development Doctrine, on which local settlement policies/programmes are based, and give an overview of UNHCR local settlement programmes of the 1980s. This section identifies developmental activities that refugee assistance (of local settlement) can effectively manage and ones that it cannot.

4.1.1 Key Principles of the Refugee Aid and Development Doctrine

In summary, the Refugee Aid and Development Doctrine is two-fold:

Burden-sharing: International community should support refugee-hosting countries and communities with development programmes in order to alleviate burdens caused by massive refugee influx.

Refugee self-reliance: Refugee assistance should include development-oriented activities in order to improve the quality of refugee life, promote refugee self-reliance, and integrate refugees into host communities.

This sub-section will explain the key principles of the Refugee

Aid and Development Doctrine, that is, burden-sharing, self-reliance and integration.

Burden-sharing: The first principle means opportunities for additional assistance for host governments. Hence, the first point primarily concerns the development of host countries with little direct reference to refugee protection, although it may still contain the implicit importance on refugee protection. That is to say that supporting refugee-hosting communities is expected to promote peaceful coexistence of refugees and locals by ameliorating burden imposed on local communities.

Self-reliance: The second principle directly addresses the value of refugee protection, advocating for such refugee rights as those regarding education, free movement and employment. Self-reliance[95] is a condition in which refugees are able to live without external aid. Achieving self-reliance, therefore, means that refugees are able to cover the cost of food, basic social services such as education and health, and purchase essential domestic items. Self-reliance further refers to refugees' mental capacity to make decisions about their own lives.

In this connection, promotion of self-reliance inevitably encourages refugee participation[96]. Involving refugees in planning, implementation and evaluation of the assistant programme can

---

[95] A synonym for self-reliance is self-sufficiency. A clear distinction between the two may be elusive. However, we may safely say that self-sufficiency refers to more material sufficiency as in "food self-sufficiency" while self-reliance includes both material sufficiency, psychological satisfaction and capacity .

[96] Harrell-Bond (1986) was one of the first researchers who criticised refugee assistance as an imposed assistance and emphasised the need for an assistance that encourages refugees involvement in the planning and implementation of assistance and thus enhance refugees' capabilities. Although the situation described in her work may appear to be obsolete now, the essence of her points, i.e., the importance to refugees key actors in refugee assistance remain valid in today's refugee assistance.

thus be considered essential to self-reliance. The second principle of the doctrine, then, is to provide opportunities for refugees to increase the control over their lives and dignity in exile.

Integration: Recently, the terms "integration" and "local integration" arc more frequently used than "local settlement." The UNHCR programme manual[97] defines local settlement as one of durable solutions that provides opportunities for refugees to become more self-sufficient and get integrated into the economic and social life of the host community (see Chapter 2). However, recent UNHCR documents[98] use "local integration" instead.

Neither "local integration" nor "local settlement" has any formal definition in international refugee law. UNHCR Statute, which was adopted in 1950, uses "assimilation"[99]. However, the word has a connotation of one group (e.g., a refugee group) having to become more or less indistinguishable from other members of the society by losing or hiding their original culture (Kuhlman, 1991: 6). Possibly because of its negative connotation, the word is no longer used in any recent UNHCR documents. By contrast, "integration," meaning that migrants (or refugees) maintain their identity but still become part of the host society (Kuhlman, 1991:6), may be more appropriate and is most frequently used in recent documents.

Crisp (2004: 1) suggested the definition of local integration as a "process which leads to a durable solution for refugees" and which is related to legal, economic and social processes. UNHCR's documents consider it rather as the "end product" that requires "refugees to adapt to host society without having to forego their own cultural identities, host society to welcome refugees, and public institutions

---

[97] *UNHCR Manual,* Chapter 4, 1995.
[98] For example, *Local Integration,* Global Consultation on International Protection, 4th Meeting, EC/GC/02/6, 24 April 2004.
[99] *Statute of the Office of The United Nations High Commissioner for Refugees,* 1950, Chapter II, 8 (c).

Local Settlement

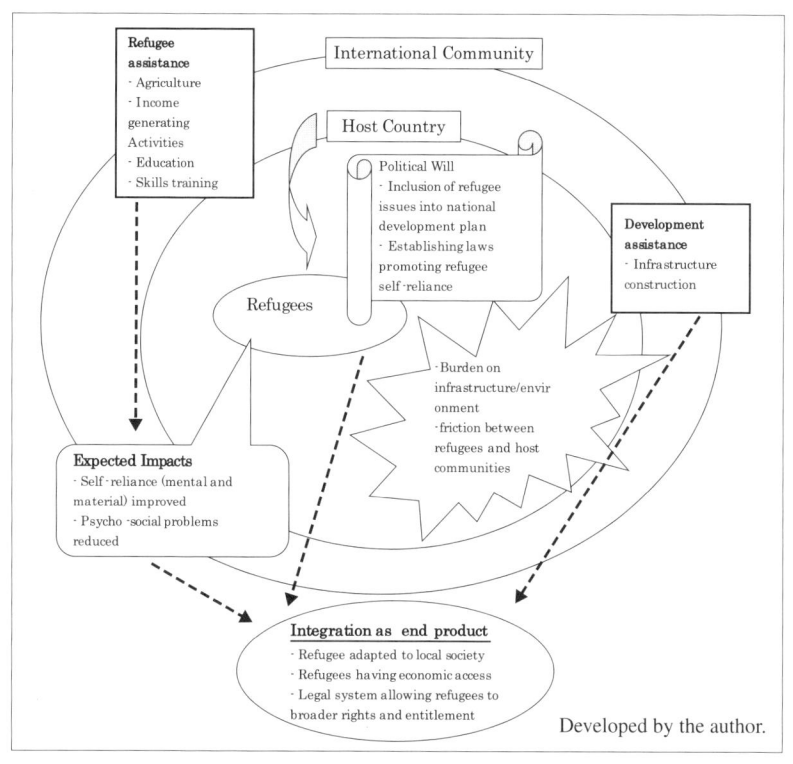

Figure 4-1: Local Settlement Programme

to meet their needs and its goes through legal, economic and social and cultural process"[100].

For the purpose of this study, as defined in Chapter 2, local integration will be used as one of the durable solutions, or goals, in which refugees are part of the local society. Local settlement can be regarded rather as a refugee policy and/or programme that promotes the process of local integration. Figure 4-1 shows the concepts of

---

[100] *Local Integration*, Global Consultation on International Protection, 4th Meeting, EC/GC/02/6, 24 April 2004.

local settlement and local integration in refugee-in-environment model[101].

4.1.2 Overview of Local Settlement

In concert with international debates on linking refugee assistance with development, various countries attempted to promote assistance programmes increasing refugee self-sufficiency through the 1970s and 1980s. Those countries include Malawi, Somalia, Zambia, Tanzania, Sudan, Uganda, and Pakistan.

Land-abundant nations such as Zambia, Sudan, Uganda, and Tanzania chose agriculture-based rural settlement projects. In Africa, 117 settlements were established and 84 of them were still operating as of 1982 (Stein & Clark, 1990). For example, Zambia offered an agriculture-based local settlement programme for some 20,000 Mozambican refugees in the late 1980s. Most of the Mozambican refugees, given agriculture land (2ha/family), seeds, and agriculture tools, became self-sufficient in food by 1992[102]. The programme also included construction of schools, clinics and roads, creating employment opportunities for both refugees and local Zambians.

Other countries, such as Pakistan and Malawi, offered opportunities for them to be engaged in small-scale business and employment. Frequently cited in this category is Income Generating Projects for Refugee Areas (IGPRAs) in Pakistan from 1984 to 1994. It was a joint project with the World Bank, UNHCR, and the Pakistani government to support Afghan refugees and the host country. The US$85-86 million project created employment opportunities for both Afghan refugees and local Pakistanis with nearly 300 projects in the areas of afforestation, irrigation, flood protection,

---

[101] Chapter 5 will discuss integration in more details.
[102] UNHCR, *The State of the World's Refugees*, 1995, p. 168.

Local Settlement 121

road repair/construction and skills training courses[103].
By 1988, over 200 refugee settlements were established worldwide with a population exceeding 1 million. Eighty percent of them were in Africa (Armstrong, 1988). UNHCR allocated a significant portion of its budget to local settlement programmes in the 1980s (see Figure 4-2)[104]. All through the 1980s, local settlement programmes in Africa constituted 40% to 70% of the total

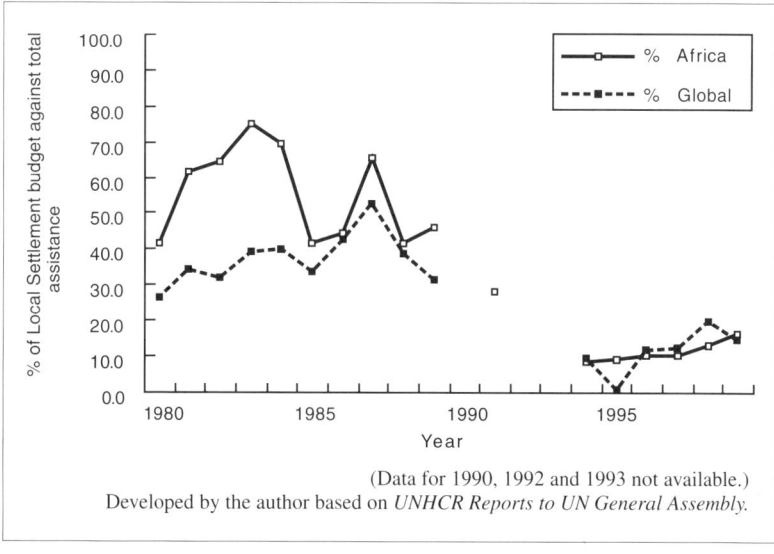

(Data for 1990, 1992 and 1993 not available.)
Developed by the author based on *UNHCR Reports to UN General Assembly*.

Figure 4-2: UNHCR Budget: Local Settlement Programme Against the Total Budget

---

[103] Ibid, p. 161; WB, P*ost-Conflict Reconstruction: The Role of the World Bank*, 1998, p. 37.
[104] *UNHCR Report of the United Nations High Commissioner for Refugees*, A/36/12, A/37/12, A/38/12, A/39/12, A/40/12, A/41/12, A/42/12, A/43/12, A/44/12, A/44/12/Add.1, A/45/12, A/46/12, A/51/12, A/52/12, A/53/12, A/54/12 and A/55/12, 1981-2000. UNHCR budgets mentioned in this section are all from these issues of the reports.

disbursements, much higher than the global average of 25% to 50%. These percentages dropped dramatically in the 1990s reflecting the decreased interest of international communities in protracted refugee caseload in Africa and also the increased opportunities for repatriation. In 1995, for example, local settlement programmes formed only 8.8% of the UNHCR's total expenditure for Africa and 2.4% of its worldwide expenditure. Not many African countries retained local settlement programmes in the 1990s. With the repatriation of some 1.7 Mozambican refugees[105], countries of asylum that offered local settlement programmes shrunk their budget dramatically in 1996, two years after the end of massive repatriation.

The local settlement budget in Tanzania dropped from over US$1 million in 1989 down to US$0.2 million in 1996. There was a similar drop in Zambia from US$3.1 million down to US$0.5 million over the same time period. Similarly, many other countries such as Kenya, Burundi, and Zimbabwe shifted their attention from local settlement to care and maintenance programmes. The exception was Uganda, which continued to offer local settlement programmes for Rwandan and Sudanese refugees all through the 1990s.

The above overview has shown the temporal trends of local settlement programmes. So, this is a convenient point to examine the activities of local settlement programmes in comparison with care and maintenance assistance in refugee camps. Figure 4-3 compares the project budgets for Kenya, which predominantly provided care and maintenance refugee assistance, with Uganda, which is one of the few countries that continued implementing local settlement programmes in the 1990s. Both countries hosted relatively similar profiles of refugees, including Sudanese and Somalis. Their budget

---

[105] Number of repatriated refugees is from UNHCR, *The State of the World's Refugees*, 2000.

size in 1999 was similar, in its total amount as well as cost per capita. However, the difference is the composition of the two budgets. In Uganda, activities to improve refugees' self-sufficiency, such as education and crop production, constituted 27 % of the total budget whereas in Kenya, budget for such activities was limited to 10%. By contrast, material assistance under "domestic needs" (e.g., provision of kitchen utensils, plastic sheet and other domestic items or cash allowances) and "special food" (e.g., supplementary food for vulnerable individuals) is higher in Kenya than Uganda[106].

The budget comparison, presenting sector-level differences, does not provide adequate information on differences in approaches between care and maintenance and local settlement. Some sectors, such as water, do not stand alone either as developmental or relief-oriented sectors. Rather, their detailed activities and approaches determine whether a programme is developmental or relief-oriented. Take the case of water, which, in relief operations, should focus on the supply of adequate and clean water by, for example, operating water tankers to refugee camps.

In local settlement programmes, the water sector activities may pay more attention to refugees' self-management, mobilising refugee communities for management of wells and water fee collection. Similarly, the shelter/infrastructure sector under care and maintenance programmes may simply mean the procurement of plastic sheeting for makeshift tents, or health services may merely provide medical care in refugee camps. The same sectors in local settlement, by contrast, may include the construction of access roads and clinics for both refugees and locals to use, and training for local and refugee health workers.

---

[106] UNHCR's food budget does not include the cost of food that is regularly distributed to each refugee family. The World Food Programme (WFP) supplies food for UNHCR and its partners to distribute to refugees.

124   *Linking Refugee Aid with Development*

	Kenya	Uganda
Type of Assistance	CM	LS/CM
Number of refugees	217,500	218,190
Project Budget (US$)	11,203,434	12,500,330
Cost/person (US$)	51.51	57.29
	%	%
Community Services	2.0	2.6
Crop Production	0.0	4.2
Education	6.9	16.1
Fishery	0.0	0.1
Forestry	0.9	2.4
Income Generation	0.1	0.9
Livestock	0.0	0.3
Domestic Needs	5.8	1.4
Special Food	0.6	0.0
Health	10.9	7.8
Legal Assistance	1.8	0.8
Operational Support	16.4	17.3
Sanitation	0.4	0.3
Shelter/Infrastructure	4.5	3.6
Logistics/Transport	7.7	18.4
Water	3.7	2.2
Others	38.3	21.6
Total	100.0	100.0

Developmental activities included community services, crop production, education, fishery, income generation, and live stock.
Material assistance included domestic needs and special food.

CM: Care and Maintenance
LS: Local Settlement

Uganda
- Developmental activities: 27%
- Material assistance: 1%
- Other activities: 72%

Kenya
- Developmental activities: 10%
- Material assistance: 1%
- Other activities: 84%

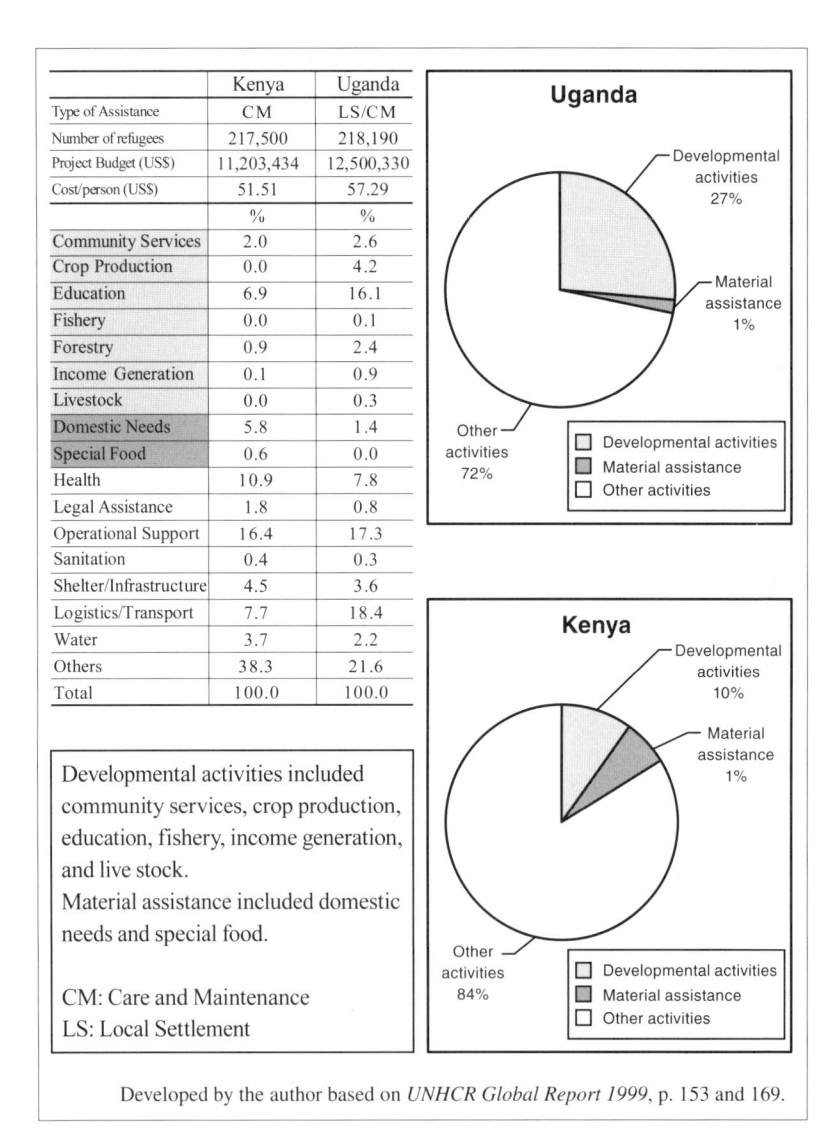

Developed by the author based on *UNHCR Global Report 1999*, p. 153 and 169.

Figure 4-3: Comparison between Care & Maintenance and Local Settlement Programmes–Kenya and Uganda (1998)

It is therefore necessary at this point to further examine the details of assistance activities and its approaches. Following the discussions in the preceding chapters, this section will consider developmental refugee assistance from two perspectives:

Development of refugees: Developmental activities to promote refugee self-reliance and

Development of host communities: Developmental activities to contribute to the development of host communities.

4.1.2 Activities for Development of Refugees

Activities to improve refugee self-reliance often include the following activities:

Agriculture
- Crop production
- Animal husbandry (rabbits, chickens, goats, cows, etc.)

Small Business (Income-Generating Activities)
- Micro-credit schemes for small business (shops, barbers, tea houses, carpentry, dress-making/tailoring, mechanics, etc.)
- Grant schemes for small-business

Human Development
- Leadership training
- Vocational training/skills training
- Education

Previous experiences prove that crop production produces certain achievements. Armstrong (1988) reported on a case from Tanzania (Armstrong, 1988: 61), which showed an increase in refugee household income generated through crop production over five years of period in the 1980s. Average annual earnings from official crop sales in a refugee settlement in rural Tanzania increased from 190 Tanzanian Shilling (Tz Shilling) per family in 1981/82 to 1682 Tz Shilling in 1985/86 (Armstrong, 1988: 66). Another study by

Armstrong (1991: 80) on the same subject reported that refugees' crop production contributed to food stability in surrounding areas and provided a major stimulus to the local economy. Similarly, according to UNHCR's global reports in 2001 and 2003, some 24% of Sudanese refugees in Uganda became independent from food aid in 2001 and the number increased to 56% in 2003.

At the same time, previous studies indicate that the impact of crop production on refugee self-reliance was limited. Studies on Sudan (Harrell-bond, 1986; Kibreab, 1987) and Tanzania (Armstrong, 1988, 1991; Kibreab 1989), and UNHCR's reports on Uganda[107] all point to lack of land, poor quality land, and bad weather (e.g., lack of rain) as constraints on crop production. With inadequate income that largely depended on crop production, refugees had to continue depending on external aid for agriculture input such as tools and seeds, much less the cost sharing of other services. Even the Tanzanian case, which reportedly had a positive impact on regional economy, was no exception to these problems. Armstrong (1991:83) concluded that refugees' crop production was not sustainable because of the constraints listed above.

It is safe to conclude from these findings that crop production contributes to the improvement of refugee self-reliance but it does not have sufficient impact to make refugees independent from external aid. If general refugee populations have to rely on external assistance for their agricultural activities, it can be reasonably assumed that vulnerable refugees, such as families with disabled or older persons and female-headed households, are even worse-off.

There is little information on the effectiveness of animal husbandry. Judging by this author's own experiences, however, it may be reasonable to say that raising small animals such as rabbits or bee-keeping may be useful if properly targeted at vulnerable people

---

[107] *UNHCR Global Report*, 2001, 2002 and 2003.

who could not leave their house to spend many hours a day on a farm. They can keep small animals or bees near their houses and, also, small animals and bees are not such a heavy labour as crop production. On the other hand, possibilities for keeping cattle and other big animals that require vast grazing land may be extremely limited because land scarcity is an increasingly serious problem in most refugee situations.

Small businesses or non-agriculture based income generation activities in refugee projects do not yield much success. There are no thorough studies available on refugee's income-generating activities, but this author's personal observations in refugee work suggest that refugee projects in small business rarely created a broad impact.

Microcredit schemes, especially, are too complex to bring immediate measurable output for many refugees. Managing microcredit schemes requires special skills, implementing a long-term process from selecting participants, to identifying appropriate businesses, to training refugees on basic business skills, to distributing loans, to monitoring activities and finally collecting loans. Therefore, it is not only the qualification of aid workers in refugee assistance that is a challenge, but also the fact that microcredit schemes do not fit the short project cycle of refugee assistance.

On the other hand, the need for some type of income-generating activities is high because of the increasing number of refugees who are not well suited to fit crop production. Vulnerable persons (e.g., female-headed households, older persons, unaccompanied minors and people with disability) cannot engage in heavy physical work; female-headed families with children may not be able to stay on a farm for many hours a day. Another group are refugees with more urban backgrounds or those with higher education who prefer jobs other than agriculture.

This is an area whether refugee programmes have not adequately responded to the needs of refugees and where development programmes can possibly respond better. If refugee assistance is to include small-scale business projects, it should be on a limited scale for targeted populations. For example, a grant scheme combined with basic skills training may benefit vulnerable refugees. For urban refugees, refugee programmes based on rural settlement do not seem to be able to offer many benefits. More solid development programmes in employment creation are therefore crucial to support the process of self-reliance of both refugees and local populations.

The other three categories of activities, namely leadership training (see Figure 4-4), vocational/skills training, and education are important for human development of refugees. Although the activities do not contribute to an immediate increase in household income in their countries of asylum, activities in this category are investments in the future. Refugees with education and skills can contribute to the development of their home country once they return.

Taken by the author.

Figure 4-4: A woman refugee in leadership training

Unfortunately, refugee projects do not allocate much funding for these activities that are not life-saving and that do not have an immediate impact on refugees' self-reliance partly due to funding shortage and also due to priority-setting among UNHCR activities.

4.1.3 Activities for Development of Host Communities

The previous chapters considered infrastructure projects as development assistance for host communities. This chapter will further examine the types of infrastructure projects and add capacity development activities:

Public Facilities
- Construction/rehabilitation of schools and clinics
- Construction/rehabilitation of community centres and women's centres
- Construction/rehabilitation of roads and bridges

Water
- Construction/rehabilitation of water supply systems (e.g., wells, boreholes)
- Construction/rehabilitation of small-scale irrigation systems (e.g., canals)

Capacity Development
- Workshops on refugee protection for government officials of host countries
- Implementation of refugee assistant projects by existing public services in host countries

Construction of facilities such as schools and hospitals is one of the aid programmes that some may criticise as just giving "boxes" for visibility but not reaching the needy. However, more attention should be paid to the advantages in improving accessibility of basic services in local communities. Moreover, the construction of social infrastructure that provides opportunities for refugees and locals to interact can contribute to the harmonious coexistence of the two communities.

Multi-purpose centres such as community centres and women's centres may need to be approached with more caution. Unlike clinics and schools, community centres or women's centres do not have specific purposes. Nevertheless, aid workers are apt to build one in a refugee settlement or nearby communities without much forethought. They may be simply hoping "refugees and local people should come here for discussion," "women should talk about their problems here," or "women's activities will attract donor funds."

If a project starts with such simplistic thinking but without seriously assessing needs, the construction of multi-purpose centres may find no users or end up in failure. Refugees normally need room for various activities including food distribution, registration of newly arrived refugees, religious rites, pre-schools and schools. Multi-purpose centres should be planned based on such needs and located accordingly (see Figure 4-5).

Taken by the author.

Figure 4-5: Multipurpose centre in a refugee settlement in Uganda. It is used for food distribution, kinder-garden and meetings.

Clean water is often a matter of vital importance and one of the most needed aid activities in many countries. While water projects have much potential for benefiting needy locals as well as refugees, thorough assessment of both technical and social aspects is essential to achieve success. Take the example of an irrigation project. A community upstream may control the water supply for another community downstream. Unless the project includes the co-management of the irrigation scheme with the two communities, it may cause conflicts between them.

Another element to consider is gender. The importance of incorporating gender perspectives into water projects is broadly recognised in aid communities (for example, Wijk van, 1998; Tsujita, 2003; UNDP's resource guide, 2003). Culturally, fetching water remains one of the tasks primarily of women and children in many countries. For women who do not have other chances to go out, washing and collecting water at wells and rivers serves as an important occasion for socialisation. The location of wells should, therefore, consider not only hydrological studies but also women's daily activities.

Unlike water projects, the construction of bridges and roads may not always be manageable in refugee programmes. Small-scale projects on feeder/access roads may not create any problem. However, the construction of main roads and bridges may not be manageable in refugee programmes. Such large-scale infrastructure development requires complex technical assessment. In addition, the project cycle of such large-scale development does not fit that of refugee assistance.

The last two activities in the above list in page 129 are intended for the capacity development of host governments in responding to a refugee crisis. The integration of refugee services into locally existing services should further lead to the equalisation of services between refugees and locals.

For example, in Uganda, health services for refugees were handed over to a district health department from an international NGO. The district department began supervising public clinics in both local communities and refugee settlements in 2000. The handover process involved, apart from refugees and aid agencies, various local actors, namely elders, both local and central government officials, and politicians. It was rather a complicated process for a refugee programme. However, it helped to raise overall awareness on refugee affairs among district officials. Furthermore, health services were all integrated into the public welfare system leaving few discrepancies between services offered to refugees and locals.

4.2 Developmental Refugee Assistance in Place of Development Aid?

The previous section gave an overview of the developmental activities in refugee local settlement programmes and identified activities that refugee assistance may effectively manage. As seen, some developmental activities are intended to help refugees while others contribute to host communities. Do these developmental activities in refugee programmes replace development aid in host communities? This section will consider this question.

4.2.1 Limitation of Refugee Assistance

Debates on Refugee Aid and Development often stress refugees as (potential) contributors to the development of host countries. The ICARA process in the 1980s promoted refugee self-reliance through productive activities for the development of host countries. The Programme of Action of ICARA II[108] promoted local settlement,

---

[108] *Report of the Secretary-General*, A/39/402, 1984.

when voluntary repatriation was not immediately feasible, so that refugees could "contribute to the overall development of the area." The Convention Plus process is even more vocal about this point. UNHCR' EXCOM Standing Committee describes refugees as "agents of development"[109]. Also existing among aid workers in both refugee assistance and development aids is the notion that UNHCR or refugee programmes are getting into more and more development business, as discussed in Chapter 1.

Does the Refugee Aid and Development Doctrine then encourage developmental refugee assistance programmes to replace development aid by development actors? The answer is no. As shown in Figure 4-1, the local settlement policy can be complete only with the combined efforts of refugee aid and development programmes. Indeed, major international conferences such as Development Assistance Committee (DAC) in 1981 and ICARA II in 1984 recognised the important fact that both bilateral and multilateral development organisations should play a leading role in development of host countries and the integration of refugees (for example, Koizumi, 1998).

There is historical background to UNHCR's taking up of developmental activities for the refugee-hosting communities. As mentioned in Chapter 3, development actors were not adequately present on the scene contrary to the expectation made at the two ICARA conferences. Consequently, refugee programmes took up infrastructure development not only in refugee settlements but also in refugee-hosting communities. Gorman (1990/1993: 69) states that there were strong expectations of some governments and

---

[109] *Economic and Social Impact of Refugee Populations on Host Developing Countries as well as Other Countries: Partnerships with Bilateral Development Agencies*, EXCOM Standing Committee, 24th Meeting, EC/52/SC/CRP.10, 31 May 2002, para. 1 and 9.

NGOs for UNHCR, rather than UNDP, to take the leadership role on ICARA II follow-up. Gorman (1991b/1993: 163) further states that UNHCR's aggressive promotion of Refugee Aid and Development was its reaction to "a tepid UNDP response." T. Betts (1984/1993:19) sees it differently, stating that UNHCR had a strong interest in offering developmental aid to refugee-hosting developing countries (and even other developing countries).

It is not possible to prove the above points either way. In all probability, the truth may be the combination of the two: There must have been external pressures for UNHCR to respond quickly to the needs which arouse from refugee presence, as well as internal ambition of UNHCR to meet such expectations.

However, developmental activities within refugee programmes are limited in their impact on the macro economy (Callarmard, 1994). Cassen and Associates (1994: 36), taking WFP's programmes as examples, acknowledged the value of developmental activities organised by humanitarian agencies as they can serve as the *"direct* relief of poverty". They, however, pointed out that such activities do not address the longer-term issues, and, therefore, argued that striking a balance between assistance targeted at acute needs, a longer-term development, and policy reform is needed. The above arguments appear to remain valid in refugee situations, and the existence of comprehensive and longer-term development programmes is crucial in achieving the objectives of the Refugee Aid and Development Doctrine and local settlement policy/programmes.

Essentially, issues concerning host communities are principally development problems. As repeatedly emphasised in the ICARA process, lack of basic infrastructure, public services, or employment opportunities is the manifestation of underdevelopment, which cannot be solved without longer-term development plans. Thus, UNHCR's small-scale infrastructure projects no way make such a significant impact as full-scale development programmes[110].

Chambers (1986/1993), an authority on rural development and a leading advocator for the poorest, asserted that the local poor are often the "hidden losers" of the negative impact of large-scale refugee influx. Although his view has some merit, the question here is who should respond to the issue of the local hidden losers? Can or should refugee programmes manage the issue? It bears repeating that, based on discussions here and in previous chapters, the issue is beyond what refugee programmes, even more development-oriented ones such as local settlement, can address.

Refugee influx exacerbates the problems that were already existing in a host community, but the presence of refugees is not the root cause of underdevelopment of a host community. Developmental activities in refugee programmes, which are like patchwork activities on small-scale infrastructure, can only mitigate problems aggravated by refugee influx but, obviously, cannot address more complex development issues.

4.2.2 Roles of Refugee Assistance

Section 4.1 identified activities that refugee programmes can effectively manage and others that they cannot. Table 4-1 shows differences between humanitarian aid and development aid, while Table 4-2 shows the advantages and disadvantages of developmental refugee assistance.

---

[110] UNHCR indeed acknowledges such limitation. *The State of the World's Refugees*, 1995.

Table 4-1: Comparison Between Humanitarian Aid and Development

	Principles	Beneficiaries	Duration of Assistance	Project Cycle	Assistance Activities
Humanitarian Assistance	Humanity, neutrality, impartiality (Non-political nature)	Victims of natural and man-made disasters (Refugees)	Until solutions are found for the victims. Normally, assistance is regarded for short-duration, can be one-shot assistance.	Short-term Often one-year.	Food and other material assistance. Health, water and primary education for individual victims.
Development Aid	Conditionality can be added. (It may reflect political interests of donors.) Accordance with national priorities of aid recipient countries.	A country, or a region in general	Long-term development plan. Sustainability is often a key.	Longer-term planning, often multi-year project cycle.	Broad ranges from loan, capacity-development, governance, to rural development. Individual assistance is not its usual aid modality.

Developed by the author.

Local Settlement

Table 4-2: Advantages and Constraints of Developmental Refugee Assistance

Type of Developmental Refugee Assistance	Advantages	Disadvantages/Constraints
Agriculture	• Crop production contributes to food security and improves food self-reliance. • Raising small animals can be an alternative income-generating activity to crop production.	• Increase in crop production is limited because of lack of land, its poor quality and bad weather. • Cattle keeping need large grazing land. • Control of disease among animals may be difficult.
Small Business	• Grant schemes may help vulnerable refugees.	• Credit schemes requires skills and longer process to manage, and thus may not fit refugee projects.
Human Development	• It provides refugees with skills and knowledge that they can utilise once they return home.	• It is not placed as high priority among refugee assistance and thus does not attract adequate donor funds.
Public Facilities	• Sharing of clinics/schools may promote harmonious coexistence of refugees and locals. • Construction of clinics and schools contributes to well-being of local populations.	• Construction of large infrastructure such as roads and bridges does not fit refugee programmes. The latter lacks adequate technical expertise, funds and project duration that are essential to the large infrastructure projects.
Water	• It is most needed in many countries. • It can benefit both refugees and locals.	• Thorough preparation is needed to ensure that the water project equally benefits different gender, ethnic and/or religious groups.
Capacity Development	• Awareness of refugee affairs rises among government officials. • Capacity of government offices in dealing with refugee protection/assistance improves. • Incorporation of refugee assistance into public services ensures equal services for refugees and locals.	• It requires longer process to involve public services than NGOs.

Developed by the author.

Characteristics of refugee assistance shown in Table 4-1, such as short-cycle of projects and limited timeframe of assistance, cannot effectively manage challenges accompanying usual development activities. Developmental activities in refugee assistance (or ones organised by humanitarian agencies), therefore, consequently face constraints shown in Table 4-2. Considering these, it is obvious that developmental refugee projects cannot improve overall socio-economic conditions of communities or countries hosting refugees.

Instead, developmental activities within refugee programmes should be principally targeted at the interests of refugees. Their contribution to host communities inevitably remains limited. In other words, the primary role of refugee assistance programmes should be focused on the well-being and human development of refugees, rather than blurred into the development of host countries. This point should be recognised not only by aid workers but also by local stake holders.

On the other hand, development programmes could focus their aims on overall development of a concerned community/country and play a vital role to improve its overall socio-economic conditions. Such a problem may start with a community-based small-scale project to respond to acute needs in host communities, such as lack of water or damaged roads. They should and can eventually develop small-scale initiatives into a larger plan, for example, on the vitalisation of the local economy in a concerned region, establishment of a road network, or improving health programmes[111].

---

[111] A good example of this kind of programme is a rural development project in eastern Chad by Japan International Cooperation Agency (JICA). As of this writing (Nov. 2005), JICA is implementing a rural development project to support Chadian communities that host some 200,000 Sudanese refugees. JICA is Japan's ODA implementator in the field of technical cooperation.

4.2.3 Need for Development
In the previous section, it was stated that development intervention is particularly needed in the areas related to economic development such as employment creation and income-generating activities. Some other areas that require development intervention will be explored below.

Programmes related to human development should be one of the first to come to mind. Earlier discussions have mentioned that services on education and skills/vocational training are not available to all refugees. At the same time, it is important to recognise that local populations are least likely to have access to adequate education–either formal or non-formal. Therefore, in some refugee situations, skills training courses of refugee projects are extended to local populations. This is, however, probably not a good direction to pursue. The Refugee Aid and Development Doctrine aims to integrate refugee issues into national development plans, but not vice versa. It would be more logical if a development programme on such activities as education and vocational training were brought into a local community and were extended to refugees.

What is typically weak, if not entirely lacking, in refugee projects is local capacity development. Implementing refugee projects, especially those oriented to development requires local capacity. As Hall (2003: 25) points out, it is often wrongly assumed that local institutions exist which can manage refugee assistance. The reality is quite to the contrary. Existing local institutions and governmental offices normally need additional resources and training on refugee protection, project management, planning, and financial control. Although refugee projects may contribute to this area, for example, by organising training courses on refugee protection, they can not, however, adequately address issues related to governance that are indeed closely related to refugee protection.

As such, linking refugee aid with development cannot be

achieved without active involvement of development actors. In other words, without them, refugee-related problems in developing countries cannot be solved. As Callamard (1991/1993) remarked, local settlement programmes without the existence of development intervention would not make the linkage of refugee aid and development. Instead, it may become an alternative but limited development assistance that refugee programmes promote in refugee-hosting areas.

Then, what prevented development actors from working in refugee-hosting communities in the past? Why did a gap between humanitarian aid and development programme exist?

These points were often debated in the 1990s. Although the debates were often in the context of returnee aid and development, most of the points are also applicable to the situation of refugee-hosting countries. UNDP's report lists six factors as constraints in responding to complex crises in post-conflicts[112]. These are (a) differences in planning approach between relief and development, (b) inflexibility of development assistance and inability to convert pledges into concrete assistance, (c) constraints of funding, (d) lack of donor coordination, (e) funding mechanism and financing structure and (f) lack of incentives and organisational structure for cooperation within the UN.

---

[112] UNDP Rwanda, *Linking Relief to Development*, June 1998. The report was based on cases of Rwanda, Mozambique, Cambodia, and Central America, which were the cases of returnee integration in countries of origin. Nevertheless, the points raised are pertinent to refugee situations. Other documents that mentioned similar points include: UNHCR document *Returnee Aid and Development* (1994), Danish Ministry of Foreign Affairs' research (2000), Suhrke (1994) and Fukada (1999). Of them, the UNDP's report well summarised the factors that hinders the linkage of relief and development. Moreover, the analyses of this report, made by a development agency, has more value than others that were made by donors, humanitarians or researchers.

Although the above points remain true not only for the UN but also aid organisations in general, there has been some progress regarding these issues in recent years. At least, with regard to post-conflict situations (or the returnee aid and development context), there has been growing consensus that development actors should support the reconstruction process and respond to it more quickly. Development organisations are reforming their own systems to enable them to act faster and more flexibly. Afghanistan is a good example. After the fall of the Taliban in Afghanistan in December 2001, the World Bank already started its study before the end of the year, and in 2002, many development organisations went to Afghanistan for assessment.

The challenge remaining is that, unlike post-conflict situations, protracted refugee situations do not seem to offer sufficient incentives for development actors to come in. Mostly, refugee-hosting communities are on the periphery of a country that is not a priority in national development. Then, development organisations, the work of which should be in accordance with national development priorities, even lose justification for supporting refugee-hosting communities.

4.2.4 The Future

What motivates development actors to assist refugee-hosting communities? What should be also improved in developmental refugee assistance of local settlement?

Earlier, Chapter 3 suggested that humanitarians, especially UNHCR as a mandated refugee protection agency, should repackage the Refugee Aid and Development Doctrine in concepts more familiar to development actors and donor governments. In relation to it, at the country and project level, efforts to incorporate refugee-related issues to national development plans or PRSPs should continue.

UNHCR's study on Poverty Reduction Strategy Papers (PRSPs)

in 2004[113] reveals that only two out of twenty PRSPs include refugees in their strategies, i.e., Armania and Serbia & Montenegro. If refugee-hosting developing countries claim to be burdened, they should mainstream refugee issues into their national development plans. UNHCR, as a refugee agency, needs to encourage more persistently countries of asylum to incorporate refugee issues into their PRSPs or related government documents.

On the side of refugee assistance, the local settlement policy needs to have measurable objectives. Simply stating the integration of refugees and refugee self-reliance as objectives is ambiguous. What can be realistically achieved in a certain given refugee situation should be clearly assessed and presented. Furthermore, to achieve set objectives, developmental activities in refugee assistance should also be targeted at appropriate activities and apply appropriate approaches. The analysis of this chapter identified developmental activities that are more effective and ones that are less effective in the refugee assistance. Refugee assistance should focus its developmental activities on ones that humanitarian aid agencies can effectively manage.

This chapter, however, did not sufficiently examine the integration and self-reliance as the objectives of local settlement and refugee participation as an approach towards reaching such objectives. It is therefore appropriate to discuss these issues in Chapters 5 and 6.

4.3 Summary

This chapter reviewed the local settlement as a policy and a programme derived from the Refugee Aid and Development Doctrine. Analysis of the project activities of local settlement con-

---

[113] UNHCR, *Poverty Reduction Strategy Paper: A Displacement Perspective*, October 2004.

cluded that development intervention is indispensable to link refugee aid and development. It also argued that refugee assistance, however development-oriented it may be, should primarily focus on the protection and well-beings of refugees, but not be blurred into development of a host country. Further, the absence of incentives for development actors to come into refugee situations was pointed out. It suggested that humanitarians and UNHCR should incorporate development theories into the concept of refugee protection.

This chapter also urged that local settlement at the country and project level needs concrete and measurable objectives based on any given situation and organise activities suitable to refugee assistance with appropriate approach. In this regard, the analyses of this chapter identified developmental activities that refugee assistance can effectively manage and that should be principally targeted at the well-being of refugees and the peaceful coexistence of refugees and locals.

It is, therefore, necessary to further examine issues related to "concrete objectives" and "appropriate approach" in subsequent chapters.

Chapter 5
Developmental Refugee Assistance in Local Settlement

The last chapter gave an overview of the refugee assistance activities of local settlement. It identified different roles in local settlement between developmental refugee assistance and development aid: refugee assistance for keeping the well-being of refugees in priority, and development aid for improving socio-economic conditions of refugee-hosting areas. This chapter will proceed to further examine the aims of developmental refugee assistance in local settlement. Chapter 4 pointed out that refugee self-reliance is one of the objectives of local settlement and local integration as its potential end product, or, an ultimate goal. It was also noted that refugee participation is an approach that leads to self-reliance and integration.

These development-oriented objectives and this approach have so far been used in refugee assistance without much review and some refugee aid workers as well as observers believe in them without question. It is apparent that the uncritical application of these developmental objectives to refugee situations, in some past projects, has resulted in unrealistic objective setting. It is necessary to recall the fact that development aid and refugee assistance are different in many ways (see Table 4-1). Although Chapter 3 acknowledged the validity of the Refugee Aid and Development Doctrine as an idea, the idea needs to be operationalised. In this regard, Chapter 4 concluded that developmental refugee assistance in local settlement should have concrete objectives and appropriate approaches. The uncritical adoption of developmental objectives and approach in refugee situations causes ambiguity in policy, misunderstanding among stakeholders and infeasible planning of projects.

It is, therefore, essential to revisit these development-oriented objectives and approach, and to bring more practical viewpoints into refugee assistance under local settlement. Based on this notion, Sections 5.1 and 5.2 will examine self-reliance and integration as the objectives of local settlement. Then, Section 5.3 will examine a participatory approach in refugee situations. What can a refugee programme of local settlement practically achieve, and how? Chapter 5 will attempt to answer these questions.

5.1 Self-reliance and Integration: Developmental Objectives in Refugee Assistance?

This section will examine the two objectives of local settlement from a refugee assistance view point. The section will first examine the types of self-reliance and varying levels of each type of self-reliance. The section will argue that "perfect" self-reliance is not an achievable objective in most of the refugee situations and, instead, a local settlement project in each given situation should clearly identify the level of "partial" self-reliance that the project is aimed at. This section will go on to similar discussion on integration. Integration as an objective should not remain as an abstract concept. Three integration processes will be examined and factors that influence the processes will be identified.

5.1.1 Self-Reliance
The first topic to be examined is "refugee self-reliance". What

does it mean? Do local settlement programmes offer opportunities for refugees to become independent from external aid?

In Chapter 4, self-reliance was defined as a status in which refugees are able to live without external aid. It was further stated that self-reliance included both material self-sufficiency and psychological capacity. The latter can be further broken down into the capacity of individual refugees in managing their lives and that of the community in administering itself.

The question, then, is what degree of self-reliance can refugee projects reasonably expect to achieve? UNHCR remains ambiguous about this point but simply mentions the aim "to attain self-reliance"[114] or that "refugee self-reliance is the key element."[115] Even at a project level, the target of self-reliance is not always specific[116].

Which level of self-reliance do local settlement programmes expect refugees to attain? Do they realistically assume that refugees can become entirely independent from external aid?

Table 5-1 presents types and indicators of self-reliance. Economic self-reliance may include more hierarchical order than the other two types of self-reliance. Social and psychological self-reliance, on the other hand, are not suitable to present hierarchy. Instead, the table presents some indicators of these types of self-reliance.

---

[114] UNHCR, *New Approaches and Partnerships for Protection and Solutions in Africa: Addressing Protracted Refugee Situations in Africa*, Informal Consultations, 14 December 2001.
[115] *Protracted Refugee Situation*, EXCOM Standing Committee, 30th Meeting, EC/54/SC/CRP.14, 10 June 2004.
[116] The case of Uganda will be discussed in subsequent chapters.

Table 5-1: Indicators of Self-Reliance

	Indicators
Economic Self-Reliance	**Perfect Self-Reliance** Refugees are independent from external assistance.
	Indicators for Partial Self-Reliance Refugees are independent from food assistance. And/or they are able to partly share the cost of basic services such as water, education and health.
	Refugees are independent from food assistance but receive inputs for agriculture and/or other income generation activities.
	Refugees are on reduced food assistance.
	Refugees depend on full ration of food assistance.
Social Self-Reliance	**Perfect Self-Reliance** Refugees are able to decide on the administration and management of their communities. No involvement of aid workers and host governments required.
	Indicators for Partial Self-Reliance Refugees can mobilise themselves to help vulnerable persons in their communities.
	Refugees have their own committee(s) or system on self-management.
	Refugees participate in assessment, planning, implementation and evaluation of projects.
Psychological Self-Reliance	**Perfect Self-Reliance** Refugees are able to decide on their life, pursue their plan and attain psychological well-being.
	Indicators for Partial Self-Reliance Refugees feel that they are developing their own potentials for themselves.
	Refugees feel that they are contributing to their community and/or local community.
	There are less psycho-social problems among refugees.

Developed by the author.

This section will examine each category of self-reliance. The following shows the summary of the three categories of self-reliance and related refugee assistance activities.
1. Economic self-reliance: This concerns refugees' capacity in providing or purchasing food and basic goods and services. The self-reliance in this category largely depends on the outcomes of productive activities such as crop production, employment and other income generation activities.
2. Social self-reliance: This concerns the capacity of refugee communities as a group in making decisions and helping each other. Focused on this self-reliance are activities in leadership training, self-management of wells, community activities to help vulnerable individuals, or activities relating to project assessment and implementation.
3. Psychological self-reliance: This concerns refugees' capacity in gaining control over their own life. This is similar to and interlinked with social self-reliance, but is more focused on individuals rather than a community as a whole. Human development activities, such as education and skills training, are expected to enhance this category of self-reliance.

How to look more closely at the economic self-reliance? Banki (2004: 2) suggested that perfect self-reliance may be attainable in the long run but it cannot be an objective for an intermediate term. In this author's view, perfect self-reliance cannot be a feasible objective in refugee assistance.

The most serious impediment to economic self-reliance is the insufficient income generating opportunities. Many researchers identify the scarcity of arable land, lack of non-agriculture income generating opportunities, lack of employment and unfavourable climate conditions as factors that hinder the process of economic self-reliance in East Sudan, South Sudan, Tanzania and Southwestern Uganda (Armstrong, 1988; Bulcha, 1987; Smyke & Smyke, 1988; Meeren, 1996; Bulcha, Kibreab & Nobel, 1987; Chambers, 1979, 1982; Harell-Bond, 1986; Kibreab, 1987; Kok, 1989). The same situation in Northern Uganda will be discussed in subsequent chapters.

The above studies found that refugees in local settlements, in spite of improvement in food self-sufficiency, had to continue depending on external aid. Even in the case considered most successful, i.e., Tanzania's agriculture-based settlement programme from the 1970s to the 1980s, average income per refugee family in the late 1980s (2312 Tz Shillings) did not reach the level of an average rural Tanzanian family of 1977 (2936 Tz Shillings) (Armstrong, 1988: 61).

Another point to consider is the vulnerability of refugees in settlements. Among refugees, there are those who prefer to stay outside organised settlements for various reasons. Among them, some have their ways to financially support themselves without assistance[117]. Residents of refugee settlements, in the first place, may not include the most able people among refugee populations. Damme (1999) found that refugee camps in Guinea between 1992 and 1995 became almost vacant because able refugees were search-

---

[117] Assistance here means services such as education, health, water, food, etc., but does not refer to legal assistance or protection. As opposed to assistance, protection should be provided regardless of refugees' economic status. Those who opt not to be included in the assistance may have their own business, stay with relatives in the country of asylum or depend on remittance from relatives abroad. This does not mean that all the refugees outside settlements are better off than those in settlements. Rather, the point here is that those who have business potentials or social network may be already out of assistance.

ing for employment outside the camps and only vulnerable refugees remained there.

Vulnerable refugees including those with disabilities, older persons or female-headed households are also disadvantaged in agriculture, which requires heavy physical labour. Coupled with the fact that income generating opportunities are limited, it is inevitable that increasing the level of individual (refugees') household economy reaches its limit well below the perfect level.

Given these constraints, it can be reasonably said that refugee local settlement programmes can help refugees increase the level of self-reliance but perfect self-reliance is not attainable. Nevertheless, it is worth noting that productive activities such as carpentry and tailoring, even if not immediately increasing economic self-reliance, may create a positive impact on refugees' psychological well-being.

There are not many studies on refugees' social and psychological self-reliance. As Bulcha stated (1987:74) [118], this may be because many assume that social or psychological self-reliance will be automatically attained when economic self-reliance is attained.

Concerning social self-reliance, the optimum level that the figure indicates is not at all possible for any group of people to attain unless they have their own autonomous society that is free from government rules. Laws and administration of a nation binds its people. The degree of social self-reliance that refugees may achieve, in this respect, depends greatly on overall policy of the country of asylum and legal rights that refugees may enjoy there. For example, ensuring free movement increases refugees' psychological satisfaction and confidence (Bulcha, 1987: 81).

---

[118] Bulcha does not distinguish self-reliance (or self-sufficiency) from integration. Rather, his concept of integration is a combination of self-reliance and integration that this paper defines.

Refugee participation in assistance programme may be another factor in increasing the degree of refugees' social self-reliance. One can reasonably assume that refugees would feel more empowered in a programme where they participate in the decision making process of aid activities compared with one in which the government of a host country and aid agencies decide on all the details. While recognising the positive impact of the participatory process on refugees' self-reliance, it is also important to point out that participation in refugee assistance needs further examination. The next chapter will take up issues relating to participation.

Psychological self-reliance is difficult to measure. Researchers in the 1980's (for example, Harrell-Bond, 1986; Armstrong, 1988; and Kibreab, 1989) were critical about the impact of local settlement on refugees' well-beings, reporting that local settlement is not refugees' priority but rather their primary interest is, understandably, returning to their home. A more recent study (Ayoo, 2000) also quoted a refugee's comment that local settlement is an imposed policy. Then, doesn't a local settlement programme contribute to refugees' well-being? It is premature to draw such a conclusion.

Although it is quite understandable that refugees' primary interest is voluntary repatriation and not local settlement in a country of asylum, it is also narrow-minded to conclude that local settlement programmes do not contribute to refugees' psychological well-being. First of all, it is necessary to note differences between the expectations of refugees and the aims of aid programmes. Refugees, understandably, compare their life with normal life that they could have lived at home while aid programmes mainly concern the improvement of asylum life. Therefore, it is just reasonable and natural that refugees have dissatisfaction as long as they are in exile.

Secondly, also it must be noted that one's psychological status does not always match what he/she expresses. Since there is no stringent study on refugee psychology in camps/settlements, it is not possible to present academically proven data. To speak of personal experiences, however, this author has observed positive changes in refugees' psychology in local settlement programmes. In 1996 in Uganda, many refugees in transit centres had many complaints, tended to be confrontational with aid workers, and were opposed to going to a settlement. However, as time went by, in 1998 and in 1999, refugees began to look more relaxed in their attitude, logical in presenting their views and to be more confident in what they were doing.

An example of an opposite situation is from my own experience in Europe. In a country where I worked in the late-1990s, refugees had stayed in collective centres already for several years. There was no particular work or other activity that could occupy them. Refugees were not aggressive but apathetic and continued mourning the dead and the lost. This is not to imply that local settlement can solve all the refugee problems, but based on my own observations of different refugee situations, it is apparent that local settlement programmes, provide more productive opportunities for refugees, and, therefore, contribute to refugee's well-being.

Hoeing's study (2004) supports my observations. Her study was based on interviews with Sudanese refugees in Uganda. It found that refugees in a local settlement programme in Uganda became to gain positive self-image, felt empowered and attained new skills/knowledge. As Hoeing stated, there are not many studies focused on refugees' strengths. This is certainly an area for future research.

5.1.2 Integration

Chapter 4 reviewed UNHCR's definition of local integration as one of durable solutions in which refugees are adapted to the host society, the host society welcome refugees, and public institutions serve both refugees and locals. It was also recognised that integration goes through legal, economic and social and cultural processes. This definition, however, is certainly not satisfactory and it is necessary to examine each aspect of integration, its determining factors and impacts.

Khulman (1991) identified five groups of factors that determine integration and presented a comprehensive model as seen in Figure 5-1.

Kuhlman's model serves to understand the inter-dependence among various factors. In the process towards integration, various factors mutually affect one another. For example, government policy is seen as an independent variable in the model, while among the

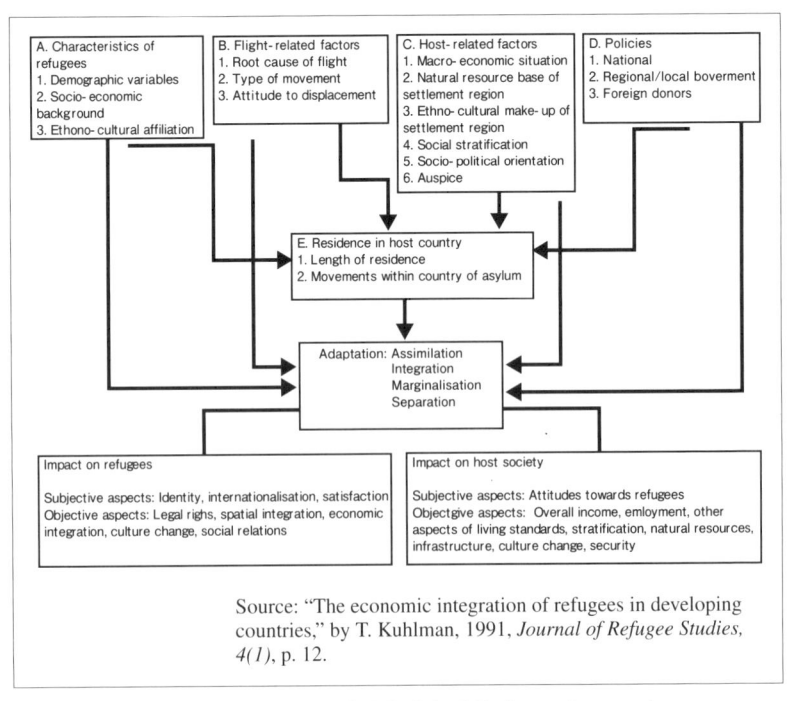

| A. Characteristics of refugees
1. Demographic variables
2. Socio-economic background
3. Ethno-cultural affiliation | B. Flight-related factors
1. Root cause of flight
2. Type of movement
3. Attitude to displacement | C. Host-related factors
1. Macro-economic situation
2. Natural resource base of settlement region
3. Ethno-cultural make-up of settlement region
4. Social stratification
5. Socio-political orientation
6. Auspice | D. Policies
1. National
2. Regional/local boverment
3. Foreign donors |

E. Residence in host country
1. Length of residence
2. Movements within country of asylum

Adaptation: Assimilation
Integration
Marginalisation
Separation

Impact on refugees	Impact on host society
Subjective aspects: Identity, internationalisation, satisfaction Objective aspects: Legal righs, spatial integration, economic integration, culture change, social relations	Subjective aspects: Attitudes towards refugees Objectgive aspects: Overall income, emloyment, other aspects of living standards, stratification, natural resources, infrastructure, culture change, security

Source: "The economic integration of refugees in developing countries," by T. Kuhlman, 1991, *Journal of Refugee Studies*, 4(1), p. 12.

Figure 5-1: Kuhlman's Model of Refugee Integration

impacts or dependent variables, is refugees' legal rights, which are indeed part of national policy on refugees. Similarly, refugees' emotional aspect (refugees' attitude to displacement as a determining factor and refugees' level of satisfaction as impact) and economic status of host country (macro-economic condition of the host county as a determining factor and job obtained/overall income as an impact) appear as both independent and dependent variables.

In other words, the initial states of refugees and host country/communities affect the subsequent process of self-reliance and integration, while the whole process itself affects the status of refugees and that of host countries/communities. Therefore, it can be said that the process of local settlement, or one toward integration, is a dynamic one in which refugees and local communities/country create mutual impacts.

Recognising the comprehensiveness of Kuhlman's model, his determining factors seem to need reclassifying in a simpler manner. For example, flight-related factors seem to be either insignificant or reasonably merged into characteristics of refugees. It remains true that the root cause of flight affects refugees' well-being. However, differences among refugees with different causes of flight may not be as significant as other factors. Similarly, the type of movement does not seem to be important enough to highlight. Refugees' attitude to displacement, which seems to be more important as a dependent variable than independent, could be part of the characteristics of refugees if it is to remain as an independent variable.

Kuhlman identified security as a possible impact or a dependent variable. It can be argued, however, that this should be an independent variable, or, otherwise, an external factor. The process of integration does affect security to a certain degree, such as the level of coexistence (or friction) between refugees and locals. Then, these impacts should be stated as such (friction or coexistence). Security should rather reflect the level of anti-government activities or crimes which affect the process of self-reliance and the level of integration.

More important for the purpose of this study is to identify the determining factors where refugee assistance can intervene: what could be the expected outcomes and how to organise assistance towards the identified objectives[119]?

Self-reliance is an important constituent of integration. Without feeling confident in one's own economic and social situations, one can not feel like a member of society. However, it is also obvious that self-reliance per se is not sufficient for integration. To achieve integration, host communities and country accept refugees while the latter has willingness to adapt them to a new society.

Social and cultural process: It is generally assumed that relations between refugees and locals will be positive where both groups share ethnicity, language and/or religion. Researchers (for example Bulcha, Kibrab & Nobel, 1987; Kok, 1989; and Smyke & Smyke, 1988) have tended to agree on this point, and aid workers generally receive more or less similar impressions (for example, during the Kosovo crisis in 1999, ethnic Albanian refugees from Kosovo were comparatively better received in Albania than in Macedonia, which is a predominantly Serbian society.).

It should not be taken for granted that refugees and locals with cultural/ethnical affinity will stay close to each other. For example, some may assume that African refugees and their hosts in border lands, originally from the same ethnic group and artificially divided by colonial governments, can live like a family without problems.

---

[119] Interestingly, Kuhlman stated that type of refugee assistance is not a crucial factor, or at least less important than the refugee policy (Kuhlman, 1991: 10). This view seems to be rather obscure. Assistance is also given for a government to formulate refugee policies. Also, if the characteristics of assistance are negligible to refugees, why, in general, do people blame aid agencies for refugees' dissatisfaction?

Gingyera-Pinycwa (1998: 10-11) warned of such misconception, stating "there would appear to be in the minds of African refugees a rather strong fixation with, or even affection for the territories in which they were born and brought up, despite all that may be said about the artificiality of Africa's colonially carved-out territories." Supporting this view are observations on refugee settlements (for example, Kibreab, 1989; Bulcha, Kibreab & Nobel, 1987; and Ayoo, 2000). Many refugees consider their life in asylum as temporary, with the hope to return to home soon. Similarly, local populations may develop assistance fatigue and friction may develop even in a situation in which locals are accommodating and tolerant at the initial stage of refuge influx.

The implication of this on refugee assistance is that assistance programme should include activities to help refugees go through adaptation process and gain skills/knowledge useful once they return home, and address peaceful coexistence of the two communities.

Bulcha's study on Eritrean refugees in East Sudan (1987) identified other social factors that influence the integration of refugees. He found that homogeneous (local) societies are less capable of absorbing non-natives than heterogeneous societies and that women refugees are more isolated and less integrated than men. Bulcha also found that those who continued to support anti-governments movement in their country of origin tended to have little interest in the host community. However, findings are mixed concerning whether refugees in settlements are better integrated than those who are "self-settled."[120]

Legal process: The Convention Relating to the Status of Refugees (1951) and its Protocol (1967) are the legal instruments that provide the basis for protection and assistance given to refugees.

---

[120] Self-settled refugees are ones who do not live in a camp or settlement but stay independently or with relatives/friends.

Whether a country of asylum is a party to these instruments can be considered an indicator to show how that nation regards refugee issues. However, it should be noted that whether a nation accedes the convention or not does not necessarily determine how the nation treats refugees. Pakistan, for example, has acceded neither the convention nor the protocol, but is well known for having accepted millions of refugees from Afghanistan since 1977 (for example, Farr, 1991/1993).

National laws affect the type of refugee assistance and daily activities of refugees. Not only laws on refugees but also ones on land and public administration determine issues such as free movement, access to land, access to employment and access to education and other public services.

Should the legal process lead to the naturalisation of refugees as the final stage of integration? "Yes" in theory, but "no" in practice. Ultimate integration in a legal sense should mean that refugees attain citizenship in the country of asylum. For example, the Tanzanian government adopted a mass naturalisation policy for Rwandan refugees in 1978, which continued over 10 years (Gasarasi, 1990)[121]. This is, however, an exceptional case (Khulman, 1994: 135). In general, governments of countries of asylum are hesitant about giving citizenship to refugees (Gorman, 1990/1993: 70). Possibly because of that, UNHCR is less assertive about this point, stating that "(the integration) process should lead to ... *perhaps* [emphasis added] ultimately the acquisition of citizenship in the country of asylum"[122].

---

[121] The process is documented in Gasarasis' study (1990), according to which, the programme failed due to government bureaucracy.

[122] *Framework for Durable Solutions for Refugees and Persons of Concern*, EXCOM Standing Committee, 28th Meeting, EC/53/SC/INF.3, 16 September 2003. However, local integration without possibility for citizenship remains questionable as a durable solution.

It may be understandable that the government of a country of asylum decides not to absorb a great many refugees as its citizens. Once political problems are settled in the country of origin, naturalisation should be considered on an individual basis for those whose protection remains at risk in their home country.

Economic process: Economic process is closely related to the first two processes described above. The level of refugees' social integration and the ranges of economic rights that national laws grant greatly affect the economic aspect of integration. If refugees are obliged to stay in a camp, they have no chance for economic improvement. Or, if refugees are prohibited from certain economic activities (e.g., fishing at a local river), their integration will be limited.

Determining factors and actors: As such, the process towards integration largely depends on factors in the host country. As seen, legal instruments of a host country provide the framework on possible ranges of integration. Social and cultural aspects either facilitate or hinder the process towards integration. The next obvious step, then, is to consider to the integration of assistance systems.

So far, discussions on integration have focused on the individual level. However, integration of individual refugees would not go far without changes in the systems of refugee assistance. More precisely, locally existing systems, public or private, incorporate refugees into their client group; the government of the country of asylum should include refugee issues in their development agenda. Otherwise, refugee integration does not progress far because integration can not be achieved only through individual efforts but rather it requires a more systematic approach from key actors of refugee assistance, especially, from the government of the host country.

Anderson and Woodrow (1988) similarly made the criticism that humanitarian assistance often ignores the capacity, resources and culture of affected communities, sets up parallel systems for assistance and thus hampers the development process. As long as a system of refugee services is parallel to a local or national system, refugees are isolated from national plans and the local system does not improve its capacity to respond to refugee situations. This may further result in conflict between locals and refugees.

Anderson and Woodrow's main point was the criticism against the traditional way of delivering humanitarian assistance. It is indeed important for aid workers to note that they should not do harm while attempting to help people. It should be noted, however, that political will of a host government is equally important for refugee integration.

In sum, then, integration is a goal of local settlement. The optimum level of integration may be a situation in which refugees are socially adapted to a host community, suffer no discrimination and have contacts with local people through daily activities at work places, markets, clinics and schools, and thus local populations consider refugees as part of their community. The local system provides basic social services for both nationals and refugees. Economically, refugees are self-reliant and their economic activities contribute to the development of the host country. Legally, national laws grant refugees access to employment, free movement and other basic human rights equal to citizens (see Table 4-6).

Determining factors can be summarised as:
- Characteristics of the two communities including social and cultural aspects,
- Levels of refugees' self-reliance and economy,
- Security
- Laws and policies of a host government.

As such, it can again be seen that for the integration of refugees, assistance targeted at refugees plays only a partial role. Concerted efforts from a host country/community and development actors are essential to the goal towards the integration process.

Therefore, refugee assistance, or more precisely, UNHCR, may consider shifting its emphasis more from the delivery of services to broader advocacy and coordination. It should address policy issues at a national level, encouraging a host government to adopt generous refugee laws/polies and promote coexistence at a local level. Outside the refugee assistance arena, networking with development actors is indispensable.

This is not to say that UNHCR should reduce its assistance activities. Rather, they are important protection tools. In reality, no one will listen to an actor that can not deliver visible assistance but preach on human rights, even those of aliens. However, it is important to consider that the agency further strengthen its capacity in coordination and advocacy.

Another implication of the analysis in this chapter is the need for accurate assessment for the realistic setting of objectives. For example, where local communities are more antagonistic and national laws do not allow any employment of refugees, activities of refugee assistance programmes would also be limited and, thus, the objective of the programme should not be too ambitious. Rather, in such a situation, UNHCR could focus their resources more on government capacity building.

On the other hand, if the local community has potential for agriculture development and is in need of labour force, refugees' economic opportunity is much greater (for example, the case in Tanzania in the 1980s presented earlier) and their presence can truly contribute to the development of the local economy. In such a situation, a refugee programme may expect that refugees will attain higher levels of self-reliance and integration.

Unlike development programmes that require detailed assessment, refugee programmes, which often hurry to implementation, tend to lack adequate analysis and appropriate planning. This tendency may result in idealistic, optimistic but fallacious objective setting. "Careful analysis in a short period" is indeed a contradictive concept and a challenge to refugee aid practitioners. However, if promoting developmental refugee assistance such as local settlement or refugee self-reliance, UNHCR and other refugee assistance agencies need to obtain skills and re-establish a system to assess issues related to development of refugees and locals.

5.2 Participation: Developmental Approach in Refugee Assistance?

The discussion in Chapter 4 explained the concept and objectives of the local settlement policy with the focus on their developmental aspects in refugee projects. Integration and self-reliance are more development-oriented objectives than those in relief-oriented refugee assistance which focuses on the survival of refugees.

As the objectives and activities of refugee assistance became more developmental in the 1980s, the approach shifted from a directive, give-away style to a more participatory one. In this section, the appropriateness of the participatory approach as applied to refugee context will be examined.

5.2.1 Participation in Refugee Assistance

The actors of traditional or relief-oriented refugee assistance are few: the government of a host country, UNHCR, WFP and other agencies implementing assistance activities[123]. As explained in

---

[123] Most implementing agencies are non-governmental organisations (NGOs), some of which may be affiliated with governments of third countries. In some countries, however, governmental agencies of a host country implement all the assistance activities.

Chapter 2, the government of a host country, together with UNHCR, is a major decision maker, making the overall policy. WFP supplies food for refugees. Implementing agencies, often under an agreement with UNHCR, organise assistance activities such as distributing food, providing health care, or setting up a water system with refugees being mere recipients of assistance.

In developmental refugee assistance, with its aim to enhance refugees' potentials and contribute to development of local communities, involvement of local communities and the refugees themselves becomes indispensable. Generally, the participatory approach to refugee assistance includes two aims: (1) to reflect the views of refugees and locals in designing assistance projects; and (2) to have refugees and locals participate in implementing assistance projects.

In the 1980s, researchers and observers on refugee assistance criticised the mode of refugee assistance which excluded refugees from participating in decision-making (for example, Harell-Bond, 1986; or Bulcha, Kibreab and Nobel, 1987). Today, it is a common practice for UNHCR and aid agencies to get views of refugees through interviews and meetings while assessing their needs, available resources, and the community structure. Similarly, local representatives get involved in the planning process of refugee assistance by participating in meetings and workshops. In addition, both refugees and locals may take more active roles than merely being interviewed by participating as members of an assessment team.

In the implementation process, refugees are often encouraged to establish a committee to manage their own communities. Refugee committees normally function for the purpose of problem-solving and decision-making within their community. Elected refugee leaders work as representatives of their community when negotiating with aid agencies, the host country government and UNHCR. Many other refugees may also work as community workers, health volunteers or agriculture extension workers in the refugee community.

As such, refugee assistance attempts to involve refugees, as well as locals, in the process from planning, to implementation and evaluation. However, the participatory approach, which originates in rural/community development, seems to pose certain limitations in its application to refugee assistance.

One of the immediate questions on participation in refugee context is on time frame. The more people a project involves, the longer the whole process takes. The time required for a participatory approach does not seem to fit the short cycle of refugee assistance projects. Rural development plans (in development context) may require an implementation period of 5-10 years. The first year may be spent solely on preliminary assessment and consensus-building. Detailed data on a project site (villages) are collected and workshops are held to decide on project objectives, directions, and activities.

Refugee projects, on the other hand, cannot afford such long preparation. Instead, they are expected to produce some visible results from the first year, such as constructing clinics, organising non-formal education, or establishing other community-based activities. Naturally, such a short process in refugee assistance may not ensure the consensus of all the stakeholders that participatory development usually attempts to achieve.

Such an issue as the limitation of participation has not been cricically discussed in the community of refugee aid practitioners and observers. Rather they seem to believe naïvely that it is a good thing. This author has often come across researchers and project evaluators who make comments such as "Not all stakeholders were informed of the objectives of this project," "Some local authorities felt not consulted on the project," or "Refugees should be consulted more." This, then, begs the question: How broadly and how often should people be consulted within a given limited time frame?

A second question concerns the level of decision making that refugees and locals can be reasonably involved in. Some refugee aid practitioners tend to insist that refugees should decide on and organise activities without any restriction or obligation to aid agencies (e.g., free from reporting responsibility or without regard to policy priorities). Likewise, some observers of a refugee assistance programme state that refugees should be allowed to decide on major policy matters such as whether or not refugee assistance should be camp-based or individual based[124].

Such a notion seems to be based on Chamber's idea of "putting the last first" (1983), or the idea that aid projects should not be elite-oriented or donor-driven but for the interests of the poor. Advocates of these ideas also seem to be followers of Pretty's argument (1994) that functional participation is a minimum requirement to ensure sustainable development (see Table 5-2). Noda (2003: 68), for example, suggests that a project should not be called participatory when external actors, though based on local information, set its objectives.

Those who insist on the ultimate level of participation can be called "puritans" of participation. Contrary to the opinion of these "puritans" of participation, it may be more realistic to say that Pretty's functional level, instead of self-mobilisation level, may be the level of participation that refugee assistance can realistically aim at.

---

[124] Camp-based assistance in this context means that assisted refugees should live in an organised camp or settlement, while individual-based assistance does not specify any particular location for refugees and they find their shelter on their own.

Table 5-2: Hierarchy of Participation

Typology	Components
Self-mobilisation	People participate by taking initiatives independent of external institutions to change systems. Such self-initiated mobilization and collective action may or may not challenge existing inequitable distribution of wealth and power.
Interactive participation	People participate in joint analysis, which leads to action plans and the formation of new local institutions or the strengthening of existing ones. It tends to involve interdisciplinary methodologies that seek multiple perspectives and make use of systematic and structured learning processes. These groups take control over local decisions, and so people have a stake in maintaining structures or practices.
Functional participation	People participate by forming groups to meet predetermined objectives related to the project, which can involve the development or promotion of externally initiated social organization. Such involvement does not tend to be at early stages of project cycles or planning, but rather after major decisions have been made. These institutions tend to be dependent on external initiators and facilitators, but may become self-dependent.
Participation for material incentives	People participate by providing resources, e.g., in return for food, cash or other material incentives. Much on-farm research falls in this category, as farmers provide the fields but are not involved in the experimentation, yet people have no stake in prolonging activities when the incentives end.
Participation by consultation	People participate by being consulted, and external agents listen to views. These external agents define both problems and solutions, and may modify these in the light of people's responses. Such a consultative process does not concede any share in decision-making, any professionals are under no obligation to take on board people's view.
Participation in information giving	People participate by answering questions posed by extractive researchers using questionnaire surveys or similar approaches. People do not have the opportunity to influence proceedings, as the findings of the research are neither shared nor checked for accuracy.
Passive participation	People participate by being told what is going to happen or has already happened. It is a unilateral announcement by an administration or project management without any listening to people's responses. The information being shared belongs only to external professionals.

Source: "Alternative Systems of Inquiry for a Sustainable Agriculture," by J. Pretty, 1994, *IDS Bulletin*, 25(2), p. 41.

In this author's view, the puritans' idea of participation seems to ignore both accountability and policy priorities. It also ignores the realities in refugee assistance and thus the inevitable limitation of participation in refugee context. While refugees are assisted within the policy framework of a country of asylum and their assistance programmes depend on external donors, refugees as beneficiaries of the assistance are also responsible for what they choose to do with the funds and may have to follow the overall policy of a country of asylum. In any society, laws and regulations bind people; public budgets limit the ranges of public services. While individual citizens and refugees should be allowed to freely express their opinions, such freedom does not endorse "autonomic" decision by aid beneficiaries.

This point of reality leads on to the third question that concerns the neutrality and credibility of the participants' opinions or what is called "local knowledge" in participatory development. That the participatory approach reflects the views of the refugees and locals seems to be based on two assumptions: the representatives of the locals and refugees always reflect the rest of their respective communities and their opinions are always right and appropriate. Are these reasonable assumptions?

In Chapters 1 and 2, politicised leaders who victimised vulnerable refugees were discussed. Chapter 1 also explored the difficulties that refugee leaders have in being objective or garnering consensus within their own community. Such examples illustrate situations in which refugee leaders, whether they are genuine or not, may not always be able to represent the views of the most vulnerable people in their community or may not always have "correct" views.

All these realities call for a critical review on some issues concerning participation in refugee assistance: What should be expected from the participation approach in a refugee context? Who should participate? What kinds of skills are required for aid workers in order for them to apply the participation effectively in the refugee context?

As stated earlier, there is not much critical debate within the refugee aid community. In the development arena, however, legitimate criticism has appeared against conventional notions on participation. Following is a brief overview of how the participatory approach became mainstreamed in international development. The next sections will examine experiences and critiques in applying the participatory approach to refugee situations.

Through the 1960s and the 1970s, the participatory approach was advocated in the context of rural development (Sakata, 2003; Mansuri & Rao, 2004). In the 1980s, participation began to receive broad attention from development workers and donors, with the traditional top-down development approach being recognised as ineffective. The idea to include "the poor" and "locals" in the development process gained growing consensus in the development arena by the mid-1980s when elite-oriented development or big development was accused of performing poorly (Mansuri & Rao, 1994: 7). Chambers (1983), claiming the participation a new paradigm of development, is generally considered as the focal advocator or the authority of participation who promoted the application of the idea to rural development (Cleaver, 2001; Cooke & Kothari, 2001a; Sato, 2003a).

Participation is generally considered effective in incorporating local ideas into development projects (Mosse, 1994: 498), benefiting the poorest (Mansuri & Rao, 2004: 7) and leading people to self-reliance (Kumar, 2002: 27; Sakata, 2003: 39). It is often referred to as a development concept (e.g., participatory development as a concept), used as an approach (e.g., participatory rural appraisal) and it produced tools (e.g., mapping).

On the other hand, since the 1990s, development researchers have exchanged critical debates on participation (for example, Cooke

& Kohtari, 2001a; Leeuwis, 2000; Mosse, 1994; Sato, 1994, 2003b). The critics have questioned the effectiveness of participatory approach, its assumptions and its methodologies. Among the debated points are effectiveness in targeting the poor and fairness of "local" people's perspective. Though concerns were presented previously over participation as particularly observed in refugee situations, some of the critiques on participatory development do share common issues and are quite applicable to the refugee context as well.

In the remainder of this section, by referring to debates on participatory development and cases of refugee assistance, the limitation of participation in refugee assistance, its feasible application and the skills that are required for aid practitioners will be explored. The purpose of the discussion in this section is not at all to reject participation but to revisit its approach with an attempt to make it more realistic and useful in a refugee context.

5.2.2 Level of Participation

Levels of participation in refugee assistance vary mostly from passive to functional participation of Pretty's hierarchy. Many situations are even at the consultation or information-giving level. Very rarely does it get closer to the interactive level.

The level of influence that refugees could make in the above example (Box 5-1) is limited compared with some arguments of the "puritans" that "good" participation should empower locals (or refugees in this example) to decide on the direction and objectives of a project. This example illustrates factors that limit the level of participation. Those include: (1) the participatory assessment mission, i.e., JFAM, can only make "recommendations" within the set refugee policy, i.e., local settlement in which able refugees should be engaged in agriculture; (2) the limited duration of assessment does not give adequate time to reconcile opposing views between refugees and

Box 5-1: Limitation of Participation–Sudanese Refugees in Uganda

In August 2000, the Joint Food Assessment Mission (JFAM) consisting of the government of Uganda, WFP and UNHCR visited Sudanese refugee settlements. The mission was to assess the household food security in the settlement and decide on the level of food assistance that WFP would provide. Periodically, food assistance had been reduced based on the findings of previous JFAMs.

The mission spent two days on visiting two refugee settlements in one district. The assessment team, including refugee representatives and local administrators, interviewed both locals and refugees on their life, food situation and refugee assistance. It also reviewed data on the nutrition status of refugees and the crop yield from refugees' agriculture activities.

Refugees claimed that the climate of the last season had not been favourable to crop production, and other income generating opportunities were extremely limited. Locals claimed that they were just as poor as refugees and some were even worse-off. They also argued that refugees were lazy, not working on the farm. Reviewing all the claims and data, the mission concluded that the shortage of rain had seriously damaged crop production. They further recommended that food assistance should not be reduced, and additional emergency food rations be given to those who were seriously affected by the drought.

A week later, WFP had to announce the reduction of food assistance due to the lack of food that donors contributed to the organisation.

Adapted from *Uganda News*, Shimizu, 2000.

locals; and (3) available resources (food donated by donors to WFP) finally determines the level of food assistance.

The distinct feature of participatory refugee assistance, in comparison with development, is the heterogeneity of the "participants" or "community." Mansuri and Rao (2004: 39-40) refer to rural development cases in which social heterogeneity has negative impacts on cooperative behaviour. In the participatory process in refugee assistance, the elements associated with the heterogeneity appear more distinctively. The "participants" or "communities" referred to in refugee assistance represent two characteristically different groups, namely refugees who are aliens and locals who are citizens of the host country. Therefore, one refugee situation already includes two distinctly heterogeneous groups.

Furthermore, the refugee group is quite diversified. People from different villages and with various ethnic backgrounds are placed together in a refugee settlement/camp and regarded as one refugee "community" but the refugee community is more diversified than communities that usual rural development programmes may deal with.

Given these features, consensus building, which is normally a long process, takes even longer in a refugee assistance context. On the other hand, as repeated, time allowed for refugee assistance is much shorter than usual development process. Therefore, it is challenging, if not impossible, to go through an adequate participation process as recommended by many advocators for participatory development.

Besides, limited participation is not only a matter of feasibility, but also a matter of necessity or even appropriateness. I would further argue that such a sophisticated process or high level of participation may not be required in refugee assistance. The government of a host country (or together with UNHCR) may establish overall policies on refugee assistance, just as the host country government establishes other national policies in areas such as education or social services. Returning to the case in Box 5-1, the conclusion of JFAM cannot go beyond the set policy that promotes refugee self-reliance through agriculture-based activities. It could not decide that all the refugees should abandon agriculture activities and continuously depend on full food rations, even if some refugees preferred such an option.

Purist advocates of participation may argue that nationals have their representatives in the parliament but refugees do not. They might therefore claim that there should be a way to allow the latter to get directly involved in the high-level policy making process. This argument, however, seems to ignore the fact that political rights of aliens are usually limited compared with a country's own citizens. The role of refugees (and refugee assistance) can and should indeed make a positive influence on national laws and policies. However, it is a long-term process. At least for in the short term, it is more reasonable to assume limited direct participation of individuals on making national policy and that the influence of refugees and locals remains within the predetermined legal and political framework.

The puritans' argument also seems to be based on the assumption that refugee leaders may always properly represent the rest of their members of the community. To the contrary, neither development researchers nor refugee experiences support such an assumption. This point will be discussed in a subsequent section.

Considering the above, it is reasonable to conclude that the functional participation of Pretty's typology is the realistically optimum level and, perhaps, interactive participation may be more ideal.

Another example from Afghanistan (Box 5-2) may well explain the limitation of "local" influence through participation. The case of Afghan returnees in Box 5-2 presents the combination of higher and lower levels of participation. Although a community had power to decide on beneficiaries, choice over construction materials highly depended on an external aid agency, i.e., UNHCR. Besides, the type of project (i.e., shelter, but not clinics or schools) was already decided before returnees and locals were consulted, or even before refugees returned to Afghanistan. Again, this would be a functional level of participation, according to Pretty's definition.

One may propose that aid agencies should give out cash for communities to decide on their own projects and, in this way, the projects would become more participatory[125]. This argument appears sound at first. Upon a closer examination, however, this alternative approach, which claims to have a higher level of participation, brings up several issues.

Box 5-2: Limitation of Participation–Shelter Projects for Refugee Returnees in Afghanistan[126]

UNHCR planned, as its project for 2002, to construct 40,000 shelters for Afghan refugees returning from neighbouring countries. Because of a long lead time, mass procurement of shelter materials had to be initiated already in December 2001. The large-scale shelter project, requiring a significant amount of wood, was expected to cause a negative environmental impact but a positive economic one locally. Based on the results of an expert study and the organisation's own assessment, a decision was made to use both international and domestic markets.

---

[125] A possibility for this option was actually discussed within UNHCR.
[126] The situation in Afghanistan in 2002 concerns returnees but not refugees in an asylum country. Nevertheless, as the essence of participation in this example remains relevant to the refugee situation, it is presented in this paper. In 2002, some 1.8 million Afghan refugees and IDPs returned home.

> In March 2002, a large number of Afghan refugees started to return home under UNHCR's repatriation programmes. Representatives from the Afghan administration, UNHCR's implementing partners (NGOs) and local shuras (traditional Afghan forums for decision-making) formed a committee in each village to implement the shelter project. Their tasks included selection of beneficiaries, monitoring the distribution of shelter materials, and confirmation on the completion of construction. Construction work was principally the beneficiaries' responsibility, while most of the construction materials were provided through the aid project.
>
> Afghans traditionally used logs for beams, but internationally supplied beams were sawed flat. UNHCR partner agencies talked with returnee communities and shelter committees to assess which communities would accept the foreign type of wood. Most of the communities received beams according to their preference. One community received beams of substandard quality that UNHCR and its partners had failed to screen out. The community questioned the reliability of a supplier and proposed to use one that they trusted. UNHCR staff, explaining the bidding procedure, counter-proposed to replace the unsatisfactory beams with the right ones that would be procured through a supplier of UNHCR's choice.
>
> Developed by the author.

If all the communities had voluntarily chosen shelter as their project[127], the procurement of beams, which would have also been organised by communities, would have mostly depended on local markets. Then, the environmental impact of cutting down significant amounts of trees in that country would have been more serious. Furthermore, assistance standards would have been foregone, running the risk that one community would provide expensive shelters for a handful of people while another community provided sub-standard shelters for many people.

Contrary to the above hypothesis (i.e., to disburse cash directly), if communities had voluntarily chosen different activities and if all the aid agencies had applied a "high-level" participatory approach, there would have been no coherence among communities and the central government would have lost the overall picture on what was being done at local levels. The situation, in which the government had no control over its regional development, would possibly result in the absence of a central development plan.

The final point concerning the limitation of participation is on resources. Whatever control or influence refugees and locals may have, external assistance is bound by the resources available. In the case of Uganda, the assistance project was not able to provide more food than what was available from WFP. Likewise, allocation of shelters may be decided according to the resources available and the number of returnees per region.

The analysis of the cases reconfirms the earlier argument that expecting a high level of participation is not only unrealistic but also less meaningful or less appropriate in the refugee context. The level of participation is not the most important issue in refugee assistance.

---

[127] Choosing shelter as an assistance project was based on a preliminary assessment among Afghan refugees in Pakistan that found shelter as one of in the highest needs.

Rather, it seems more important to consider how to effectively use a participatory approach within constraints given.

It can be drawn from the discussion so far that it is essential for aid workers to be able to make appropriate judgements on who should be involved in a process and when. Aid workers must also be able to make sound analysis of conflicting views among different stakeholders. It is not necessary (or even possible), as the puritans contend, that locals (or refugees) decide on everything to make a "good" participatory project. As Mohan (2001: 164) suggests, we should not fall into a dichotomy between experts' knowledge and that of locals/refugees, but rather aim for combined knowledge. The next obvious question, then, is how and when to combine the knowledge (input) from experts/authorities and locals/refugees.

Based on the above arguments, it can be reasonably said that key actors including government and main agencies in refugee assistance should be the ones to determine the overall policy and direction of assistance programmes. At the same time, the appropriateness of such "expert" decisions should be cross-checked by improving "downward accountability" (Mansuri and Rao, 2001:55). To ensure the downward accountability, locals views and those of refugees are essential. The implementation of the programme requires the participation of locals and refugees. Furthermore, the views of refugees and locals should be reflected on the evaluation of the programme, which the policy makers (or experts) should utilise in revising the policies.

Similarly, at a community level, aid agencies should better understand different interests among the main actors. UNHCR Guidelines on Development Assistance for Refugees published in 2005[128] suggests focusing on common interests at the early stage, rather than presenting all the issues to all the stakeholders. A paral-

---

[128] UNHCR, *Handbook on Development Assistance for Refugees,* 2005.

lel system to formal committees might be required to cross-check leaders' opinions with the rest of the refugees. Alternatively, individual consultations, apart from formal workshops, may be more appropriate to assess different interests among leaders or stakeholders.

5.2.3 Credibility of Leaders, Local Views and Refugees' Opinions

Publicly questioning the credibility of refugees' opinions creates psychological discomfort among refuge aid workers. This reaction is similar to a situation in which development researchers are uncomfortable about criticising locals. Critics of participation point out the fact that practitioners fear criticising local practices (Cleaver, 2001:47), they accept local knowledge as objective truth (Kothari, 2001:145), and they romanticise the poor without objective grounds (Mohan, 2001:60). Hickey & Mohan (2004: 9) state that this tendency of aid workers, assumed to be westerners in their writings is the consequence of post-colonial guilt.

Fear of criticising refugees involves something more than guilt. As discussed in Chapter 2, present societies are not necessarily favourable to refugees (or immigrants). Campaigns against refugees (and immigrants) are seen in many places in the world. More than a few citizens develop stigma against refugees even before meeting any. Under such circumstances, aid workers' criticism of refugees may result in further setbacks in refugee protection.

As such, it is not easy, and may even be inappropriate for refugee aid practitioners to make public criticism of some refugee behaviour. However, without looking at the reality, discussions on refugee participation would remain superficial and naïve. The problems related to militarised or politicised leadears who wrongly control other refugees were discussed earlier. The previous chapter also presented a situation where refugee leaders might not properly represent their communities and fail to provide neutral opinions.

How to apply a participatory approach in such situations needs to be discussed. In the development context, researchers have already posed questions on the appropriateness of leadership and the quality of information collected through participation. Mosse's study (1994: 508) concludes that the Participatory Rural Appraisal (PRA)[129] process, far from gathering neutral local knowledge, tends to exaggerate the selective presentation of opinion because of the influence of power and authority as well as gender inequality. He argues that the perspectives and interests of the most powerful people of a community are likely to dominate the PRA process. As Mosse states, more complicated is the fact that the domination would appear not through competition or confrontation but through the expression of consensus.

Similarly, Shepherd (1998: 185) warns of the over-reliance of community leaders. Sato (2003a: 24) even cautions about the appropriateness of a leader that a community or an institution "democratically" chooses. Mansuri and Rao (2004) reviewed a number of World Bank's community-based projects. Their analysis reveals that participatory projects are not particularly effective at targeting the poor. They also find that participatory projects and top-down projects are equally susceptible to political manipulation.

Taking these findings into consideration, it is reasonable to suppose that a participatory approach does not necessarily ensure the neutrality of opinions or the most accurate information on the poor. Instead, a participatory approach may reinforce local power

---

[129] There are a number of participatory approaches. Rapid Rural Appraisal (RRA) appeared first, and developed into Participatory Rural Appraisal (PRA). It is a body of methods to empower locals to share their knowledge, plan and act. These methods include meetings, workshops, and group discussions. They also include research methods of applied anthropology, farming and eco-systems (Kumar, 2002).

relations.

Conflicting interests among actors: As stated earlier, stakeholders of refugee projects develop different expectations. Shimizu (2005: 33) highlights differences in perception among actors of a refugee project in Uganda (see Table 5-3). Similarly, Jacobsen (2001: 11), studying a refugee programme in Tanzania, discusses different interests among stakeholders. As Jacobsen states, even each individual group does not hold the same interests but holds competing interests and agendas within themselves. Jacobsen (2001: 10) argues that the willingness of the local population to accept a refugee (local settlement) programme depends on who may benefit from it and, particularly, whether "the interests of the most powerful would be satisfied".

Further, a participatory approach, by definition, involves many people through workshops and interviews. By doing so, a participatory approach can raise high and even unrealistic expectation among stakeholders of a project. Both development researchers and refugee aid workers reported on such situations[130]. At this point, it may be helpful to review the studies of development researchers on this matter.

The participatory process often creates public events such as workshops and meetings among stakeholders. Mosses (2001:19) points out that the public nature of the participatory approach involves politics reflecting local relationships of power and authority. Leeuwis (2000: 946) further argues that participatory development could lead to unproductive development intervention due to an inability to handle conflicts. Leeuwis demonstrated in the study that

---

[130] For example, Sato (2003a: 23) mentions high expectations that participatory development process may raise. On the side of refugee aid, UNHCR in its global reports of 2001and 2002 list unrealistic expectations among stakeholders as one constraint.

stakeholders are not necessarily willing to compromise through the participatory process and are "unable and/or unwilling to take other actors' viewpoints and interests seriously."

Table 5-3: Different Perceptions among Actors of A Refugee Project

	Refugees	Local People	Government	UNHCR
About Self	• Victims	• Under-developed region, poverty	• Policy maker on refugee assistance	• Coordinator, facilitator
About Refugees and Refugee Assistance	• Anxiety about uncertain future • Wish to return home • Wish to return to normal life	• Jealousy about refugee assistance • Refugee assistance as a tool for development • Anxiety over refugee presence	• International protection • International communities should share burden of refugee assistance.	• International protection • Gradual reduction in cost of refugee assistance
About Local Settlement Programme	• Imposed	• A tool for development	• To improve quality of refugee life and development of own citizens	• To improve quality of refugee life

Adapted from "Nanminshien to Chiiki Kaihatsu," by Shimizu, 2005, *Cross-border Kara Miru Kyosei to Fukushi*, p. 19.

Such problems as those noted above may even be magnified in refugee situations as the UNHCR handbook published in 2005 suggests[131]. The increased complication is due to the unique status of refugees as aliens compared with development situations where all the stakeholders are the citizens of a concerned country. A study

---

131 UNHCR Handbook on Development Assistance for Refugees (2005), its first handbook on linking refugee aid and development, points out that challenges in refugee participation are even greater than in development situations.

done by Mansuri & Rao (2002:39-43) suggested that heterogeneous communities where people have multiple and conflicting identities could be less egalitarian or transparent than homogeneous communities because of competing incentives for a project.

Refugee assistance projects, by nature, inherit the problems of the heterogeneous communities. Refugees as aliens may first focus their efforts on their survival in asylum while local populations do not want to be disrupted by their presence. On the political side, naturally host country government may not be as interested in refugees as in its own nationals. The host country's positions may not even be coherent within itself: A local government may take a different position from the central government. Moreover, some countries may not have written policies on refugees.

Speculation over the presence of refugees is likely to magnify inherited conflicts in opinions among local actors. Furthermore, if any politicised elements are involved in refugee communities, power relations among locals, among refugees and between locals and refugees become more complicated. Under such circumstances, the participatory process in refugee situations can be more susceptible to politics and manipulation than in the usual development process.

Coordination: All the debates so far are related to the complexity and importance of coordination. In traditional relief-oriented assistance, or care and maintenance, coordination could be simple. As relief-oriented assistance activities are less participatory with little relation to local communities, many activities can be decided among a small number of actors: the host country government, UNHCR, and UNHCR's partner agencies which are implementing assistance projects. Consultations with refugees can also be less frequent.

A developmental, and thus participatory, approach creates more complex inter-relations among actors. Should participatory refugee assistance then be abandoned? No. In spite of its limitations, it is important to recognise the participatory process as the only way to reflect the needs of refugees and local voices on assistance and to help refugees empower themselves. What can be the wayforward? Mohan (2001: 164) urged that aid workers should "move beyond the bounded notions of self/other and insider/outsider." It is important to seek the balanced knowledge of experts, locals and refugees, or a combined participation and top-down approach.

It is then imperative for aid workers to acquire skills to assess power relations among stakeholders and crosscheck the leaders' claims. As suggested in the section 6.2, some situations may need a parallel system to formal committees to crosscheck information. Apart from a refugee committee, health volunteers or traditional births attendance, for example, could provide voices of ordinary refugees in a community.

While urging improved assessment by aid practitioners, the responsibilities of leaders of refugee and local leaders should not be overlooked. The point that Mansuri & Rao (2004:55) urged with regards to downwards accountability is: Both political and community leaders should be accountable and answerable to their own people.

5.3 Summary

This chapter first examined the two main objectives of local settlement, namely self-reliance and integration. Discussions in this chapter identified three categories of self-reliance and their indicators. It is essential that a project in each given situation should have clearly defined objectives. The chapter further examined determining factors of integration and concluded that integration should occur not only at the individual level but also the system level. The analysis of the integration process confirmed the conclusion of the previous discussions: To promote integration, the government's role in a country of asylum is crucial. Finally, the discussion in this chapter suggested the need for refugee aid to play a more active role in advocacy and coordination.

Then, this chapter analysed the applicability of the participatory approach, which originally appeared in the context of community/rural development, to developmental refugee programmes. This chapter has shown that the most important aspect of participation in refugee assistance is not increasing the level of participation, but rather improving the quality of participation. For an improved participatory approach, aid workers should be able to assess different interests among stakeholders and make sound judgements on whom to involve, when, and how.

Effective participation further calls for "down-ward accountability" at all levels from policy makers to locals/refugees, from aid practitioners to beneficiaries, from leaders to other members of the (refugee) community. Finally, these new challenges may require a shift of focus in UNHCR roles from implementation of assistance projects to coordination among broader ranges of actors.

Chapter 6

Case Study–Part I:
Uganda's Local Settlement Refugee Programme

The previous chapters have explored the validity of the Refugee Aid and Development Doctrine and examined local settlement as refugee policy and as an aid programme. It was concluded that the doctrine includes values important to refugee protection and assistance. The discussions further deduced that local settlement programmes could be effective only with the concerted efforts from both refugee aid and development actors. The previous chapters also identified factors determining the level of refugee integration and self-reliance. The important role of host country governments was also recognised. The previous chapter highlighted the distinctive features of a participatory approach in refugee situations in comparison with development situations.

Based on these previous discussions, Chapters 6-7 will present a specific case in Uganda to understand its local settlement programme.

6.1 Model, Objectives and Methodologies

This section will explain the conceptual model, objectives and methodologies of this case study.

6.1.1 Conceptual Model

In relation to integration and self-reliance, cultural/social, political, legal and economic aspects of the integration process have been discussed in earlier chapters. It was noted in the previous chapter that these factors could not be clearly divided between independent and dependent variables, but most of them are, in fact, mutually dependent on each another. Figure 6-1, based on Khulman's integration model (see Figure 5-1) and local settlement in Person-in-

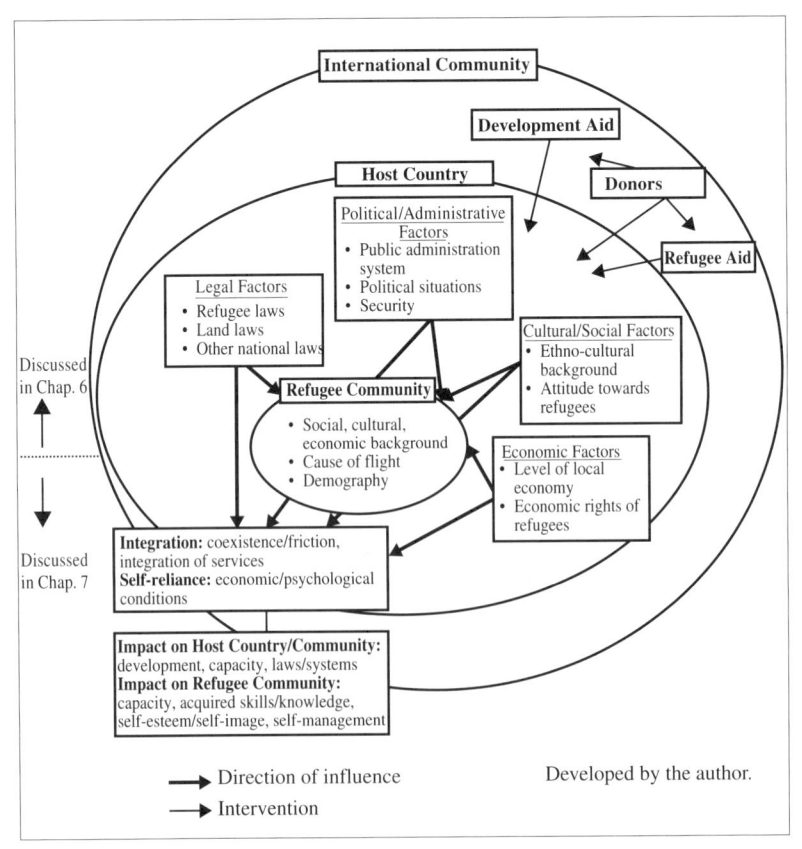

Figure 6-1: Interrelations Among and Between Actors in Local Settlement

Environment model (see Figure 4-1), presents interrelations between and among these factors, their impact, and directions of external assistance/actors.

The conditions in host countries such as laws, public administration systems, economic conditions and local attitudes to refugees may influence the process of integration and the level of self-reliance that refugees may achieve. However, these factors are not independent from the process of local settlement and their status may change through the integration process. The impact of the local settlement may appear as changes in laws, policies or locals' perception of refugees. Therefore, items listed as determining factors may again appear as impact or as indicators of self-reliance and integration.

External assistance, including assistance targeted at refugees and also at development of a refugee-hosting area/country, may affect the integration process either positively or negatively. It is clearly desirable to seek out such methods of assistance so as to maximise positive impacts and mitigate negative consequences.

6.1.2 Objectives of the Case Study

One reason for selecting Uganda for the case study originally comes from my personal experiences with Sudanese refugees in northern Uganda from 1996 to 1998 and 1999 to 2001. The programme was both criticised and praised. My own curiosity also was aroused surrounding concept, approach, and overall achievements or failures of this programme. My daily work in refugee situations and questions arising out of it drove me to embark on this study.

Even putting aside my personal experiences in the country, Uganda, as a country promoting local settlement policies for 50 years, offers a good case to understand typical local settlement programmes. Uganda has a long history of receiving refugees, dating back to the 1940s, even before the establishment of the modern concept of refugees in 1951. Since then, Uganda, starting with a British colonial government in its pre-independence period until 1956, has promoted refugees' "self-sufficiency" by encouraging them to engage in agriculture in remote and isolated camps (Gingyera-Pinycwa, 1998: 5-6). Uganda is one of the few countries that maintained local settlement programmes throughout the 1990s when most countries had abandoned this policy.

Sudanese refugee caseload was, on the other hand, a typical case of protracted refugee situation (at least until January 2005 when the government of Sudan and the Sudanese People's Liberation Army signed a peace accord). Therefore, examining Uganda's policy and its assistance of Sudanese refugees will provide useful suggestions on opportunities and limitations that the local settlement policy could offer for protracted refugee cases in Africa.

This study will examine Uganda's local settlement programme for Sudanese refugees from 1996 to 2001 with the focus on the Arua District in West Nile, northern Uganda. The programme offered during this period was characterised as a transition from relief to rural settlement, and to what was called Self-Reliance Strategy (SRS)[132]. The objective of the case study is to understand the local settlement case of Uganda: How are the conclusions of the previous chapters manifested in the case of Uganda? What policy implications can be drawn from the case?

This study is therefore what Stake (1995: 3) calls an "instrumental case study." Normally, case studies are not meant for producing generalisations. However, as Stake wrote (1995: 7-8), a case

---

[132] Later in 2004, Uganda's refugee programme further evolved into Development Assistance for Refugees (DAR). Based on the definition given in the previous chapters, the term "local settlement" is used in this case study as a general term for a policy and a programme that promotes settlement of refugees in a country of asylum.

study can increase the confidence of readers/researchers' generalisations, or modify the existing "grand generalizations." Stake (1995: 7) also stated that "petite generalizations" can be established if some patterns occur regularly throughout the case.

This case study targets the former. Discussions in the previous chapters led to several conclusions on the Refugee Aid and Development Doctrine and local settlement policy/programmes. Of them, interrelations among various factors in the local settlement process are reflected as part of the model presented in Figure 6-1. Other conclusions concerned the doctrine, the concepts of integration and self-reliance as well as the approaches of participation. Following, then, is a summary of previous points:

1. The Refugee Aid and Development Doctrine is meaningful as a refugee aid doctrine because it aims to improve the situation of both refugees and locals of host communities. From a refugee protection viewpoint, the doctrine is valuable especially because it recognises the refugees' rights beyond survival and promotes the well-being of refugees.

2. Neither self-reliance nor integration is a single static status but they both include varying degrees and go through a dynamic process. Assistance programmes should therefore be clear about which level of self-reliance/integration is being targeted.

3. Developmental (or development-oriented) refugee assistance may have some positive impact on refugee-hosting areas. Nevertheless, the impact in this regard is limited. Therefore, local settlement policy can be materialised only through the concerted efforts of both development and refugee aid actors.

4. Participatory refugee assistance may not reach very high levels of hierarchy. Overall policies and programme framework may be set by the key policy makers instead of

jointly by all stakeholders. Participation of refugees and locals is, nevertheless, essential for gaining better understanding about their views and needs.
5. Participation is not a perfect approach but rather includes certain limitations, such as its long timeframe, faulty or otherwise poor representation of leaders, and reinforcement of power relations. Aid workers should balance their own expert knowledge and the views of participants.

The particularities of the Uganda case will show how the various factors were inter-related and how the above points manifested themselves in the case.

Chapter 6 will provide information on refugee communities, and examine how cultural/social, economic, political/administrative and legal aspects of host communities affected the implementation process of local settlement in the Arua District, Uganda. Chapter 7 will then examine the impact of the local settlement on its host country/community as well as refugees (see Figure 6-1).

6.1.3 Methods

The case analysis is based on two major sources, namely literature review and my own experience with Sudanese refugees in Uganda from 1996 to 1998 and from 1999 to 2001. The former consists of news articles, reports and other documents by the UN, Uganda government, aid agencies, researchers and observers. The information obtained during my stay in Uganda was through observations, meetings and direct communications with refugees, local people, aid agency workers, government officials, and researchers. Structured or semi-structured interviews with individuals or focus groups, methods traditionally used in qualitative research, were not conducted particularly for this study, mainly because of ethical reasons and issues relating to validity. These ethical and validity matters are explained in more detail below.

During my nearly five years in northern Uganda, many assessment missions and researchers visited refugee settlements. They stayed in the settlements for varying periods from 2-3 days to over one month. Some missions were directly linked with future policies on refugee assistance. Some were evaluations of projects, which would not necessarily influence the programme in the immediate future but rather in the longer term. Others were academic researchers that had no link with policy makers[133]. From these researchers and aid practitioners, refugees received and answered many similar questions on multiple occasions. Using refugees as subject of yet more research this time, my own, did not seem to be ethically sound, especially when my research was not going to bring them any immediate benefit.

The issue relating to validity comes from my position in the refugee settlements in Uganda. Even if refugees and locals had accepted my academic research, they all knew that I was an aid worker. Consequently, there would be strong bias in their answers. Their responses would have more likely prompted a particular vision which they felt I, as an aid worker, should know. Considering this, it became apparent that my conducting field interviews would not specifically help to improve the quality of the case study.

Rather, just as Jacobsen and Landau (2003: 101) stated, observations of refugee situations for an extended period such as I did may help to increase validity. Instead of preparing a set of questions, I talked with refugees or observed them on various occasions such as food distribution, registration, meetings, cultural events, workshops, project monitoring and even security incidents where refugees were killed. On such occasions, most of my conversations with refugees

---

[133] Unfortunately, most of the researchers that I met in Uganda did not send me either draft or final versions of their papers.

were aided by local assistants who spoke the refugees' languages. The local assistants also worked as cultural informants, explaining to me behaviours and cultural values of Sudanese and Ugandans.

6.1.4 Limitation of the Case Study

This case study is not free from general problems relating to research on refugees. Jacobsen and Landau (2003) pointed out weak representation due to insufficient sampling in most refugee studies. Though I said that I had conversations and made observations on various occasions, it is not possible to rule out that those who wanted to talk to me consisted of a select group of people, who were more vocal and active, but who might not have represented fully the entire refugee population. (As discussed in Chapter 5, this is one of the typical limitations of "participation.")

Another weakness is insufficient information from donors and development actors in the study. The data collection mostly depended on refugees, humanitarian organisations, local authorities and Ugandan government offices, while views of development agencies and donors might not be adequately reflected.

Efforts were made to compensate for the shortcomings by using multiple sources of information. Nevertheless, I remain open to different views and interpretations of the case presented in this study.

6.2 Uganda: General Background

This section provides an overview of Uganda and Uganda's refugee assistance. The section will begin by explaining the history of Uganda's refugee assistance, and the origin of its local settlement policy. Then, the section will go on to explain the poverty of refugee-hosting areas, and examine the relationships between Sudanese refugees and local Ugandans from cultural, economic and political viewpoints.

6.2.1 History of Uganda's Refugee Assistance[134]

The history of refugee assistance in Uganda dates back to 1942 when the country received more than 7,000 Polish refugees under the British Protectorate Government. Since then, Uganda has been receiving refugees mainly from neighbouring countries (see Figure 6-2). From the 1950s to 1960s, the country received refugee influxes of southern Sudanese, ethnic Tutsi Rwandans and Congolese.

Uganda's refugee affairs in more recent years were dominated by Rwandans and Sudanese. Following civil turbulence in Rwanda in 1994, ethnic Hutu Rwandans fled into southwestern Uganda. From southern Sudan, civil war between the government of Sudan and the Sudanese People's Liberation Army (SPLA) caused massive displacement of people to northern Uganda (as well as within Sudan). In the mid-1990s, a major influx occurred from southern Sudan to northern Uganda. According to UNHCR, 170,800 Sudanese refugees lived in Uganda as of 2001. Of them, 156,800 were under the assistance of UNHCR[135].

Uganda historically encouraged refugees to engage in agriculture. In 1942, the British Protectorate Government encouraged Polish refugees to cultivate their own food in isolated areas. This is partly because the British wanted to segregate the European refugees from local Ugandans, but also because they wanted refugees to become self-sufficient as fast as possible.

Gingyera-Pinycwa wrote (1998:7) that the initial policy formulated by the British government laid the foundation for subsequent

---

[134] The history on Uganda's refugee assistance is based on Gingyera-Pinycwa (1998) unless otherwise noted.
[135] *UNHCR Global Report*, 2001.

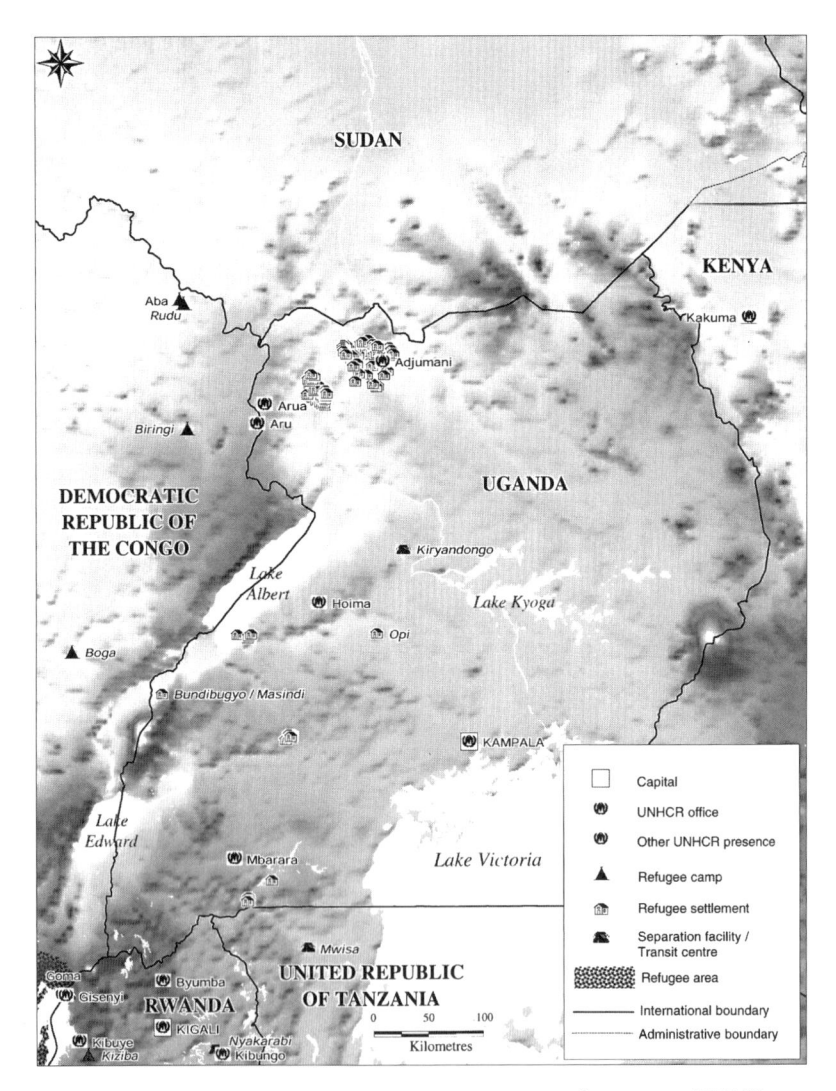

Source: www.UNHCR.org

Figure 6-2: Map of Uganda

refugee policies in Uganda which, even now, places refugees in rural, often isolated, and agriculture-based camps. British policy must certainly be one of the factors that influenced Uganda's present refugee policy. Considering the history of Refugee Aid and Development debates reviewed in Chapter 3, however, it may be more accurate to say that while Uganda's policy evolved based initially on the British influence, it was more inspired by later trends of African countries that attempted to seek development of their countries in conjunction with refugee assistance.

6.2.2 Social and Economic Situations of Uganda and the Arua District

Areas hosting refugee settlements in the Arua District are one of the most impoverished areas in Uganda, which itself is a poor country categorised as a Least Developed Country (LDC). Before looking into the situation of the Arua District, the following paragraphs will first give an outline of the general situation in Uganda.

Uganda relies on the primary industry for its economy. Agriculture and fishery account for 40-50% of its GDP with 83% of its labour force engaged in agriculture. Though Uganda's economy grew annually by five percent on average in the 1990s, its social and economic indicators were not outstanding.

For example, 75% of the government's development budget, or US$2.4 billion from 1998 to 2001, depended on external aid[136]. UNDP reported that Uganda's human development is ranked at 158th out of 174 countries[137]. Its Human Development Index (HDI) [138] was 0.404 in 1996, increased to 0.508 in 1998 and decreased again to

---
[136] The United Nations System in Uganda (UNSU), *Uganda: Promise, Performance and Future Challenges*, 2000; CIA, *The World Factbook 2002-Uganda*, 2002.
[137] UNDP, *Human Development Report*, 1999.
[138] HDI considers life expectancy, education level and standard of living. The

0.4496 in 2000. In 1996, 44% of the total population was below the poverty line, meaning income of less than US$1/person/month. According to UN's assessment in 2000[139], life expectancy at birth (1998) was 40 years, infant mortality rate per 1,000 live births (1996) was at 84, and only 49% of the population had access to a health facility within five kilometres (1998). It also reported that only 44% of people in rural areas had access to safe water.

A positive development was Universal Primary Education (UPE) that the government introduced in 1997 to ensure free primary education. UPE increased enrolment rates of eligible children from 55% to 85%. The downside, however, was a decrease in quality. In some places, the pupil-teacher ratio soared to 300:1 a year after the introduction of UPE[140].

Overall, Uganda's economic, social and human developments are low, and refugee-hosting districts including the Arua District are located in the poorest region of Uganda. The above assessment reported that the HDI of the central region that included the capital town Kampala was 0.497, while the north including the Arua District was as low as 0.317. Similarly, the population below the poverty line constituted 30% in the central region but 60% in the north. Table 6-1 shows the gap in HDIs between Arua and Kampala. The Arua District remained at the bottom from 1996 through to 2000. Similarly, Table 6-2 presents the gaps shown by other poverty indicators.

It should be kept in mind that the refugee-hosting area in the case study, i.e., the Arua District in northern Uganda, is a marginalised region within a country that suffers from underdevelopment. It should be further noted that refugee settlements were located in

---

indicator varies from 0 (lowest) to 1 (highest). Information on HDI is from: *UNDP Uganda, Uganda Human Development Reports* 1996, 1998 and 2000.
[139] UNSU, *Uganda: Promise, Performance and Future Challenges*, 2000.
[140] Ibid.

particularly rural and impoverished areas even within the district. Refugee settlements were isolated from towns. There was neither public transportation to connect the settlements with towns nor proper shops except for small local markets that dealt with food and basic domestic items such as matches and candles. It cannot be overemphasised that the refugee-hosting communities are the poorest of the poor.

Table 6-1: Human Development Index in Uganda

	1996	1998	2000
HDI Uganda	0.404	0.508	0.496
HDI Kampala	0.65	0.652	0.5933
HDI Arua	0.31	0.417	0.3830
Rank of Arua	35th/40 districts	42nd/45 districts	45th/56 districts[141]

Developed by the author based on *Uganda Human Development Reports*, UNDP, 1998, 2000, and 2002.

Table 6-2: Distribution of Human Poverty by Rural, Urban and Regional Comparisons (2000)

Region	Not expected to survive to age 40 (%)	Illiteracy rate (%)	No access to safe water (%)	No access to health care (%)	Children moderately underweight (%)
Rural	44.2	41	49.0	31	23.6
Urban	35.3	13	13.0	4	12.4
Central	38.2	23	49.0	20	19.9
Eastern	39.9	41	34.3	26	22.5
Northern	47.1	54	34.9	35	25.0
Western	46.8	35	42.0	30	23.7
Uganda	42.9	37	43.0	26	22.8

Source: *Uganda Human Development Report*, by UNDP, 2002.

---

[141] The number of districts increased because of the creation of new districts between 1996 and 2000.

6.2.3 Social and Cultural Relations between Refugees and Locals

People in northern Uganda are generally thought to be generous to Sudanese refugees and understanding of their plight. This is mainly because of ethnic affinity between southern Sudanese and northern Ugandans, and free cross-border contacts in their daily lives. Further details of the characteristics of this area will be given below.

Southern Sudan and northern Uganda share the same ethnic groups and languages. Some tribes such as Kakwa, Lugbara and Madi are thought to be originally from Sudan and currently live in both Sudan and Uganda (Nzita & Niwampa, 1993; Allen, 1994). The international boundary was, in the first place, artificially drawn in the Uganda-Sudan borderland where people originally lived without the concept of two different nations. Therefore, there have been constant movements of people between southern Sudan and northern Uganda, including merchants travelling for commerce and people in search of jobs (Allen, 1996; Merks, 2000).

Furthermore, northern Ugandans and southern Sudanese shared refugee experiences. In the 1960s, southern Sudanese fled into northern Uganda due to civil strife and stayed in northern Uganda until the mid-1970s when a peace accord was signed in Sudan. During those days, Sudanese refugees were assimilated into Ugandan society in many ways. Not only were they accepted in business and education, they also gained employment in both private and public services, even in the military (Pirouet, 1988: 241). Recruitment for the Ugandan Army was, for example, extended to Sudanese refugees in Uganda, and even into southern Sudan in the 1960s and 1970s (Woodward, 1988).

Then, later, northern Ugandans had to flee to southern Sudan and Zaire (the present Democratic Republic of the Congo) when Tanzanian troops proceeded to West Nile in 1979. Ugandan refugees were hosted in southern Sudan until 1988 when most of them returned to Uganda. Then, in the 1990s, there was another massive refugee flow from southern Sudan to northern Uganda. These Sudanese are the main refugee populations of this case study. Ugandans' own experiences as refugees in southern Sudan seemed to help them open up to Sudanese refugees. Local people often said, "As I was also a refugee in Sudan, I can understand and so we accept them [Sudanese refugees]."

The shared ethnicity, language and experiences seemed to work as a positive factor in relations between Sudanese refugees and Ugandans in northern Uganda. Although they did not share the same religion–southern Sudanese are predominantly Christian while most Ugandans in the north are Muslim–, religion did not seem to affect the relations between Sudanese refugees and Ugandans. Their amicability was even more apparent in comparison with the situation in southwestern Uganda where serious tensions were often observed between Rwandan Hutu refugees and local Ugandans.

The local settlement process and this basically positive relationship between Sudanese refugees and local Ugandans will create mutual impact. This will be examined in Chapter 7.

6.3 Uganda: Political and Administrative Aspects of Local Settlement

This section will examine the political and administrative aspects of local settlement. It will first give an overview of Uganda's local settlement, its development from a rural settlement programme to the Self-Reliance Strategy (SRS)[142] and illustrate how refugee policies were developed (or not developed) through the official pro-

---

[142] In this study, local settlement is used as a general term, while rural settlement and Self-Reliance Strategy are specific terms used in Uganda.

cess with the Ugandan government and UNHCR. Particularly, the process of officialising the SRS as a national/district policy was much affected by the decentralisation process that was progressing in Uganda in the late 1990s. Security incidents that occurred during the early days of the settlement programme also negatively impacted its implementation.

6.3.1 From Rural Settlement to Self-Reliance Strategy

The Sudanese refugees of this study had to flee to northern Uganda because of the clash between the Sudanese government and the SPLA in 1993. By 1994, the Arua District in West Nile had received some 100,000 refugees in transit camps in its northern area called Koboko (Payne, 1998: 7). Other districts on the eastern side of the Nile (Acholi region) also received over 100,000 refugees.

Responding to this refugee influx, the government of Uganda, together with UNHCR, decided to set up an agriculture-based local settlement programme for these southern Sudanese. The programme originally aimed (1) to improve refugee self-sufficiency mainly through agriculture activities and (2) to integrate services in refugee settlements into locally existing systems[143]. The government, with assistance from UNHCR, established refugee settlements in three districts in the north including the Arua District, and another district in the west.

UNHCR's report[144] described the beginning of Uganda's local settlement programme and its objectives as follows:

---

[143] UNHCR, *Northern Uganda: Review of Rural Settlement Programme for Sudanese Refugees*, Internal report based on the UNHCR Programme & Technical Support Section mission 23 January-13 February 1996.
[144] Ibid. Refugee statistics as of 1995 are also quoted from the report.

> The government of Uganda and UNHCR have established the policy of the creation of refugee rural settlements with the objectives of the promotion of refugee self-sufficiency and refugee integration within the local socio-economic structures. (UNHCR PTSS mission report, 1996: 2)

The first objective of Uganda's rural settlement, i.e., self-reliance, sought to improve refugees' food self-sufficiency through agricultural activities combined with the gradual decrease of UN (WFP) food aid. The second objective, i.e., integration, included the application of the national standard to refugee services in terms of health, education and construction. It further aimed to transfer the implementation body of refugee services from NGOs to public service offices.

As of the end of 1995, three settlements, namely Ikafe, Rhino Camp[145] and Imvepi, were established on a combined total of 79,900 hectares of land. 56,354 refugees lived in Ikafe and Rhino Camp settlements and an additional 41,644 persons were to be transferred to Imvepi settlement from transit camps located in Koboko, near the Uganda-Sudan border.

The government of Uganda, UNHCR and its implementing agencies jointly administered settlements (see Figure 6-3). Refugee affairs were previously under the responsibility of the Ministry of Local Government (MoLG) but later transferred to the Office of the Prime Minister (OPM). Its Settlement Commandants were placed at each settlement, responsible for overall administration, including security, registration of refugees, and issuance of travel permits.

---

[145] This name may sound confusing and merits explanation. That area was called "Rhino Camp" even before there was any refugee settlement. Rhino Camp Settlement, therefore, means a settlement in Rhino Camp.

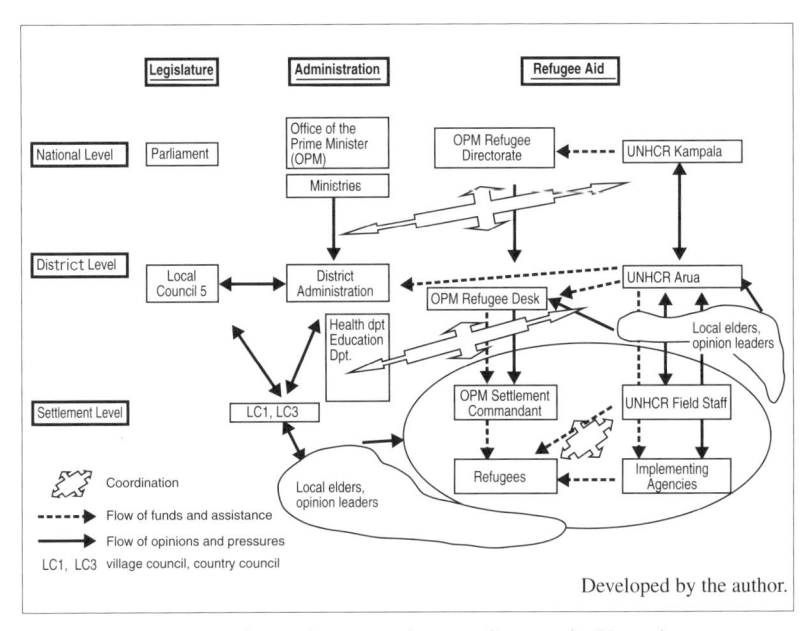

Figure 6-3: Refugee Assistance System in Uganda

UNHCR in partnership with the Ugandan government coordinated the refugee programme with other government offices and implementing agencies. UNHCR also provided most of the funds required for the implementation of assistance projects and the provision of protection. The implementing agencies, under an agreement with UNHCR and the government, delivered assistance, such as the distribution of food and aid items, agriculture, education, health services, water, demarcation of land and community services. They also provided income generation activities.

A major move came in 1998, when the government of Uganda and UNHCR launched a four-year programme called "Self-Reliance Strategy (SRS)" with the overall goal to "improve the standard of living of the people in Moyo, Arua and Adjumani districts, including refugees[146]." In July 1998, the first Round Table discussions were held to outline the SRS concepts. The Round Table participants included UNHCR, other UN agencies, district representatives, NGOs and some members of parliament. The SRS strategy paper was co-issued by the government and UNHCR in May 1999 and the Second Round Table was held in June 1999. In these years, SRS appeared to gain support from key government offices.

According to the SRS strategy paper, the objectives of the programme were:
- To empower refugees and nationals in the area to the extent that they will be able to support themselves.
- To establish mechanisms which will ensure integration of services for the refugees with those for the nationals.

The emphasis was again on promoting the self-reliance of refugees and the integration of refugee services into locally existing structures, just as in the former rural settlement programme. The difference, however, was that the SRS was no longer a policy merely on refugees, but it now emphasised the development of the entire refugee-hosting areas. (This idea was the same as the initial African concept of the Refugee Aid and Development in the 1970s-1980s.)

Hence, SRS was no longer an issue simply between OPM and UNHCR but now concerned broader ranges of stakeholders including local councils, local administrations and local authorities. Workshops and seminars were held at community, district and national levels to disseminate the concept of SRS for central and local authorities, as well as donors and development organisations. However, development actors and donors were not adequately

---

[146] Office of the Prime Minister & UNHCR, *Strategy Paper: Self Reliance for Refugee Hosting Areas in Moyo, Arua and Adjumani Districts, 1999-2003*, May 1999. The goal and the objectives of SRS were also quoted from this document.

involved in SRS, and the lack of development programmes limited its impact on the development of host areas, as well as the refugees' economic self-reliance. This will be discussed in Chapter 7.

Concerning the integration of services, it was decided that the refugee health services in Imvepi should be transferred from an international NGO to one of the district departments of Arua called District Health Services[147]. In the latter part of 1999, coordination meetings were frequently held among district representatives, OPM representatives, UNHCR, implementing agencies and refugees to prepare for the handover.

Then, in December, the Local Council V (i.e., Arua district assembly) adopted the principles of SRS. With the adoption of the SRS principle by the district assembly, it became an officially recognised policy in the Arua District.

The initial momentum of SRS was, however, soon lost. At the national level, SRS was not adopted by either the parliament or the cabinet. OPM expressed concern over certain issues related to SRS. Discussions between UNHCR and OPM did not yield much progress, and it became "stalled" in 2000[148]. SRS was not revitalised until 2001 when the newly appointed First Deputy Prime Minister and the Minister for Disaster Preparedness and Refugees indicated to all the refugee-hosting districts that the strategy was an official government policy and instructed them to proceed with implementation[149]. The stalemate at the national level was very much linked, among other reasons, with the decentralisation process that the government was implementing during the same period.

---

[147] District Health Services was later renamed District Directorate of Health Services (DDHS).
[148] Government of Uganda and UNHCR, *Self-Reliance Strategy (1999-2003) for Refugee Hosting Areas in Moyo, Arua and Adjumani Districts, Uganda*, RLSS Mission Report. 2004/3, p. 3.
[149] Ibid., p. 3.

6.3.2 Decentralisation

The initial stage of SRS coincided with the promotion of decentralisation in the government of Uganda. The decentralisation process, which had begun in the early 1990s, brought fundamental restructuring in 1998. As a result, more authority was moved from the centre to the districts. The latter became responsible for formulating District Development Plans, drawing up budgets and delivering services such as health, education and road construction[150]. However, the roles of the central government and those of local governments had not been concretely defined[151]. With details undefined, the decentralisation process created discord between local and central governments over the refugee programme.

The transfer of authority from the centre to the districts, on the one hand, meant that district departments, rather than OPM, came to hold authority over the managing of health, education and other services in and around refugee settlements. On the other hand, refugee affairs in general remained the responsibility of the central government, that is, OPM. They, apart from being the policy maker on refugee matters, remained responsible for the protection and registration of refugees as well as the security and management of refugee camps. As such, SRS started under the "dual systems" (Kaiser, 2000) on refugee assistance: Both local and central governments began claiming authority over the refugee programme. Not surprisingly, such dual systems added practical problems and political issues to the implementation of SRS. Especially, the handover process of the refugee health programme to the District Health Services was much affected by the dual systems.

---

150 UNSU, *Uganda: Promise, Performance and Future Challenges*, 2000.
151 Both the joint mid-term review by OPM and UNHCR on SRS in 2004 and an independent evaluation (Ayoo, 2000) highlighted this point. Also, at various meetings that I attended in Uganda, participants from local communities and administration expressed the same view.

One of the most frequently debated issues was the legal justification for UNHCR's financial support to the District administration. OPM occasionally raised questions on whether or not "fiscal transfer[152]" (from UNHCR) to the district was legal. This question was raised repeatedly. Although the "Strategy Paper on Self-Reliance Strategy" [153] issued in 1999 urged OPM to take the decentralisation process into account, and later in 2000, SRS secretariat further endorsed the district's implementation of refugee programmes[154], the strategy paper and the endorsement by the secretariat had no legal binding. OPM even expressed their disagreement on the district's implementing health services for refugees (Ayoo, 2000: Appendix three), while the district Local Council V Chairman was clearly unsatisfied with OPM's attitudes (Ayoo, 2000: 18).

Since there was no established division of authority between the centre and the district, many other issues that might concern both OPM and the District administration required consultation among all the parties, including OPM, the district leaders, other local authorities and UNHCR. Consequently, the consensus-building process became much more complex than earlier days when MoLG or OPM had been the central body deciding on refugee affairs. But in general, the District administration, empowered by decentralisation, became more keen to support SRS and eventually led to the adoption of the SRS principle at the district assembly.

---

[152] Personal communication from an OPM official.
[153] Office of the Prime Minister & UNHCR, *Strategy Paper: Self Reliance for Refugee Hosting Areas in Moyo, Arua and Adjumani Districts, 1999-2003*, May 1999.
[154] UNHCR Uganda, *Draft Guiding Principles for Harmonizing Interactions Between the OPM, UNHCR, Districts, and Donors and Other Partners in The Framework of the Self-Reliance Strategy For Refugees in Uganda*, December, 2000.

In contrast, the process of legalising the Self-Reliance Strategy at the national level was more gradual than at the district level. Following the joint statement on SRS by the Minister for Disaster Preparedness and Refugees/OPM in 1999 and UNHCR Representative for Uganda, SRS secretariat consisting of members from OPM and UNHCR was established. Nevertheless, unlike the district of Arua, neither the national parliament nor the cabinet took up SRS officially as a national policy (as of 2001). As mentioned earlier, SRS thus fell into a deadlock. UNHCR lost its partner advocate of SRS at the national level and sound legal grounds for it, but still had to work among concerned ministries, government offices and refugee-hosting districts without clear policies on the respective responsibilities.

Public sector reform such as decentralisation goes through a long political and administrative process during which issues including division of roles and responsibilities are decided upon. In Uganda's case, it became impossible to get refugee services fully integrated into the locally existing public system unless the status of the latter became more clearly defined.

6.3.3 Security

The security situation in West Nile (including the Arua District) was devastating from late 1995 to the first quarter of 1997. During this period, the local settlement programme in the Arua District existed only on paper. The reality was more like a relief operation. Frequent security incidents on refugee settlements as well as transit camps prevented refugees from working on the farm, and even if they managed to cultivate the land, they could not enjoy the harvest as rebels looted refugees' crops. The psychological impact on the refugees was also not negligible.

A rebel group called the West Nile Bank Front (WNBF) attacked local villages, planted mines, and ambushed travellers. According to a report by the US government (1997), some 200 deaths attributed to WNBF were reported during these two years. Rebels also attacked refugee transit camps and settlements. The most serious attacks on transit camps in Koboko occurred in April and June 1996. After these two attacks, some 25,000 refugees, afraid to stay in the remote camps, fled into a town[155]. The town soon became packed with refugees who took shelter under trees, in half-built houses and under the eaves of shops and restaurants. What made the crisis even more disastrous was a shooting incident among Ugandan soldiers that occurred at a bar in the town, resulting in deaths of some refugees. On the same night, rebels attacked the Rhino Camp Settlement. Later in the same month, Ikafe and Imvepi Settlements were also attacked. Most of the aid workers including UNHCR and its partner agencies had to evacuate themselves from their offices in Koboko and the settlements to Arua town. After that, they could visit the settlements only rarely.

The final blow on refugees was in late February 1997 when rebels attacked Ikafe Settlement, killing seven refugees. Next attacking Imvepi Settlement, rebels cut the ears off of six refugees (Payne, 1998: 34). These incidents displaced some 50,000 refugees from Ikafe, Imvepi and even Rhino Camp Settlements to towns in Koboko and Yumbe, near the Sudan-Uganda border. Refugees said, "We would like to die in our own home rather than in a foreign country."

In early March, many refugees did return to southern Sudan. Some others were stranded in villages and towns near the border for another few months until they eventually decided to return to the settlements. At the same time in southern Sudan, SPLA along with the Ugandan army killed WNBF as well as Sudanese soldiers, resulting in the final defeat of WNBF (Moro, n.d.). This military operation

---

[155] Information on insecurity incidents against refugees is based on Shimizu (1997) and the author's experience in nothern Uganda, unless otherwise specified.

brought peace to the Arua District and the local settlement programme finally started in earnest.

The impact of insecurity on the refugees was severe, causing tremendous fear and anxiety among them. The refugees' normal life was totally disrupted. The refugees' farms were destroyed and crops were looted by the rebels. Transfer of refugees from transit camps to the settlements came to a halt. Refugees in the settlements, understandably, mostly abandoned agriculture land while the refugee programme had to reallocate funds from agriculture activities to the distribution of relief items such as household items and plastic sheeting. During this period, the local settlement programme existed only on paper; in reality, this became a case of emergency relief.

Another point to note on security is that refugees were not victims of circumstances, but they were specifically targeted. Since governments of Sudan and Uganda were not on good terms, the Ugandan rebels were believed to be supported by the Sudanese government while SPLA was supported by the Ugandan government. For example, an SPLA leader was seen moving in a Ugandan military vehicle. He also appeared frequently at meetings with refugees, the government and UNHCR. Many even believed that refugee camps in Koboko harboured SPLA soldiers (Payne, 1998: 29). Therefore, refugees, who were thought to be supporters, or at least, sympathisers of the SPLA, became the targets of rebel attacks.

Similarly, the return of refugees to Sudan might not have been as straightforward as first thought but could have been an effect of political manoeuvres. Many believed that the SPLA strongly influenced the return, which coincided with its military advancement in southern Sudan (USA government report, 1997; Payne, 1998; Ayoo, 2000). For example, the SPLA in the Arua District reportedly transported refugees to Sudan (Payne, 1998: 36).

It was noted earlier that common culture and ethnicity generally worked positively for relations between Sudanese refugees and locals in northern Uganda. However, it is equally worth noting that such positive factors could be reversed by politically-oriented groups as explained in this section.

6.4 Uganda: Legal Aspects of Local Settlement

In comparison with many other countries, Uganda's national laws were generally quite reasonable with regards to refugees. However, the Land Act, which was adopted in 1998, hindered the progress of refugee self-reliance. This section will first cover the general legal aspects related to refugees in the Arua District, and then, specifically examine the impact of the Land Act on the local settlement programme.

6.4.1 Legal Aspects of the Refugee Programme

Uganda is often described as a country generous to refugees. As a matter of fact, the country reasonably granted (Sudanese) refugees basic rights and access to basic public services. For example, refugees were allowed to work. Uganda's Control of Alien Refugees Act, Cap 64 (1960) permits the employment of refugees at the "appropriate rate of wages prevailing in Uganda[156]." It was also usual for refugee children to go to local schools. On their graduation, refugee children received Uganda's official certificates just as local children did.

With regard to refugee movement within the country, the Ugandan government demanded that refugees obtain a travel permit from a Settlement Commandant when temporarily leaving their respective settlements. Some may see this policy of the Ugandan government as restriction on free movement (Hovil, 2003: 7). Taking

---

[156] *The Control of Alien And Refugee Act*, Cap. 64, Uganda, 1960, 15.

a closer look, however, a system to register refugees' movements may be required in order to understand the population and better manage assistance to them. For example, some refugees visited their relatives in another settlement and stayed with them for some time. Without knowing about the registered population and their visitors, it would not be easy to arrange certain types of assistance, such as food distribution, or to assess household food security.

In addition, for Sudanese refugees, the travel permits rule was applied in a rather relaxed way. Even if Sudanese refugees travelled without a permit, the authority, normally, did not impose any penalty. This was a complete contrast with Hutu Rwandan refugees in the southwest, where refugee travellers without permits were detained at a police station. In sum, for Sudanese refugees, the travel permit rule did not impose any serious restriction on their movement.

With regard to naturalisation, however, refugees had no opportunity except through marriage with a Ugandan national. The Uganda Citizenship Act, Cap 58[157] provides that citizens from African states are entitled to apply for Uganda citizenship after five years of residence in Uganda and its constitution[158] provides that all the immigrants who entered legally may apply for citizenship after 10 years of residence. However, according to the Control of Alien Refugee Act, Cap 64, these provisions for naturalisation do not apply to refugees[159].

Similarly, the Aliens (Registration and Control) Act prohibits any aliens from participating in politics in Uganda[160]. Uganda's local assemblies were called Local Councils (LCs) that were established from Level I to V[161]. Copying this system, refugee communi-

---

[157] *The Uganda Citizenship Act*, Cap. 58, 1962, Part II, 3(a).
[158] *Constitution of the Republic of Uganda*, 1995, Chapter Three, 12(b).
[159] *Control of Alien Refugee Act*, Cap. 63, 1969, 18(2).
[160] *The Aliens (registration and control) Act, Uganda*, 1984, para. 6.
[161] LCII and LCIV are set for administrative purposes with no local assembly

ties established Refugee Welfare Councils (RWCs) as non-formal self-help committees, the structure of which was equivalent to LC III at Uganda's sub-county level. While the RWC regularly invited local members of LC I and LC III to their councils, refugees were not allowed even to observe LC I and LC III.

Such a ban from political participation could be seen as a restriction on refugees' activities. During my stay in northern Uganda, refugee representatives and NGO aid workers occasionally expressed such a view. Some people demanded the refugees' right to vote. Though their argument had some merit, it was also reasonable to look at its practical side. The total local population of the Arua District was estimated to be 734,000[162]. The population of Sudanese refugees, on the other hand, varied from 50,000 to some 100,000 from 1993 to 2001, which constituted 6.8% to 13.6% of Ugandan population of the district. It was neither realistic nor fair to expect the government of the country of asylum to grant eligibility for the election and right to vote to such a large number of refugees.

It can be said that Uganda's existing laws permitted reasonable rights and opportunities for Sudanese refugees. The single but still important improvement expected was the passage of a new refugee bill that had been in draft form ever since the enactment of the constitution in 1995. The refugee bill, which was still under consideration as of 2004, was expected to give stronger thrust to the implementation of SRS (and, thus, to stop the disputes over it). A draft of the bill was not available to the public, but it appeared to contain articles that would promote refugee self-reliance and ensure support for refugee-affected areas[163]. Compared with the Control of Alien

---

attached.
[162] The figure is based on Government of Uganda's home page, accessed on 22 March 2003.
[163] Government of Uganda and UNHCR, *Self-Reliance Strategy (1999-2003) for Refugee Hosting Areas in Moyo, Arua and Adjumani Districts, Uganda*, RLSS

Refugee Act, which some criticised for lacking guidance on refugees' employment and work (Macchiavello, 2003), the bill was expected to ensure better opportunities for refugees and support the development of refugee-hosting communities once the parliament passed it as a new law.

6.4.2 Land Act

More problematic were laws regarding land. When the settlement programme started in 1994, not all the refugee settlements were officially gazetted as government land but some were traditionally owned by communities. During my stay in northern Uganda, no one from UNHCR or OPM could identify documents that could justify the use of the land for existing refugee settlements.

Stories from various sources, however, suggested that the refugee-hosting communities and the government, i.e., Ministry of Local Government, had reached an agreement allowing the government to use, free of charge, the land for refugee settlements as long as refugees stayed in Uganda. In exchange, the agreement had been that once refugees returned to their home, the government would return the land to the communities together with infrastructure developed on it.

Such an arrangement based on the traditional concept of community land brought about complex issues in 1998 when a new Land Act was adopted. This act speficied that the land belongs to individuals, not to communities[164]. With this provision, justification to use non-government land for refugee settlements came into question. The act states that land issues fall under the jurisdiction of local districts, not the central government[165]. This means that OPM

Mission Report, 2004/3, p. 28.
[164] The Republic of Uganda, *The Land Act*, 1998, Part II, 3.
[165] Ibid. Part V. 77.

alone would not have authority to decide on the problems related to the land for refugees but should consult with district authorities who might have different interests.

The Land Act hindered the allocation of additional land for newly arrived refugees and newborn babies. Moreover, individual Ugandans began claiming ownership of land that refugees had already been cultivating. In some case, refugees were prevented from working on farms claimed by Ugandans. Such incidents increased in frequency every year. The issue grew so serious nationwide (for example, Bagenda, Naggaga and Smith, 2003) that OPM began to embark on their own research in 2001 in an attempt to find a better solution.

Chapter 7

Case Study–Part II:
Uganda's Local Settlement Refugee Programme

Chapter 6 began by presenting the conceptual model (see Figure 6-1) showing interrelations among refugee communities, host communities/country and external aid system in the framework of refugee local settlement policy. The chapter also presented the case of local settlement in the Arua District, Uganda. The situation of the host country/communities and its impact on local settlement were discussed from legal/political, social/cultural and economic viewpoints. The process of the local settlement programme in the Arua District, Uganda was also explained.

The case study continues in this chapter, by first reviewing a participatory approach in the case of Uganda. The participatory process in this case study experienced problems similar to those that were discussed in Chapter 5. Later in this chapter, the result and impact of refugee local settlement on refugees and local communities will be examined (see Figure 6-1).

7.1 Participation Process

This section will explain how all stakeholders got involved in the local settlement programme, what problems occurred and how these problems were tackled. Chapter 5 discussed the limits of a participatory approach noting especially that its application to refugee situations poses a considerable challenge. Issues similar to those discussed in Chapter 5 also came up in the case of Uganda.

Local stakeholders were never satisfied with the level of their participation in the programme. Both refugees and local authorities felt that their views were not adequately reflected in the process of the programme planning and implementation. Such dissatisfaction caused concern of local authorities. Unclear objectives of the programme even worsened the situation causing confusion and anxiety among local authorities as well as refugees.

7.1.1 Participation of Stakeholders

There is no systematic data available about the frequency and locations of the meetings and workshops that were held in relation to the implementation of the local settlement and SRS projects. Based on my knowledge, however, there were three levels of communication on SRS: at the national level involving the central government and the head offices of concerned agencies, particularly UNHCR and WFP, implementing agencies and donors; at the district level involving district administration, members of Local Council V, Refugee Desk from the Office of the Prime Minister and UNHCR Sub-Office Arua; and at the settlement level involving UNHCR's implementing agencies, UNHCR's field staff, Settlement Commandant from the Office of the Prime Minister, and Local Councils I and III. Participation of refugee representatives was largely at the settlement and district levels. In addition, a small number of refugee representatives participated in some national-level meetings.

Settlement coordination meetings took place monthly. Apart from those regular meetings, there were additional meetings including Joint Food Assessment, ad hoc communications, field visits of UNHCR and government officers along with various workshops.

The total number of all these meetings and workshops was not insignificant. It is reasonable to say that Sudanese refugees and stakeholders of refugee assistance were no less consulted on refugee projects than Ugandans on their own public services.

Nevertheless, a common criticism across all evaluations and reports was the lack of information flow to refugees and stakeholders and the inadequate involvement of stakeholders. Burnham et al. stated:

Unfortunately, this communication was problematic given the fact that the strategy had been developed by stakeholders at the Kampala level with limited input from district administrative and political leadership. This led to reluctance and distrust among various local-level stakeholders and the entire integration process had stalled. (Burnham et. al., 2003: 60)

Similarly, according to Ayoo (2000: 15, 17), the Refugee Welfare Council felt that they had no power to reflect refugees' views on the assistance project and the district perceived that not all stakeholders were "on board." Further, Ayoo's report (2000: 17, 19, Appendix three) illustrated the unrealistically high expectations of locals over SRS in terms of its potential for infrastructure development and their wish for extending refugee assistance such as income generation, agriculture and food aid to local populations. UNHCR's mid-term evaluation on the handover of the health sector[166] also commented on the lack of preparation with stakeholders.

How should this information be interpreted? While there was still significant time devoted to dialogues with stakeholders including both Ugandans and refugees, there was dissatisfaction among the Ugandan local authorities and the refugees. Theoretically,

---

[166] UNHCR Uganda, *Mid-Term Assessment Report of Basic Health Services in Imvepi Settlement, Arua District*, 7-13 August, 2000.

unlimited and unending participation until the process satisfies everyone is not at all necessary, as discussed in Chapter 5. The central government and UNHCR are to make the overall policies. The other stakeholders should be consulted for better needs assessment and implementation, but not to re-establish the policy itself or plan all details.

However, reality does not always follow theory. Rather, reality must count more than theory. If the dissatisfaction of stakeholders is the reality, ignoring their claims will eventually hinder refugee assistance and protection. The refugees are aliens. Without support from the local population, their protection cannot be achieved. In view of this, UNHCR, even more than the central government, should inevitably respond to such dissatisfaction, no matter how illogical or irrational, in one way or another.

In the case of Uganda, continuous dialogue with local stakeholders seemed to yield positive outcomes. UNHCR's reports up to 2001 stressed the "misconception" surrounding SRS and "resistance by local authority" as hindrance to the implementation of SRS[167]. The reports from 2002 onwards, however, changed in tone. For example, in 2002, it was reported that sensitisation campaigns by UNHCR and the government "proved to be very useful in dispelling apprehension[168]" and in 2003, it further noted that "a gradual positive change was observed in the attitude of the district authorities towards SRS[169]." Then, the joint evaluation with the government and UNHCR in 2004 finally recognised adequate information dissemination at all levels including the Refugee Welfare Council as well as Local Councils I, III and V[170].

---

167 *UNHCR Global Report*, 2001, p. 187.
168 *UNHCR Global Report*, 2002, p. 194.
169 *UNHCR Global Report*, 2003, p. 220.
170 Government of Uganda and UNHCR, *Self-Reliance Strategy (1999-2003) for Refugee Hosting Areas in Moyo, Arua and Adjumani Districts, Uganda*, RLSS

Another point in relation to consensus building in the case of Uganda was the lack of clarity in the initial policy. As discussed in Chapter 5, participation may involve a lengthy consensus building process with conflicting views and interests. This was also the case in Uganda where lack of clarity in the initial policy on SRS exacerbated the complexity of consensus building.

7.1.2 Ambiguity in the Initial Policy

The strategy paper on SRS, however, did not define concretely what should be achieved as self-reliance and integration. As discussed in Chapter 5, self-reliance consists of various levels, and integration goes through various processes. Uganda's local settlement, or SRS, should have clarified what it expected to achieve during the four-year programme duration. Instead, the SRS document may have simply given the impression that the programme was aimed at perfect self-reliance and that all the services for refugees should be implemented and financed by Uganda's central and local governments.

The strategy paper stated that the ultimate goal was to find ways to integrate the services for refugees into regular government structures and policies. It further emphasised the need to enhance the government's capacity to "take over this responsibility." With regards to refugee self-reliance, the document stated:

> Of equal importance is the phenomenon of diminishing donor interest in funding protracted refugee assistance programmes

---

Mission Report, 2004, p. 11. Though the situations in 2002 onwards are outside the scope of this study, this example shows the dynamics of participation in development-oriented refugee assistance. However, the information on this particular point is all based on reports from UNHCR and the government of Uganda. The final judgment may have to wait until independent researchers analyse the situation. Further, it is worth pointing out that the review in 2004 noted little information flow to the most vulnerable refugees.

and the circumstance that UNHCR is not a regular development agency. This demands innovative methods to become more efficient and *promote self-management* [emphasis added][171].

These descriptions in the document gave the impression that UNHCR was to phase out the refugee assistance in Uganda, the refugees were to be totally independent from assistance, or the government of Uganda was to take all the responsibilities, including financial responsibility, in providing assistance for refugees, and that all this was to be achieved within four years. Indeed, at the beginning of SRS some UNHCR staff members naïvely believed that refugees should achieve perfect self-reliance within four years. Others did not seriously examine what it meant in real terms to promote "self-reliance" or "integration."

Different stakeholders had different views, expectations and dissatisfactions regarding the Self-Reliance Strategy and its refugee programmes. Some district authorities felt that SRS was the exit strategy of UNHCR imposing the burden on the district. UNHCR regarded such a view as a "misconception" and stated that SRS was not an exit strategy but rather a strategy to improve the quality of asylum[172]. However, the initial document and discussions apparently contributed to such "misconception," and made consensus-building even more difficult.

7.2 Integration: The Result of Local Settlement Process

Chapter 4 defined integration as a result or a goal of local settlement. Uganda's local settlement involved two aspects of integration.

---

[171] Ibid. pp. 10-11.
[172] *UNHCR Gobal Report*, 2001, pp. 186-192.

One was the integration of refugee services into locally existing (public) systems and the other was the integration of refugees into host communities. This section will first discuss the integration of services, and, then, the integration of refugees.

Integration was, from the standpoint of refugees and refugee aid workers, the integration of refugees into local communities and that of refugees' services into local systems. From the locals' perspectives, however, integration meant rather the extension of refugee projects to local communities. In this regard, this section will also examine the impact of refugee projects on local communities.

7.2.1 Integration of Refugee Services

Integration of refugee services in the Arua District can be examined from three points: (1) whether national or district regulations/standards were applied to refugee services, (2) whether the system to deliver refugee assistance was integrated into the locally existing public services, and (3) whether financial sources were integrated into national or district development budgets. The integration concerning the first point did not face serious problems while the integration of the system and finances were much more difficult to achieve.

The integration of services started with the adoption of district and national standards to refugee assistance. Taking education as an example, the rules and standards of the Ugandan Ministry of Education and the Arua District Education Department were applied to refugee education[173]. Textbooks for primary schools at the settlements, the standards for school buildings, qualifications of teachers and examinations all followed Ugandan standards. District education officers regularly inspected schools in refugee settlements and

---

[173] Following the education system of the country of asylum is not always the case. In some refugee situations, the system of the country of origin is chosen.

refugee children received official certificates from the Ugandan Ministry of Education once they passed the final examination. Both Ugandan and refugee teachers were employed as long as they met the standard qualifications.

The same principle was applied to other sectors such as health. The Ugandan Ministry of Health categorised the level of health centres from one to five with one being the smallest and five being the largest district hospital. The number of health centres, their staffing level and functions were established depending on the population.

Concerning the integration of the refugee assistance system, as mentioned earlier, refugee health services in Imvepi Settlement were transferred from an NGO to the District Directorate of Health Services (DDHS) in 2001. The health services handover process, however, started with many difficulties. As mentioned earlier, the Office of the Prime Minister questioned the legal justification of funding the district directly from UNHCR. Even within the district administration, not all were supportive of the process at the beginning. There were many suspicions and disagreements over the idea on the handover. Some district administrators may have felt that the handover was a matter of dumping the burden onto the district. Some others seemed to have felt left out of the process.

Various meetings and joint missions to the refugee settlement helped to ease the tension and misunderstandings. By the time of handover in January 2000, main stakeholders on the district side supported taking over the refugee health services in Imvepi Settlement. Nevertheless, the process was far from perfect. The review conducted by the government of Uganda and UNHCR pointed out that the handover process (not only in this specific case but also other cases in Uganda) did not give adequate time and sufficient dialogue among the stakeholders[174].

---

[174] Government of Uganda and UNHCR, *Self-Reliance Strategy (1999-2003) for*

Following the handover of health services from an NGO to DDHS, two health centres, along with their equipment and staff, were transferred from the international NGO to the District[175]. However, the official status of refugee health workers in the district system remained unclear. DDHS provisionally treated them as project staff. While salaries and allowances were paid by DDHS with UNHCR's funds, whether they were entitled to other benefits as Ugandan public servants remained an unresolved question. In summary, the integration of the system had to go through a rather long negotiation process, but even so, some issues were not resolved.

In terms of finance, UNHCR continued supporting most of the costs of health services. It was unrealistic to assume that the district would raise revenue to afford the total cost while the country depended on external assistance for its national budget. Additional funds from donors, however, were not forthcoming to the government of Uganda or the Arua District administration to help manage its refugee programmes. Unfortunately, the reduction of humanitarian assistance (e.g., food reduction) did not lead to the increase of development funds for the district of Arua that took up new tasks such as health services in the refugee settlements. UNHCR reported:

> ...there remains a serious problem in getting the ... donors to promise or provide regular development resources to districts that are willing to integrate services of refugees in their district development plans. The obvious saving on food aid and ongo-

---

Refugee Hosting Areas in Moyo, Arua and Adjumani Districts, Uganda, RLSS Mission Report, 2004, p. 24.
[175] Later, the health sector in Rhino Camp Settlement was also transferred to DDHS. Further, the education sector was transferred to the District Education Officer (DEO).

ing reduction in UNHCR budget would more than compensate for the additional expenditure by the districts (e.g. in education, health, agriculture, income generation etc.), but there is no simple mechanism of transferring savings from humanitarian budgets to development budgets[176].

Therefore, UNHCR had no option but to fund the District administration (namely DDHS). This case also made obvious that some areas such as financial resources would not be "integrated" in the near future. It can therefore be said that the integration of services, as well as refugee self-reliance, made reasonable progress in this case but that complete integration–implementation and financing by the government of Uganda–within a short time frame (i.e., four years) was not at all feasible.

The above described the state of the integration in the Arua District as a result of local settlement (as of 2001). The integration also created its own impact on both of the refugee programme and district administration, namely DDHS.

The immediate impact was decreased quality of services. Though performance of DDHS was thought to be generally satisfactory,[177] official assessment revealed that it did not retain the same level as that of the NGO[178]. Before the handover, refugees were, indeed, doubtful about the transfer. They expressed their concern over (potential) decrease in quality of services at a meeting that I attended with refugee leaders, district administrators, OPM representatives, UNHCR, and representatives from other aid agencies in

---

[176] UNHCR Uganda, *Country Operations Plan 2002*, 21/08/01 version, p. 11.
[177] UNHCR Uganda, *Mid-Term Assessment Report of Basic Health Services in Imvepi Settlement, Arua District*, 7-13 August, 2000, p. 8.
[178] Government of Uganda and UNHCR, *Self-Reliance Strategy (1999-2003) for Refugee Hosting Areas in Moyo, Arua and Adjumani Districts, Uganda*, RLSS Mission Report, 2004, p. 16.

1999[179]. Unfortunately, some drawbacks were actually observed after 1 January 2000. Unauthorised absence of senior district medical officers (e.g., a doctor) from health centres in refugee settlements were reported to UNHCR more than once. According to one DDHS official, it was difficult for the district office to ensure medical professionals in such remote areas as refugee settlements because none of the doctors or other senior staff was willing to work there.

Another typical downside in integration was the abolishment of community health workers. Community health workers in the refugee project had been engaged in outreach activities, such as vaccination campaigns, patient referrals from a village to a nearby health centre, and follow-up on the chronically ill. They had not only ensured health services at a grassroots level, but also had been helpful in advocating for the most vulnerable.

To "standardise" the service, the outreach service had to be discontinued because the district health system did not include such services. A concern over a possible downturn in service delivery was raised at coordination meetings in 1999. The joint review by the government of Uganda and UNHCR in 2004, however, did not particularly comment on this issue.

The above problems, again, presented the difficulties, if not the limitations, of integration in an under-developed region. The situation of the local community (on health services) was substandard by any international or Ugandan national standard. In refugee settlements, minimum-standards were met because the refugee programme provided additional resources, for example, by giving additional allowances to medical staff who worked in refugee settlements. Once such additional allowances were removed (for the sake of integration), medical staff opted to work in more urban areas.

---

[179] The same point was also noted by the evaluation done by the government of Uganda and UNHCR. Ibid., p. 24.

A point to note was that the standards of medical services in the settlements were not extravagant, but they simply met the national standards. Therefore, "integration" or "standardisation" between services for nationals and refugees could not justify decrease of service quality. In conclusion, idealistic integration reasonable quality of services for both refugees and locals within the district's system–was impossible. Policy makers had to choose between additional allowances for medical staff and lower quality of services.

In spite of some negative observations on the performance of the district, I also noted improved capacity of the district in dealing with refugee affairs. In 2000, there was a small refugee influx from southern Sudan into the Arua District. It is standard procedure in the case of a refugee influx for UNHCR's partner health agency, an NGO in many situations, to organise medical screenings and vaccinations. This had been the case in the Arua District as well. However, in 2000, DDHS deployed a team to a place near the Sudan-Uganda border, quickly providing the initial medical screening there.

Another positive aspect was the improvement in including refugees in national/district services. A good example was the outbreak of Ebola fever that hit northern Uganda in 2000. The Ugandan Ministry of Health, together with districts' health departments in the northern region, responded to the crisis with an emergency programme. The refugee settlements in the Arua District, covered by the DDHS, also came under the protection of this national emergency programme.

7.2.2 Integration of Refugees

Although information to measure the state of refugee integration was rather limited, relations between Sudanese refugees and local Ugandans can be considered one of the important elements of refugee integration, and therefore, this point will be discussed below.

As explained in Chapter 6, relations between Sudanese refugees and local Ugandans were essentially positive. This amicable relationship seemed to be maintained during the period of this study. Wells, schools and health centres that were constructed through the refugee programme were utilised by both refugees and locals. In Rhino Camp Settlement, for example, half of the pupils attending primary schools were local children. There were no serious conflicts observed between Sudanese refugees and Ugandans.

As settlements grew and especially at the later stage of the assistance programme, however, increased problems such as disputes over land and friction over resources became apparent. For example, refugees in the Arua District were not allowed to fish in the Nile. Coupled with problems brought by the new Land Act, infrastructure that was developed in the settlements attracted the locals, who came to live close to, or even inside the settlements. Although the two populations shared health centres and schools without problems, increased population in and around the settlements heightened competition over resources such as land and animals for cultivation and hunting. Some other issues were also reported such as low labour wage of refugees compared with Ugandans and sexual exploitation of refugee women.

Obviously, information presently available does not provide sufficient basis for any conclusion on whether relations between the two groups improved or whether refugee integration progressed or not. Sensitive issues, such as exploitation, do not easily surface, and require further studies.

7.2.3 Impact on Development of Local Communities

As discussed earlier, local authorities had an expectation that refugee assistance projects would bring infrastructure development into host communities. In other words, they regarded the presence of refugees as an opportunity for development. Over 100 wells, some 20 primary schools, 6 health centres and 161 km of roads were constructed in and around the two settlements[180]. Also, 10 local secondary schools received assistance from UNHCR in the form of construction/rehabilitation of school buildings and the provision of educational materials in exchange for accepting refugee students free of charge. In addition, secondary roads and small bridges were constructed or rehabilitated in areas near the refugee settlements. UNHCR spent over US$20 million on infrastructure development in the period between 1995 and 2001[181].

Such construction projects contributed to the improvement of community infrastructure and well-being of local Ugandans. The review by the government of Uganda and UNHCR recognised the improvement of health and education services both for refugees and nationals, particularly for nationals living near the refugee settlements, "due to an increase in the number of staffed facilities, shorter distances (to schools and health centres), and more predictable supplies of drugs." The review also reported reduced transportation costs because of better road access. It was further observed that nationals moved into refugee-hosting areas because of improved infrastructure[182].

Moreover, the settlements offered local people small business opportunities and created revenue for county administration. Local people opened markets selling fish, vegetables, local snacks and basic domestic items such as soap and matches in the settlements. The markets brought tax revenue for county administration.

---

[180] Government of Uganda and UNHCR, *Self-Reliance Strategy (1999-2003) for Refugee Hosting Areas in Moyo, Arua and Adjumani Districts, Uganda*, RLSS Mission Report, 2004, p. 15.
[181] Internal data at UNHCR Uganda, Sub-Office Arua.
[182] Government of Uganda and UNHCR, *Self-Reliance Strategy (1999-2003) for Refugee Hosting Areas in Moyo, Arua and Adjumani Districts, Uganda*, RLSS

Infrastructure building projects gave contracts to local builders. In addition, refugee assistance projects created job opportunities for locals to work with aid agencies. Some skills training courses funded by refugee projects were also extended to local people.

As such, it may be said that refugee assistance projects contributed to the development of local communities. Nevertheless, it should also be noted that this level of achievement was far from comprehensive social and economic development.

UNHCR's infrastructure projects, often called Quick Impact Projects (QIPs), were aimed at small undertakings that could show visible results in a short time and usually cost less then US$50,000 per project[183]. Taking road projects as an example, UNHCR's projects only covered secondary, tertiary or access roads but not main roads. The road project of a development agency, on the other hand, would mean more than mere infrastructure construction. It may possibly consider elements of capacity development, industry development, promotion of trade, transport and communication networks. It normally organises an in-depth assessment that might take more than a year. The whole project may even take five years.

The same can be said about agriculture development and income generation. Developmental refugee assistance is more focused on quick and visible output while development programmes aim at sustainability or capacity development. The combination of the two would have been a strong push factor for the local settlement programme. Donors and development actors, however, were not forthcoming in the Arua District.

With the absence of development support, the impact of local settlement programmes on the development of host communities remained fragmental. Another downside was the politicisation of

---

Mission Report, 2004, pp. 13-14.
[183] UNHCR, *Quick Impact Projects (QIPs), A provisional guide*, 2004.

refugee assistance. Infrastructure projects of refugee assistance, no matter how small, were still significant to communities with only a few development programmes. Local leaders asked to bring infrastructure projects to their constituency. Although most such requests were based on genuine needs, some of them did not seem to consider the overall needs of the district and its relation to refugee assistance. Gingyra-Pinycwa (1998) wrote:

> ...the [national] Government's consultation with the local government has become increasingly important because the refugee issue has been politicized by local politicians who are concerned about the development implications of refugee re-settlement camps. Many people feel that refugee presence in their areas has developmental dividends, considering the special attention accorded to refugees by international agencies. (p. 9)

Another episode in which development of a settlement had rather a negative impact was a conflict between local counties in connection with tax revenue from markets in settlements. One of the refugee settlements was located on the land of three counties. Two counties disputed the boundary in relation to the location of a market in a refugee settlement. The friction escalated to the level of one group setting fire to houses of the other group (just adjacent to refugees' houses). A group also blocked a road leading to a town from the other group. The district administration intervened with no effective outcome. Though violence ceased, disputes continued.

7.3 Refugee Self-Reliance: Impact on Refugees

This section will examine the impact of the local settlement programme on refugees of the Arua District, Uganda. Based on the categories and indicators of refugee self-reliance as defined in Chapter 5, this section will examine economic, social and psychological self-reliance of the refugees. This case demonstrates that there was improvement of refugee self-reliance in terms of food self-sufficiency and psychological and social self-reliance. However, it also shows that the improvement in refugees' economic self-reliance was limited for various reasons.

7.3.1 Economic Self-Reliance

Refugees' economic self-reliance largely depended on agriculture activities. In the settlement in the Arua District, refugees, regardless of their age, were given 0.2 hectares to 0.3 hectares of agriculture land per person[184]. Refugees produced maize, sorghum, sesame, cassava and a few other crops (see Figure 7-1). Some of the refugees organised cooperatives to produce cash crops such as tobacco. Most of the crops were consumed by the refugees at home, but sesame and some other crops could be sold at markets when there was a surplus. Occasionally, buyers from Kampala even came to settlements to buy refugees' sesame.

Refugee projects provided agriculture tools, e.g., hoes and sickles, principally one time for each household. Seeds were provided through the refugee projects annually, but the amount was gradually decreased each year. Refugees were thus expected to become able to purchase replacements for the initial tools and seeds as they moved toward self-reliance. An exceptional distribution was made when rebel groups looted refugees' belongings including their agriculture tools.

As a result, 20% of all Sudanese refugees in Uganda became independent from food aid by 2000 and 24% by 2001, according to

---

[184] The size of agriculture land per person varied among refugee settlements in Uganda due to the land availability.

232   *Linking Refugee Aid with Development*

Taken by the author.
Figure 7-1: Refugee Aid Worker Showing Model Farm

UNHCR[185]. In the Arua District which had suffered from rebel insurgency until March 1997, all refugees still depended on WFP's food rations as of 2000, though many refugees received reduced rations (10-20% of the initial quantity) by the end of the year (Shimizu, 2000). Even in 2003, all the refugees in the Arua District still received some food assistance from WFP. Fifty-five percent of them were on reduced rations[186].

Apart from food, the assistance project encouraged refugees to share the cost of services such as water, health and education. The cost-sharing was, however, rather symbolic in nature. For example, refugee parents contributed US$6 per term for secondary education against the total cost of some US$60 to over US$100. Table 7-1 summarises the state of economic self-reliance against the indicators shown in Table 5-1.

---

[185] *UNHCR Global Report*, 2000 and 2001.
[186] Government of Uganda and UNHCR, *Self-Reliance Strategy (1999-2003) for Refugee Hosting Areas in Moyo, Arua and Adjumani Districts, Uganda*, RLSS Mission Report. 2004, pp. 13-14.

Table 7-1: Economic Self-Reliance

	Indicators	Results (as of 2001)
Economic Self-Reliance	**Perfect Self-Reliance** Refugees are independent from external assistance.	Not achieved.
	Partial Self-Reliance	Not achieved.
	Refugees are independent from food assistance. And they are able to partly share the cost of basic services such as water, education and health.	Not achieved.
	Refugees are independent from food assistance but receive aid for agriculture and/or other income generation activities.	Not achieved.
	Refugees are on reduced food assistance.	More than half of the refugees achieved this level.
	Refugees depend on full ration of food assistance.	Less than half of refugees were at this level.

Developed by the author.

As such, the progress of the refugees' economic self-reliance was slow in the Arua District compared to refugees in other districts in Uganda. This was, in part, due to the insecurity that prevented them from productive activities in the first two years of local settlement. Even after security was reinstated in 1997, perfect self-reliance, which requires refugees to cover not only the cost of food, but also that of basic services, did not seem to be achievable. What were the hindrances? First, as previously noted, the new Land Act made it difficult to allocate additional land while continual reuse of the same farm was reducing its fertility. Secondly, the area hosting refugee settlements chronically suffered from a lack of rain, which also significantly contributed to poor crop production. For example, the joint food assessment by OPM, WFP, and UNHCR in 2000 reported that 70 to 80 percent of the crop had been scorched by the sun or damaged for other natural reasons[187].

---

[187] ReliefWeb: Humanitarian update - Uganda, Volume iii, Issue 1. 30 Jan. 2001.

UNHCR, the government of Uganda, and aid agencies recognised these problems clearly[188]. Particularly, the implementing agencies made efforts to bring in new skills to deal with the lack of rain, added new crops that would not require much rain, or introduce animal husbandry such as keeping rabbits or bees. In spite of these efforts, however, no effective solution was found.

What about productive activities other than agriculture? Figure 7-2 shows UNHCR's budget for the Arua District in 2001[189]. Though the proportion of income generation was minimal at 2%, the education sector also included vocational training that aimed to help refugees gain business or employment opportunities.

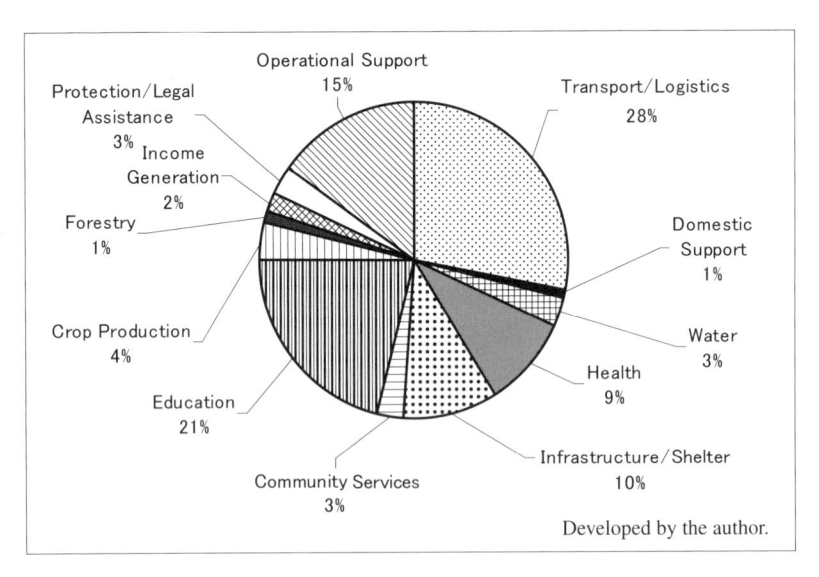

Operational Support 15%
Protection/Legal Assistance 3%
Income Generation 2%
Forestry 1%
Crop Production 4%
Education 21%
Community Services 3%
Transport/Logistics 28%
Domestic Support 1%
Water 3%
Health 9%
Infrastructure/Shelter 10%

Developed by the author.

Figure 7-2: UNHCR's Budget for the Arua District, 2001

---

[188] *UNHCR Global Report*, 2000, 2001 and 2002.
[189] Information on the initial budget of 2001 is based on an internal document at UNHCR Uganda.

Income generating activities included skills training in blacksmithing, carpentry, wood carving, brickmaking and tailoring. Vocational training at schools offered courses in mechanics, welding, electricity and carpentry. The German Development Agency, the largest implementing agency in the Arua District, further provided loan schemes with its own funds. Through these activities, the project provided many opportunities for refugees to gain skills and knowledge. Nevertheless, these efforts did not necessarily lead refugees to immediate economic self-reliance while they were staying in the country of asylum.

Some refugees could find employment at aid agencies working in the settlements as professionals or para-professionals in sectors such as education, agriculture, health and community services. These fortunate refugees were rather small in number leaving the great majority with limited employment and business opportunities. Consequently, their household income was severely restricted. Ayoo (2000: 10-11) reported that 55 percent of the refugee households earned less than US$1 per month and that another 36 percent earned less than US$27 per month.

The poverty of refugee households was not in isolation from the economy of surrounding areas. The settlements were located far from the town of Arua. Neighbouring communities appeared to be even poorer than average people of the district. The industry of the area was predominantly agriculture with many locals dependant on remittances from families and relatives (Ayoo, 2000). Only a few markets dealt with crops, fish, and basic household items such as soap and matches. Electricity was not provided and water was taken from wells.

In such a situation, refugees who learnt about electricity and mechanics could hardly find any opportunity to utilise their skills. Even for more traditional skills like carpentry and tailoring, there was little demand. Therefore, refugees had to travel to towns far away from settlements even to look for casual labour jobs (Ayoo, 2000: 8). Many refugees, especially youths, worked on local Ugandans' farms in exchange for food or cash. Others worked at construction sites in towns, helping loading and off-loading. With limited local purchasing power, access to markets and employment opportunities, refugees and locals alike could hardly earn adequate income.

The situation for women and girls seemed to be even more difficult. In the settlements, it was observed that some women operated teahouses, sold home-made snacks or were engaged in local beer brewing (see Figure 7-3). Multiple sources indicated that refugee women were involved in prostitution inside and outside of refugee settlements (for example, Ayoo, 2000). These income-generating "opportunities" did not offer much income, and some of these coping strategies were even harmful to the refugees' well-being.

Taken by the author.

Figure 7-3: Refugee Man Drinking, Women Brewing Local Beer

Based on the above information, it is reasonable to conclude that refugees in the Arua District were progressing toward economic self-reliance, but would not reach perfect self-reliance in the immediate future.

7.3.2 Social and Psychological Self-Reliance:

Section 5.1 defined social self-reliance as the capacity of refugee communities as a group to make decisions and to help each other, and psychological self-reliance as the capacity of individual refugees to gain control over their life. In accordance with Table 5-1 that presented indicators of social and psychological self-reliance, the summary of social and psychological self-reliance of refugees in the Arua district is presented in Table 7-2. The following paragraphs will first discuss the social self-reliance of refugee communities in the Arua District.

Refugees elected their own leaders and formed their own committees called the Refugee Welfare Councils. The council, modelled after Uganda's Local Council system, consisted of nine elected secretaries, representing thematic issues such as food, education, water, health or law and order. Three positions out of nine were reserved for women while some other committee members represented special groups such as youths and people with disabilities[190].

The committee members worked purely on a voluntary basis, mediating community problems, getting opinions from their communities on assistance projects, and disseminating information to them from aid agencies, UNHCR, and the government. In short, they were expected to function as representatives of the refugee community and as liaisons between their own community and aid

---

[190] Information on Refugee Welfare Councils in this paragraph is based on *UNHCR Country Operation Plan, Uganda, Planning Year 2002*, and information gained through the author's field activities.

community, namely the government of Uganda, UNHCR, and implementing agencies. As such, they frequently took part in assessment teams and project planning.

Table 7-2: Social and Psychological Self-Reliance

	Indicators	Results
Social Self-Reliance	**Perfect Self-Reliance** Refugees are able to decide on the administration and management of their communities. No involvement of aid workers and host governments required.	Not achieved.
	Indicators for Partial Self-Reliance	
	Refugees can mobilise themselves to help vulnerable persons in their communities.	Partially achieved.
	Refugees have their own committee(s) or system on self-management.	Achieved, but many refugees felt that their power was limited.
	Refugees participate in assessment, planning, implementation and evaluation of projects.	Achieved.
Perfect Self-Reliance	**Psychological Self-Reliance** Refugees are able to decide on their life, pursue their plan and attain psychological well-being.	Not achieved.
	Indicators for Partial Self-Reliance	
	Refugees feel that they are developing their own potentials for themselves.	Partially achieved.
	Refugees feel that they are contributing to their community and/or local community.	Partially achieved.
	There are less psycho-social problems among refugees.	Not evaluated.

Developed by the author.

Such refugee leaders or committee/council members, however, might not have felt that they were managing their own community. Ayoo (2000: 15) reported on refugees' views that Refugee Welfare Councils had no powers to change the already-made plan (by the government or UNHCR or both), or have it reflect refugees' views. Refugees reportedly said that the self-reliance policy was imposed on them (Ayoo: 2000). Similar to this view were opinions that I heard at meetings with refugees. Refugee leaders repeatedly emphasised the burden of cost-sharing and the reduction of food rations. Especially, they demanded that agriculture tools be re-distributed for all the families. UNHCR and implementing agencies, on the other hand, argued that the previously distributed tools had been sold in local markets and that additional food assistance should be targeted at the most vulnerable refugees instead of re-increasing the level of assistance for the entire refugee community.

My experiences with refugees, however, did not totally support the view that refugees regarded the self-reliance solely as an imposed policy or that refugee leaders had no power. It was true that reduction in assistance and failure in agriculture made them struggle. At the same time, however, the refugees' psychological and social self-reliance appeared to improve during the period observed in this study (1996-2001). I saw refugees proudly showing their farm when they had good yields, confidently arguing with the government and UNHCR, and happily dancing on festive occasions. This is not to belittle their efforts and struggles in living in exile, but rather to acknowledge another aspect of their feelings apart from complaints and helplessness.

Hoeing's research (2004) supported such a view, emphasising the psychological strengths of the refugees. Concerning the changes in attitudes, Hoeing cited words of a refugee leader:

...[refugees were] very arrogant and harsh, but bit by bit through education, through exposure to the laws of this country, continuous interaction, workshops, the community managed to understand. They managed...to have that spirit of understanding, tolerance, and unity. (p. 12)

Hoeing's research also revealed that many refugees considered themselves as independent and regarded external assistance as a supplement to their efforts. Among the quotes in this category was the following:
Actually, we are mostly not depending on DED[191] or UNHCR, that when they bring food then we can stay idle, because if you stay idle you let your life down. So, since we have nationals around we just go and ask for casual work, so that we can get something to eat. After that, DED can help by bringing additional food. (p. 12)

Apart from these quotes, Hoeing's study showed more positive views of refugees on themselves, their leadership, their tradition, and education and skills that they have acquired in Uganda. The study concluded:
Despite facing problems and experiencing frustrations the refugees have a positive self-image and do experience well-being, because they are guided and supported by their own beliefs, values, capacities, and social networks, and instead of relying solely on aid they utilize the advantages and opportunities humanitarian assistance offers. (p. 27)

It is not straightforward to interpret such contradicting information from Ayoo and Hoeing's studies above. One thing that should

---

[191] DED is the (German) acronym of German Development Agency, which, as mentioned earlier, was an implementing agency in Rhino Camp Settlement. The agency is affiliated with German government.

be noted is the time difference between the two studies. Ayoo's research was done in 2000, only a few years after the security situation calmed down. In 2000, SRS policy was ambiguous with multiple interpretations. It was not adopted at the national level. These factors may have contributed to refugees' anxiety over SRS and reduction of assistance that were reflected in Ayoo's research. Hoeing's study, however, was done in 2004. Refugees enjoyed peace for already 6-7 years and got used to working on a farm. SRS gained more national government's support than before. These positive political and security factors must have helped refugees improve their self-esteem.

During the prolonged war in Sudan, Sudanese refugees who came to northern Uganda in 1993 or later had to depend on relief assistance even before their arrival in Uganda. Some were on assistance as internally displaced persons within Sudan, or others had been assisted in Uganda as refugees earlier (Payne, 1998: 40). After fleeing into Uganda, they were again on emergency relief until 1997 when security was finally normalised in West Nile. After being exposed to continual devastating incidents and having to depend on relief for survival, it took them a long time to recover from such experiences and regain sufficient strengths to stand on their own.

Indeed, it was 1999 when I first noticed a change in refugees. I returned to Uganda from Europe after an absence of one year. In May 1999 when I went to a settlement for the first time after my return to Uganda, several refugees ran towards me with smiles and said, "Now we are OK." I had never seen such friendly attitudes and happy-looking faces during my first stay in Uganda from 1996 to 1998, when, understandably, refugees always looked angry. This episode indicated the impact of safety on refugees' well-being. It can be inferred from Hoeing's findings (2004) that several additional years were required before refugees began to feel confident in their achievements.

Another simple point is that people can have multiple feelings at the same time and they choose what to say depending on the occasion. Refugees were no exception. At meetings with aid workers, they naturally chose to emphasise their needs rather than their satisfaction. Though Ayoo was an independent researcher, her study was intended to provide an analysis for aid organisations and the government to review the programme. Because of that, refugees may have tended to emphasise their suffering and needs rather than their achievements.

The final point that we should note was a gap between refugees and aid workers. The reference point for refugees was, understandably, the normal life that they would have led in their country of origin, i.e., southern Sudan. On the other hand, what refugee assistance could offer was improved quality of life in the country of asylum, i.e., Uganda. This gap would never be filled as long as refugees had to live as refugees.

It is important for aid workers and policy makers to be aware of the limitation that refugee assistance can offer. Equally important, however, is maximising the benefit of refugee assistance in spite of any limitation. As Hoeing (2004, 27) stated, aid workers should take into consideration refugees' interests, priorities, or "inner life" when designing aid projects. By doing so, the assistance can contribute to enhancing refugees' strengths in exile instead of increasing their dependence.

7.4 Discussion

Chapters 6 and 7 examined Uganda's local settlement for Sudanese refugees in the Arua District. Conclusions of the previous chapters were illustrated in these chapters. Table 7-3 summarises the impact of Uganda's local settlement.

Table 7-3: Impact of Uganda's Local Settlement

	Factors Influencing Impact	Positive Impact	Negative Impact
Development of Host Communities	• Developmental activities in refugee projects • Support from development actors and donors	• Contribution to community infrastructure	• Impact limited • Politicisation of refugee assistance
Integration	• Political will of host government • National laws • Attitudes of local community • Ethnic/cultural affinity	• Integration of services progressed • Government capacity in managing refugee affairs improved • Relations between refugees and locals improved	• Misunderstandings and different interpretations on the policy • Competition over resources increased • Abuse of refugee women
Refugee Self-Reliance	• Opportunities for productive activities • Level of local economy • National laws • Existence/absence of development programmes • Security • Involvement of refugees • Characteristics of refugee communities	• Food self-reliance increased • Self-esteem improved • Skills and knowledge acquired • Self-management enhanced	• Burden felt

Developed by the author.

First, Uganda's local settlement during the observed period was more developmental refugee assistance than (complete) local settlement in the sense that there was little, if any, participation from development organisations. Though there was mush positive impact, the project did not create significant economic impact. This is the same as cases of the 1980s that were discussed in previous chapters.

The notable positive side was improved capacity of refugees and the local government. The most important impact was that refugees were able to become productive and increased their level of self-reliance. Another noteworthy fact is that host communities enhanced their capacity in managing refugee affairs. The construction of health centres and schools contributed to the well-being of locals in poor areas. As such, the programme had a positive impact on both locals and refugees at the project level.

However, it should also be pointed out that economic impact of the local settlement on refugees and locals was limited during the observed period of 1996-2001. Neither perfect economic self-reliance nor ideal integration was attained in Uganda. The positive impact of infrastructure construction should be recognised. Another fact, however, was that the impact of developmental refugee assistance was far from boosting the local economy. Uganda's local settlement programme which lacked the involvement of development programmes did not offer a chance for refugees' economic success or create meaningful impact on the development of host communities.

This is the same finding as in earlier programmes in Tanzania or Sudan that were discussed in previous chapters. It is not helpful to linger in the illusion that refugees will become totally independent from external aid.

Another point to note was that Uganda's local settlement did not make significant impact on the national system on refugee assistance of the host country. For example, the refugee bill was not passed during the period of this study[192]. This concerns the importance of the commitment of host governments, as discussed in the previous chapters.

Uganda's case also illustrated the challenges of a participatory approach. The process described in this case showed a complex combination of refugee assistance (e.g., demands for immediate visible output) and developmental approach (e.g., careful preparation and consensus building). This case illustrated a participatory process which required a longer consensus building process in coordinating conflicting opinions among various stakeholders. This was more complex than traditional relief oriented refugee assistance. This case further presented that the lack of clarity in the initially stated objectives added more confusion later in the participatory decision making process.

In short, the case presented here tells that local settlement is not a miracle policy for bringing immediate satisfaction to all. On the contrary, it requires a firm commitment and persistent efforts from all the actors–not only aid workers and the host country government, but also refugees themselves, local populations and donors to achieve success.

Local settlement cannot be fulfilled only by UNHCR and a government office in charge of refugee affairs. It requires more coordinated actions among various ministries and local governments of a host country, development actors and donors. Needless to say, refugees' commitment is also essential. To make local settlement effective, all the actors may need to reconsider their traditional approaches and thinking.

With broader ranges of actors involved, UNHCR as a mandated refugee agency may need to shift its focus away from implementa-

---

[192] Later in March 2006, Uganda's Parliament approved the refugee bill.

tion and more towards coordination and advocacy in promoting local settlement as a policy. UNHCR should further review their project management system and make it compatible with developmental activities. Development agencies and donors should reconsider their priorities and criteria to support the development of refugee-hosting areas. The host government needs to seriously consider including refugee affairs in their national agenda so as to invite donors and development programmes to refugee-hosting areas. Refugee and local leaders should begin to critically re-examine their roles to appropriately represent their communities.

The process of local settlement requires active participation of all actors and stakeholders. In this sense, there should be no passive recipient of aid in the process. The commitment and will of all the parties is essential for the success of the local settlement process.

Conclusion

This study examined the validity of the Refugee Aid and Development that is the aid doctrine promoting the linkage of refugee assistance with development programmes to benefit both refugees and local communities hosting refugees, and local settlement that is a refugee policy and assistance programme derived from the doctrine. The review of previous debates on the doctrine concluded that it contains values meaningful to refugee protection and is consistent with humanitarian principles. Though the doctrine evolved out of the interests of African governments to help develop their countries with international assistance for refugees, it was a rational argument that developing host countries sought assistance from international communities for burden-sharing to mitigate damage caused by large scale refugee influxes.

More importantly, the doctrine brought about a new perspective on refugees and their rights. The doctrine views refugees not as mere victims of unfortunate events but individuals with potentials to grow and contribute to the host community as well as to their own. It also recognises that rights of refugees and refugee protection go beyond mere survival but include their right to a dignified life in asylum. A perspective to strengthen latent ability is essential for any aid workers as seen in the strength perspective in social work. From the refugee protection viewpoint, it is even more crucial as dignified asylum life can be attained only when refugees regain their own internal strength and move toward self-reliance. Refugee assistance must, then, inevitably help this process.

Previous studies on Refugee Aid and Development largely

overlooked its value in refugee protection but paid more attention to development aspects. Though previous studies concluded that past attempts at local settlement had mostly failed, they did not consider the contribution of the programmes to refugee well-being. Instead, they were more focused on development aspects such as (un-)sustainability of the programmes, the absence of development actors, or stand-offs between donors and developing countries. Looking at impacts on refuges' well-being, the evaluation could have found more positive aspects. Hoeing's study (2004) is one of the few that acknowledged the strength of refugees, to which local settlement programmes may have contributed.

The above not withstanding, the study also identified a shortcoming of local settlement programmes, which is the lack of clarity in operationalising the key concepts and approaches of local settlements. "Self-reliance" and "refugee integration" as objectives of local settlement should be clearly defined in concrete terms in each given project. These objectives must not be left in the abstract. To this end, this study proposed three categories of self-reliance, namely, economic, social, and psychological self-reliance, and indicators to show varied levels of each category of self-reliance. Similarly, integration was examined through three processes, i.e., social/cultural, legal, and economic processes. Factors influencing the processes were identified, and the interrelation between self-reliance and the integration process was presented in a model adapted from social work's Person-in-Environment model.

This study challenged the conventional belief in the participatory approach that refugee assistance began applying in local settlement programmes (and other assistance programmes). While recognising the importance of the participatory approach in reflecting views of refugees and locals on the programme, the review of refugee situations warned against its naïve application. It is crucial to consider power-relations within refugees and local populations in encouraging their participation. It is equally important to note that the participatory approach in refugee situations may remain at mid-level in the hierarchy of participation, with overall policy and direction given by a host government.

Finally, the most crucial point lies in the fact that the Refugee Aid and Development Doctrine can be materialised only through concerted efforts from all the actors including refugee aid agencies, development actors, host governments and citizens, refugees and donors. So far, refugee programmes have attempted to incorporate a developmental approach (such as participation) and developmental activities (such as agriculture or small scale infrastructure construction). These attempts, while contributing to the well-being of locals and refugees, may produce only limited results on the development of host communities or the economic self-reliance of refugees. The involvement of development actors is essential to achieve the linkage and full impact. Furthermore, not only aid agencies carry responsibilities. Refugees must actively commit themselves. Host governments and donors must also maintain their political will.

The case of Uganda was presented to help understand the above points in a real-world situation. This case served to illustrate points such as the need for the involvement of development actors, the importance of the host government's role, the positive impact and the limitation of developmental refugee assistance, the challenges in a participatory approach in a refugee situation, and the need for clear objectives. The Uganda case study confirmed the importance of commitment among all the actors and stakeholders.

In this connection, UNHCR, as the UN agency mandated to protect refugees, bears a role to advocate for coordinated responses to refugee situations, especially situations that are protracted for many years. The agency may have been doing well at addressing the needs of refugee-hosting communities, but they have not presented incentives for development agencies and donors to support refugee-hosting areas. For development assistance, needs from around the world are enormous. Why do development agencies have to choose to assist refugee-hosting areas out of unending demands from every corner of the world? UNHCR has to find a tool to convince them to support refugee-hosting communities. The agency's recent attempts to join the UN Development Group and to study Poverty Reduction Strategy Papers, which are often used as a national development plan, are noteworthy. Such initiatives require persistent follow-up in order to put refugee agenda in PRSPs and priorities of international development aid.

In addition to these on-going efforts, UNHCR and humanitarian agencies need to consider re-wrapping the Refugee Aid and Development Doctrines in other aid doctrines or concepts that are more familiar to development actors. Human Security, for example, is one of those concepts that is relevant to both refugee situations and international development.

Looking at the positive side, there have been some encouraging developments in the last few years. The need for "seamless transition" from crisis to development has generally been gaining acceptance among development actors. More than ever, development agencies are more actively, flexibly and quickly engaged in post-conflict situations such as the southern Sudan situation after the peace accord in 2005 and post-natural disaster situations as seen in the Tsunami disaster in southeast Asia in December, 2004. The interventions by development actors in humanitarian-development links, so far, are mostly found in these situations but only a few in refugee asylum countries. Nevertheless, general interest among development actors in the linkage will hopefully lead to their more active collaboration in refugee situations in the future.

For example, the Japan International Cooperation Agency (JICA), Japan's ODA implementor of technical assistance, initiated rural development projects to support refugee-hosting west Chadian communities in 2005. Denmark participates in Development Assistance for Refugees in Uganda, supporting the development of refugee-hosting communities. These initiatives are not numerous, so far, but serve as good models that encourage others to follow.

Finally, because I am a refugee aid worker, some bias may have been introduced into the analysis. Though my agency generally encourages internal criticism, we, including myself, tend to over-evaluate our own efforts and justify our own actions. I am not free from the risk of being lenient on the actions that my office chose to take. In this sense, I remain open to alternative views on the situations described in this study and criticisms to the conclusions herein.

This study was mostly based on information from agencies assisting refugees, researchers on refugee assistance, development practitioners/researchers, and people from refugee-hosting countries. Information from donors, however, is scarce. Donor behaviours may need to be examined more closely in future studies.

Bibliography

Primary Sources

Refugee and Development

Addendum 2 to the report of the United Nations High Commissioner for Refugees. General Assembly. Twenty-eighth session. Supplement No.12B (A/9012/Add.2), 1 January 1974. Retrieved 6/12/04 from http://www.unhcr.ch.

Addendum to the report of the Secretary-General: Second international conference on assistance to refugees in Africa. General Assembly. Thirty-ninth session. Agenda item 100 (b) of the provisional agenda, Office of the United Nations High Commissioner for Refugees. (A/39/402/Add.2), 10 December 1984.

Addendum to the Report of the Secretary-General: Second international conference on assistance to refugees in Africa. General Assembly. Thirty-ninth session. Agenda item 100 (b) of the provisional agenda, Office of the United Nations High Commissioner for Refugees. (A/39/402/Add.1), 5 November 1984.

Addendum to the report of the United Nations High Commissioner for Refugees. General Assembly. Forty-sixth session. Supplement No. 12A, (A/46/12/Add.1), 1 January 1992. Retrieved 28/02/06 from http://www.unhcr.ch.

Addendum to the report of the United Nations High Commissioner for Refugees. General Assembly. Forty-seventh session. Supplement No. 12A, (A/47/12/Add.1), 1 January 1993. Retrieved 28/02/06 from http://www.unhcr.ch.

Addendum to the report of the United Nations High Commissioner for Refugees. General Assembly. Forty-eighth session. Supplement No. 12A (A/48/12/Add.1), 19 October 1993. Retrieved 28/02/06 from http://www.unhcr.ch.

Addendum to the report of the United Nations High Commissioner for Refugees. General Assembly. Forty-ninth session. Supplement No. 12A (A/49/12/Add.1), 20 October 1994. Retrieved 28/02/06 from http://www.unhcr.ch.

Addendum to the report of the United Nations High Commissioner for Refugees. General Assembly. Fiftieth session. Supplement No. 12A (A/50/12/Add.1), 8 February 1996. Retrieved 28/02/06 from http://www.unhcr.ch.

Addendum to the report of the United Nations High Commissioner for Refugees. General Assembly. Thirteenth session. Supplement No. 11, (A/3828/Rev.1/Add.1), 1 January 1959. Retrieved 28/02/06 from http://www.unhcr.ch.

Addendum to the report of the United Nations High Commissioner for Refugees. General Assembly. Fourteenth session. Supplement No. 11A, (A/4104/Re.v1/Add.1), 1 January 1960. Retrieved 28/02/06 from http://www.unhcr.ch.

Addendum to the report of the United Nations High Commissioner for Refugees. General Assembly. Fifteenth session. Supplement No.11A (A/4378/Rev.1/Add.1), 1 January 1961. Retrieved 6/12/04 from http://www.unhcr.ch.

Addendum to the report of the United Nations High Commissioner for Refugees. General Assembly. Sixteenth session. Supplement No.11A (A/4771/Rev.1/Add.1), 1 January 1962. Retrieved 6/12/04 from http://www.unhcr.ch.

Addendum to the report of the United Nations High Commissioner for Refugees. General Assembly. Seventeenth session. Supplement No.11A (A/5211/Rev.1/Add.1), 1 January 1963. Retrieved 6/12/04 from http://www.unhcr.ch.

Addendum to the report of the United Nations High Commissioner for Refugees. General Assembly. Eighteenth session. Supplement No.11A (A/5511/Rev.1/Add.1), 1 January 1964. Retrieved 6/12/04 from http://www.unhcr.ch.

Addendum to the report of the United Nations High Commissioner for Refugees. General Assembly. Nineteenth session. Supplement No.11A (A/5811/Rev.1/Add.1), 1 January 1965. Retrieved 6/12/04 from http://www.unhcr.ch.

Addendum to the report of the United Nations High Commissioner for Refugees. General Assembly. Twentieth session. Supplement No.11A (A/6011/Rev.1/Add.1), 1 January 1966. Retrieved 6/12/04 from http://www.unhcr.ch.

Addendum to the report of the United Nations High Commissioner for Refugees. General Assembly. Twenty-first session. Supplement No.11A (A/6311/Rev.1/Add.1), 1 January 1968. Retrieved 6/12/04 from http://www.unhcr.ch.

Addendum to the report of the United Nations High Commissioner for Refugees. General Assembly. Twenty-second session. Supplement No.11A (A/6711/Add.1), 1 January 1968. Retrieved 6/12/04 from http://www.unhcr.ch.

Addendum to the report of the United Nations High Commissioner for Refugees. General Assembly. Twenty-third session. Supplement No.11A (A/7211/Add.1), 1 January 1969. Retrieved 6/12/04 from http://www.unhcr.ch.

Addendum to the report of the United Nations High Commissioner for Refugees. General Assembly. Twenty-fourth session. Supplement No.12A (A/7612/Add.1), 1 January 1970. Retrieved 6/12/04 from http://www.unhcr.ch.

Addendum to the report of the United Nations High Commissioner for Refugees. General Assembly. Twenty-fifth session. Supplement No.12A (A/8012/Add.1), 1 January 1971. Retrieved 6/12/04 from http://www.unhcr.ch.

Addendum to the report of the United Nations High Commissioner for Refugees. General Assembly. Twenty-sixth session. Supplement No.12 (A/8412/Add.1), 7 October 1971. Retrieved 6/12/04 from http://www.unhcr.ch.

Addendum to the report of the United Nations High Commissioner for Refugees. General Assembly. Twenty-seventh session. Supplement No.12 (A/8712/Add.1), 17 October 1972. Retrieved 6/12/04 from http://www.unhcr.ch.

Addendum to the report of the United Nations High Commissioner for Refugees. General Assembly. Twenty-eighth session. Supplement

No.12A (A/9012/Add.1), 1 January 1974. Retrieved 6/12/04 from http://www.unhcr.ch.

Addendum to the report of the United Nations High Commissioner for Refugees. General Assembly. Twenty-ninth session. Supplement No.12A (A/9612/Add.1), 22 October 1974. Retrieved 6/12/04 from http://www.unhcr.ch.

Addendum to the report of the United Nations High Commissioner for Refugees. General Assembly. Twenty-ninth session. Supplement No.12B (A/9612/Add.2), 1 January 1975. Retrieved 6/12/04 from http://www.unhcr.ch.

Addendum to the report of the United Nations High Commissioner for Refugees. General Assembly. Twenty-ninth session. Supplement No.12C (A/9612/Add.3), 1 January 1975. Retrieved 6/12/04 from http://www.unhcr.ch.

Addendum to the report of the United Nations High Commissioner for Refugees. General Assembly. Thirtieth session. Supplement No.12A (A/10012/Add.1), 14 October 1975. Retrieved 6/12/04 from http://www.unhcr.ch.

Addendum to the report of the United Nations High Commissioner for Refugees. General Assembly. Thirty-first session. Supplement No.12B (A/31/12/Add.2), 14 October 1975. Retrieved 6/12/04 from http://www.unhcr.ch.

Addendum to the report of the United Nations High Commissioner for Refugees. General Assembly. Thirty-first session. Supplement No.12A (A/31/12/Add.1), 12 October 1975. Retrieved 6/12/04 from http://www.unhcr.ch.

Addendum to the report of the United Nations High Commissioner for Refugees. General Assembly. Thirty-second session. Supplement No.12A (A/32/12/Add.1), 31 October 1997. Retrieved 6/12/04 from http://www.unhcr.ch.

Addendum to the report of the United Nations High Commissioner for Refugees. General Assembly. Thirty-third session. Supplement No.12A (A/33/12/Add.1), 1 November 1998. Retrieved 6/12/04 from http://www.unhcr.ch.

Addendum to the report of the United Nations High Commissioner for

Refugees. General Assembly. Thirty-fourth session. Supplement No.12A (A/34/12/Add.1), 6 November 1979. Retrieved 6/12/04 from http://www.unhcr.ch.

Addendum to the report of the United Nations High Commissioner for Refugees. General Assembly. Thirty-fifth session. Supplement No.12A (A/35/12/Add.1), 3 November 1980. Retrieved 6/12/04 from http://www.unhcr.ch.

Addendum to the report of the United Nations High Commissioner for Refugees. General Assembly. Thirty-sixth session. Supplement No.12 (A/36/12/Add.1), 21 October 1981. Retrieved 6/12/04 from http://www.unhcr.ch.

Agenda for protection: Addendum. Executive Committee of the High Commissioner's Programme, Fifty-third session (A/Ac.96/965/Add.1), 26 June 2002.

Consideration of ECOSOC resolution 1995/56. Executive Committee of the High Commissioner's Programme, Standing Committee, 1st meeting, (EC/46/SC/CRP.12), 4 January 1996.

Economic and social impact of massive refugee populations on host developing countries, as well as other countries. Executive Committee of the High Commissioner's Programme, Standing Committee, 21st meeting, (EC/51/SC/CRP.16), 30 May 2001.

Economic and social impact of massive refugee populations on host developing countries, as well as other countries: Partnerships with bilateral development agencies. Executive Committee of the High Commissioner's Programme, Standing Committee, 24th meeting, (EC/52/SC/CRP.10), 31 May 2002.

ECOSOC resolution: Strengthening collaboration between the United Nations development system and the Bretton Woods institutions. (E/RES/1996/43), 26 July 1996.

Executive committee of the programme of the United Nations High Commissioner for Refugees, fiftieth session, summary record of the 536th meeting. (A/AC.96/SR.536), 12 October 1999.

Executive committee of the programme of the United Nations High Commissioner for Refugees, fifty-fifth session, summary record of the 583rd meeting. (A/AC.96/SR.583), 12 October 2004.

Executive committee of the programme of the United Nations High Commissioner for Refugees, fifty-third session, summary record of the 561st meeting. (A/AC.96/SR.561), 30 October 2002.
Executive committee of the programme of the United Nations High Commissioner for Refugees, fifty-third session, summary record of the 562nd meeting. (A/AC.96/SR.562), 9 October 2002.
Executive committee of the programme of the United Nations High Commissioner for Refugees, fifty-third session, summary record of the 563rd meeting. (A/AC.96/SR.563), 15 November 2002.
Executive committee of the programme of the United Nations High Commissioner for Refugees, fifty-third session, summary record of the 564th meeting. (A/AC.96/SR.564), 11 October 2002.
Follow-up to ECOSOC resolution 1995/56: UNHCR assistance activities in countries of origin. Executive Committee of the High Commissioner's Programme, Standing Committee, 2nd meeting, (EC/46/SC/CRP.16), 18 March 1996.
Follow-up to ECOSOC resolution 1996/56 on the development of operative memoranda of understanding. Executive Committee of the High Commissioner's Programme, Standing Committee, 1st meeting, (EC/46/SC/CRP.8), 4 January 1996.
Framework for durable solutions for refugees and persons of concern. May 2003. Executive Committee of the High Commissioner's Programme, Standing Committee, 28th meeting, (EC/53/SC/INF.3), 16 September 2003.
General assembly resolution: Assistance to refugees, returnees and displaced persons in Africa. (A/RES/60/128), 24 January 2006.
General assembly resolution: Charter of economic rights and duties of states. UN GAOR, Twenty-ninth session, Supplement No. 31, (Res. 3281/xxix), 1974.
General assembly resolution: Declaration on the right to development. (A/RES/41/128), 4 December 1986.
General assembly resolution: General assembly declaration and programme of action on the establishment of a new international economic order. (A/RES/3201/S-VI), 1974.
General assembly resolution: Global financial integration and strengthen-

ing collaboration between the United Nations and the Bretton Woods institutions. (A/RES/51/166), 21 February 1997.
General assembly resolution: Strengthening of the coordination of emergency humanitarian assistance of the United Nations. (A/RES/46/182), 19 December 1991.
General assembly resolution: Strengthening of the coordination of emergency humanitarian assistance of the United Nations. (A/RES/47/168), 22 December 1992.
General assembly resolution: Strengthening of the coordination of emergency humanitarian assistance of the United Nations. (A/RES/49/139), 20 December 1994.
General assembly resolutions: International conference on assistance to refugees in Africa. (A/RES/35/42), 25 November 1980. Retrieved 2/12/04 from http://www.unhcr.ch.
General assembly resolutions: International conference on assistance to refugees in Africa. (A/RES/37/197), 18 December 1982. Retrieved 2/12/04 from http://www.unhcr.ch.
General assembly resolutions: International conference on assistance to refugees in Africa. (A/RES/39/139), 14 December 1984. Retrieved 2/12/04 from http://www.unhcr.ch.
General assembly resolutions: Second international conference on assistance to refugees in Africa. (A/RES/36/124), 14 December 1981. Retrieved 2/12/04 from http://www.unhcr.ch
General assembly resolutions: Second international conference on assistance to refugees in Africa. (A/RES/38/120), 16 December 1980. Retrieved 2/12/04 from http://www.unhcr.ch
Local integration. UNHCR global consultation on international protection, 4th meeting, (EC/GC/02/6), 24 April 2002.
Ministry of Foreign Affairs, Home page, http://www.mofa.go.jp
Note on the protection of refugees in armed conflict situations. (EC/SCP/25), 4 October 1982.
Progress report on the guidelines on refugees and the environment. Executive Committee, (EC/SC.2/79), 11 September 1995.
Protocol relating to the status of refugees. 1967.
Protracted refugee situations. Executive Committee of the High

Commissioner's Programme, Standing Committee, 30th meeting, (EC/54/SC/CRP.14), 10 June 2004.

Report of the fifty-fifth session of the executive committee of the high commissioner's programme. (A/AC.96/1003), 12 October 2004.

Report of the fifty-second session of the executive committee of the high commissioner's programme. (A/AC.96/959), 5 October 2001.

Report of the fifty-third session of the executive committee of the high commissioner's programme. (A/AC.96/973), 8 October 2002.

Report of the forty-fifth session of the executive committee of the high commissioner's programme. (A/AC.96/839), 11 October 1994.

Report of the Secretary-General: International conference on assistance to refugees in Africa. General Assembly. Thirty-sixth session. Item 83(b) of the preliminary list. (A/36/316), 11 June 1981.

Report of the Secretary-General: Second international conference on assistance to refugees in Africa. General Assembly. Thirty-ninth session. Agenda item 100 of the provisional agenda, Office of the United Nations High Commissioner for Refugees. (A/39/402), 22 August 1984.

Report of the United Nations High Commissioner for Refugees, 1991. General Assembly. Forty-sixth session. (A/46/12), 1 January 1992. Retrieved 26/9/05 from http://www.unhcr.ch.

Report of the United Nations High Commissioner for Refugees. General Assembly. Thirty-sixth session. Supplement No. 12 (A/36/12), 28 August 1981. Retrieved 6/12/04 from http://www.unhcr.ch.

Report of the United Nations High Commissioner for Refugees. General Assembly. Thirty-seventh session. Supplement No. 12 (A/37/12), 18 August 1982. Retrieved 6/12/04 from http://www.unhcr.ch.

Report of the United Nations High Commissioner for Refugees. General Assembly. Thirty-eighth session. Supplement No. 12 (A/38/12), 17 August 1983. Retrieved 6/8/05 from http://www.unhcr.ch.

Report of the United Nations High Commissioner for Refugees. General Assembly. Thirty-ninth session. Supplement No. 12 (A/39/12), 24 August 1984. Retrieved 6/12/04 from http://www.unhcr.ch.

Report of the United Nations High Commissioner for Refugees. General Assembly. Fortieth session. Supplement No. 12 (A/40/12), 13

September 1985. Retrieved 6/12/04, http://www.unhcr.ch.

Report of the United Nations High Commissioner for Refugees. General Assembly. Forty-first session. Supplement No. 12 (A/41/12), 1 August 1986. Retrieved 6/12/04, from http://www.unhcr.ch.

Report of the United Nations High Commissioner for Refugees. General Assembly. Forty-second session. Supplement No. 12 (A/42/12), 27 July 1987. Retrieved 6/12/04 from http://www.unhcr.ch.

Report of the United Nations High Commissioner for Refugees. General Assembly. Forty-third session. Supplement No. 12 (A/43/12), 4 August 1988. Retrieved 6/12/04 from http://www.unhcr.ch.

Report of the United Nations High Commissioner for Refugees. General Assembly. Forty-four session. Supplement No. 12 (A/44/12), 1 September 1989. Retrieved 6/12/04 from http://www.unhcr.ch.

Report of the United Nations High Commissioner for Refugees. General Assembly. Forty-fifth session. Supplement No. 12 (A/45/12), 24 September 1990. Retrieved 6/12/04 from http://www.unhcr.ch.

Report of the United Nations High Commissioner for Refugees. General Assembly. Fifty-first session. Supplement No. 12 (A/51/12), 4 September 1996. Retrieved 6/8/05 from http://www.unhcr.ch.

Report of the United Nations High Commissioner for Refugees. General Assembly. Thirty-sixth session. Supplement No. 12 (A/36/12), 28 August 1981. Retrieved 6/12/04 from http://www.unhcr.ch.

Report of the United Nations High Commissioner for Refugees. General Assembly. Thirty-seventh session. Supplement No. 12 (A/37/12), 18 August 1982. Retrieved 6/12/04, http://www.unhcr.ch.

Report of the United Nations High Commissioner for Refugees. General Assembly. Thirty-eighth session. Supplement No. 12 (A/38/12), 17 August 1983. Retrieved 6/8/05 from http://www.unhcr.ch.

Report of the United Nations High Commissioner for Refugees. General Assembly. Thirty-ninth session. Supplement No. 12 (A/39/12), 24 August 1984. Retrieved 6/12/04, http://www.unhcr.ch.

Report of the United Nations High Commissioner for Refugees. General Assembly. Fortieth session. Supplement No. 12 (A/40/12), 13 September 1985. Retrieved 6/12/04 from http://www.unhcr.ch.

Report of the United Nations High Commissioner for Refugees. General

Assembly. Forty-first session. Supplement No. 12 (A/41/12), 1 August 1986. Retrieved 6/12/04 from http://www.unhcr.ch.
Report of the United Nations High Commissioner for Refugees. General Assembly. Forty-second session. Supplement No. 12 (A/42/12), 27 July 1987. Retrived 6/12/04 from http://www.unhcr.ch.
Report of the United Nations High Commissioner for Refugees. General Assembly. Forty-third session. Supplement No. 12 (A/43/12), 4 August 1988. Retrieved 6/12/04 from http://www.unhcr.ch.
Report of the United Nations High Commissioner for Refugees. General Assembly. Forty-four session. Supplement No. 12 (A/44/12), 1 September 1989. Retrieved 6/12/04 from http://www.unhcr.ch.
Report of the United Nations High Commissioner for Refugees. General Assembly. Forty-fifth session. Supplement No. 12 (A/45/12), 24 September 1990. Retrieved 28/02/06 from http://www.unhcr.ch.
Report of the United Nations High Commissioner for Refugees. General Assembly. Forty-sixth session. Supplement No. 12 (A/46/12), 1 January 1992. Retrieved 28/02/06 from http://www.unhcr.ch.
Report of the United Nations High Commissioner for Refugees. General Assembly. Forty-seventh session. Supplement No. 12 (A/47/12), 23 August 1992. Retrieved 28/02/06 from http://www.unhcr.ch.
Report of the United Nations High Commissioner for Refugees. General Assembly. Forty-eighth session. Supplement No. 12 (A/48/12), 13 October 1993. Retrieved 28/02/06 from http://www.unhcr.ch.
Report of the United Nations High Commissioner for Refugees. General Assembly. Forty-ninth session. Supplement No. 12 (A/49/12), 1 January 1995. Retrieved 28/02/06 from http://www.unhcr.ch.
Report of the United Nations High Commissioner for Refugees. General Assembly. Fiftieth session. Supplement No. 12 (A/50/12), 24 September 1995. Retrieved 28/02/06 from http://www.unhcr.ch.
Report of the United Nations High Commissioner for Refugees. General Assembly. Fifty-first session. Supplement No. 12 (A/51/12), 4 September 1996. Retrieved 6/8/05 from http://www.unhcr.ch.
Report of the United Nations High Commissioner for Refugees. General Assembly. (A/2011). 1 January 1952. Retrieved 6/12/04 from http://www.unhcr.ch.

Bibliography 263

Report of the United Nations High Commissioner for Refugees. General Assembly. (A/2126 and Addendum). 1 January 1953. Retrieved 6/12/04 from http://www.unhcr.ch.
Report of the United Nations High Commissioner for Refugees. General Assembly. Eighth session. Supplement No. 11 (A/2394). 1 January 1954. Retrieved 6/12/04 from http://www.unhcr.ch.
Report of the United Nations High Commissioner for Refugees. General Assembly. Tenth session. Supplement No. 11 (A/2902 and Add.1). 1 January 1956. Retrieved 6/12/04 from http://www.unhcr.ch.
Report of the United Nations High Commissioner for Refugees. General Assembly. Ninth session. Supplement No. 13 (A/2648). 1 January 1955. Retrieved 6/12/04 from http://www.unhcr.ch.
Report of the United Nations High Commissioner for Refugees. General Assembly. Eleventh session. Supplement No. 11A (A/3123/Rev.1/Add.1 and Add.2). 1 January 1957. Retrieved 6/12/04 from http://www.unhcr.ch.
Report of the United Nations High Commissioner for Refugees. General Assembly. Twelfth session. Supplement No. 11 (A/3538/Rev.1). 1 January 1958. Retrieved 6/12/04 from http://www.unhcr.ch.
Report of the United Nations High Commissioner for Refugees. General Assembly. Thirteenth session. Supplement No.11 (A/3828/Rev.1), 1 January 1959. Retrieved 6/12/04 from http://www.unhcr.ch.
Report of the United Nations High Commissioner for Refugees. General Assembly. Fourteenth session. Supplement No.11 (A/4104/Rev.1), 1 January 1960. Retrieved 6/12/04 from http://www.unhcr.ch.
Report of the United Nations High Commissioner for Refugees. General Assembly. Fifty-second session. Supplement No.11 (A/4378/Rev.1), 1 January 1961. Retrieved 6/12/04 from http://www.unhcr.ch.
Report of the United Nations High Commissioner for Refugees. General Assembly. Seventeenth session. Supplement No.11 (A/5211/Rev.1), 1 January 1963. Retrieved 6/12/04 from http://www.unhcr.ch.
Report of the United Nations High Commissioner for Refugees. General Assembly. Nineteenth session. Supplement No.11 (A/5811/Rev.1), 1 January 1964. Retrieved 6/12/04 from http://www.unhcr.ch.
Report of the United Nations High Commissioner for Refugees. General

Assembly. Twentieth session. Supplement No.11 (A/6011/Rev.1), 1 January 1965. Retrieved 6/12/04 from http://www.unhcr.ch.

Report of the United Nations High Commissioner for Refugees. General Assembly. Eighteenth session. Supplement No.11 (A/5511/Rev.1), 1 January 1963. Retrieved 6/12/04 from http://www.unhcr.ch.

Report of the United Nations High Commissioner for Refugees. General Assembly. Twenty-first session. Supplement No.11 (A/6311/Rev.1), 1 January 1966. Retrieved 6/12/04 from http://www.unhcr.ch.

Report of the United Nations High Commissioner for Refugees. General Assembly. Twenty-second session. Supplement No.11 (A/6711), 1 January 1967. Retrieved 6/12/04 from http://www.unhcr.ch.

Report of the United Nations High Commissioner for Refugees. General Assembly. Twenty-fourth session. Supplement No.12 (A/7612), 1 January 1970. Retrieved 6/12/04 from http://www.unhcr.ch.

Report of the United Nations High Commissioner for Refugees. General Assembly. Twenty-sixth session. Supplement No.12 (A/8412), 1 January 1972. Retrieved 6/12/04 from http://www.unhcr.ch.

Report of the United Nations High Commissioner for Refugees. General Assembly. Twenty-seventh session. Supplement No.12 (A/8712), 1 January 1973. Retrieved 6/12/04 from http://www.unhcr.ch.

Report of the United Nations High Commissioner for Refugees. General Assembly. Twenty-eighth session. Supplement No.12 (A/9012), 1 January 1974. Retrieved 6/12/04 from http://www.unhcr.ch.

Report of the United Nations High Commissioner for Refugees. General Assembly. Thirtieth session. Supplement No.12 (A/10012), 1 January 1975. Retrieved 6/12/04 from http://www.unhcr.ch.

Report of the United Nations High Commissioner for Refugees. General Assembly. Thirty-first session. Supplement No.12 (A/31/12), 1 January 1975. Retrieved 6/12/04 from http://www.unhcr.ch.

Report of the United Nations High Commissioner for Refugees. General Assembly. Thirty-second session. Supplement No.12 (A/32/12), 2 September 1997. Retrieved 6/12/04 from http://www.unhcr.ch.

Report of the United Nations High Commissioner for Refugees. General Assembly. Thirty-third session. Supplement No.12 (A/33/12), 12 September 1998. Retrieved 6/12/04 from http://www.unhcr.ch.

Report of the United Nations High Commissioner for Refugees. General Assembly. Thirty-fourth session. Supplement No.12 (A/34/12), 11 October 1979. Retrieved 6/12/04 from http://www.unhcr.ch.

Report of the United Nations High Commissioner for Refugees. General Assembly. Thirty-fifth session. Supplement No.12 (A/35/12), 24 September 1980. Retrieved 6/12/04 from http://www.unhcr.ch.

Report of the United Nations High Commissioner for Refugees. General Assembly. Thirty-seventh session. Supplement No.12 (A/37/12), 18 August 1982. Retrieved 6/12/04 from http://www.unhcr.ch.

Report of the United Nations High Commissioner for Refugees. General Assembly. Thirty-sixth session. Supplement No.12 (A/36/12), 28 August 1981. Retrieved 6/12/04 from http://www.unhcr.ch.

Resolution on co-operation between OAU and UNHCR. The OAU thirty-first ordinary session, (CM/RES/622), July 1978.

Resolution on the situation of refugees in Africa. The OAU forty-fourth ordinary session, (CM/RES/1040), July 1986.

Resolution on the situation of refugees in Africa. The OAU forty-fourth ordinary session, (CM/RES/621), July 1978.

Resolution on the situation of refugees in Africa. The OAU thirty-first ordinary session, (CM/RES/774), February 1980.

Resolution on the situation of refugees in Africa. The OAU thirty-second ordinary session, (CM/RES/694), March 1970.

Resolution on the situation of refugees in Africa. The OAU thirty-third ordinary session, (CM/RES/727/Rev.1), July 1979.

Social and economic impact of large refugee populations on host developing countries. Executive Committee of the High Commissioner's Programme, Standing Committee, 6th meeting, (EC/47/SC/CRP.7), 6 January 1997.

Statute of the Office of the United Nations High Commissioner for Refugees. General assembly resolution 428(V) of December 1950. Annex.

The Ministry of Foreign Affairs of Japan. http://www.mofa.go.jp/mofaj/

The Khartoum declaration on Africa's refugee crisis, September 1990. The OAU seventeenth extraordinary session of the commission of fifteen on refugees, Meeting in Khartoum, Republic of Sudan, 22-24 September 1990.

The security, and civilian and humanitarian character of refugee camps and settlements. Executive Committee of the High Commissioner's Programme, Standing Committee, 14th meeting, (EC/49/SC/INF.2), 14 January 1999.

UNDP Rwanda. *Linking relief to development.* June 1998.

UNDP. *Mainstreaming gender in water management: A practical journey to sustainability: A resource guide.* February 2003.

UNHCR policy on refugee women (Submitted by the High Commissioner). Executive Committee of the High Commissioner's Programme, Forty-first Session, (A/AC.96/754), 20 August 1990.

UNHCR. Home page, http://www.unhcr.ch (unhcr.org).

UNHCR. *A UNHCR handbook for the military on humanitarian operations.* 1995.

UNHCR. *Conclusions adopted by the executive committee on the international protection of refugees, 1975-2004 (No. 1-101).*

UNHCR. *Convention plus: Issues paper on targeting of development assistance, draft.* June 2004.

UNHCR. *Convention plus: Targeting development assistance to achieve durable solutions for refugees (a discussion paper prepared by Denmark and Japan).* High commissioner's forum, 17 February 2004.

UNHCR. *Framework for durable solutions for refugees and persons of concern.* Core Group on Durable solutions, 2003.

UNHCR. *Global refugee trends 2003: Overview of refugee populations, new arrivals, durable solutions, asylum-seekers and other persons of concern to UNHCR.*

UNHCR. *Global report.* 1998-2003.

UNHCR. *Guidelines on the protection of refugee women*, 1991.

UNHCR. *Handbook for planning and implementing Development Assistance for Refugees (DAR) programmes*, 2005.

UNHCR. *International solidarity and refugee protection.* Executive Committee Conclusion, No.52 (XXXIX), 1988.

UNHCR. *Lubbers launches forum on Convention Plus initiative*, 27 June 2003. Retrieved 18/05/05 from http://www.unhcr.ch

UNHCR. *Minimum standards and essential needs in a protracted refugee*

situation: A review of the UNHCR programme in Kakuma, Kenya. 2000.
UNHCR. *New approaches and partnerships for protection and solutions in Africa: Addressing protracted refugee situations in Africa.* UNHCR Informal Consultations. 14 December 2001.
UNHCR. *Non-refoulement.* Executive Committee Conclusions, No.6 (XXXVIII), 1977.
UNHCR. *Northern Uganda: Review of rural settlement programme for Sudanese refugees.* PTSS mission report 96/93.
UNHCR. *Note on interpreting the refugee definition and on complementary forms of protection.* Inter-office memorandum No. 38/2001.
UNHCR. *Poverty reduction strategy paper: A displacement perspective.* October 2004.
UNHCR. *Protection of asylum-seekers in situations of large-scale influx.* Executive Committee Conclusions, No.22 (XXXII), 1981.
UNHCR. *Protracted refugee situations in the African region* (Discussion Paper). 2001.
UNHCR. *Quick Impact Projects (QIPs): A provisional guide.* 2004.
UNHCR. *Quick impact projects: Lessons learnt and best practices.* Prepared by EPAU and Jozef Merks, June 2000.
UNHCR. *Reach out: A refugee protection training project, module 9, durable solutions.* 2005.
UNHCR. *Returnee aid and development.* Central Evaluation Section, 1994.
UNHCR. *The state of the world's refugees 1997-1998: A humanitarian agenda.* NY: Oxford Press. 1998.
UNHCR. *The state of the world's refugees: Fifty years of humanitarian action.* NY: Oxford Press. 2000.
UNHCR. *The state of the world's refugees: In search of solutions.* NY: Oxford Press. 1995.
UNHCR. *The state of the world's refugees: The challenge of protection.* NY: Penguin Books. 1993.
United Nations Conference on Trade and Development. *The least developed countries 2000 report.*
World Bank. *Post-conflict reconstruction: The role of the world bank.*

1998.
World Bank. *Toward a conflict-sensitive poverty reduction strategy: Lessons from a retrospective analysis.* Report N. 32587. 2005.

International Conventions

Convention relating to the status of refugees. 1951.
Geneva conventions. 1949.
International convention on the protection of the rights of all migrant and members of their families. 1990.
OAU convention governing the specific aspects of refugee problem in Africa. 1969.

Uganda

CIA. *The world fact book 2002 --- Uganda.* Retrieved 29/11/02 from http://www.cia.gov/cia/publications/factbook/geos/ug.html.
Government of the USA. *The anguish of the northern Uganda-Section 2.* 1997. Retrieved 14 June 2004 from http://www.reliefweb.int.w.rwb.nsf.
Government of Uganda and UNHCR. *Self-reliance strategy (1999-2003) for refugee hosting areas in Moyo, Arua and Adjumani districts, Uganda.* Report of the mid-term review. RLSS Mission Report 2004/03.
Government of Uganda. Home page.
Government of Uganda. *Poverty eradication action plan: 2001-2003, Vol.1.*
New vision (Uganda's daily news paper).
Relief web. httl://www.reliefweb.int,Various issues.
The Republic of Uganda. *Constitution of the republic of Uganda.* 1995.
The Republic of Uganda. *The aliens (registration and control) act, 1984.*
The Republic of Uganda. *The control of alien refugees act, Cap. 64.* 1960.
The Republic of Uganda. *The land act, 1998.*
Uganda districts information handbook: Expanded edition 2005-2006.
UNDP. *Human development report 1999.*
UNDP Uganda. *Development cooperation, Uganda: Improving the quality*

of life of the poor through safe water and sanitation, 1999 report.
UNDP Uganda. *Uganda human development reports.* 1998, 2000 and 2002.
UNHCR Uganda. *Country operations plan 2002.*
UNHCR Uganda. *Development assistance for refugee-hosting areas (DAR).* Operational manual. April 2005.
UNHCR Uganda. *Draft guiding principles for harmonizing interactions between the OPM, UNHCR, Districts, and donors and other partners in the framework of the self-reliance strategy for refugees in Uganda.* December 2000.
UNHCR Uganda. *Mid-term assessment report of basic health services in Imvepi settlement, Arua district.* 7-13 August 2000.
UNHCR Uganda. *Self-reliance strategy---Development assistance for refugee hosting areas in Uganda.* Programme document 2004-2007, working copy. September 2004.
UNICEF Uganda. *Uganda: Country programme progress report 1998.*
United Nations System in Uganda. *Uganda: Promise, performance and future challenges.* 2000.
WB Uganda. *Uganda: Country assistance strategy FY2001-2003.*

Secondary Sources

Aalberts, T. E. (2004). *The sovereignty game(s) states play: (Quasi-)states in the international order.* Paper presented at the 5th pan-European international relations conference: Constructing world orders, the Hague. Retrieved 27 February 2005, from http://sgir.org/conference.
Allen, T. (1994). Ethnicity and tribalism on the Sudan-Uganda Border. In K. Fukui & J. Markakis (Eds.), *Ethnicity & conflict in the horn of Africa* (pp. 112-139). London: James Currey Ltd.
Allen, T. (1996). A flight from refuge. In T. Allen (Ed.), *In search of cool ground: War, flight & homecoming in Northeast Africa* (pp. 220-261). Research project of UNRISD. NJ: Africa World Press & London: James Currey Ltd.
Amoo, S. G. (1997). *The challenge of ethnicity and conflicts in Africa, the*

need for a new paradigm. UNDP.
Anderson, M. B. (1994). Understanding the disaster-development continuum: Gender analysis is the essential tool. *Focus on Gender, 2(1),* 7-10.
Anderson, M. B. (1999). *Do no harm: How aid can support peace–or war.* CO: Lynne Rienner Publishers, Inc.
Anderson, M. B. & Woodrow, P. J. (1988). *An approach to integrating development and relief programme: An analytical framework.* Harvard University, Graduate School of Education, Massachusetts.
Aragaki, O. (2001). Kokusai nanmin ho no kaihatsu to kyoryoku: Nanmin nintei ni okeru syomei ni tsuite [Development of international refugee law and cooperation: Proof in the process of refugee status determination]. In Nanmin-mondai Kenkyu Foramu (Ed.), *Nanmin to jinken: Shinseiki no shiza* (pp. 163-194). Tokyo, Japan: Gendai-jinbun.
Armstrong, A. (1988). Aspects of refugee wellbeing in settlement schemes: An examination of the Tanzanian case. *Journal of Refugee Studies, 1(1),* 57-73.
Armstrong, A. (1991). Resource frontiers and regional development the role of refugee settlement in Tanzania. *Habitat International, 15(1/2),* 69-85.
Ayoo, J. S. (2000). *Socio-economic research in Imvepi Sudanese refugees settlement: Final report.* Kampala: OXFAM.
Bagennda, E., Naggaga, A., and Smith, E. (2003). *Land problems in Nakivale settlement and the implications for refugee protection in Uganda.* Refugee Law Project Working Paper No. 8.
Banki, S. (2004). *Refugee integration in the intermediate term: A study of Nepal, Pakistan, and Kenya,* (Working Paper No. 108). UNHCR.
Barkley, W. P., & Seckler, W. D. (1972=1975). Y. Shiroi (Trans.). *Kankyo keizai gaku nyumon: Keizai seicho to kankyo hakai* [Economic growth and environmental decay: The solution becomes the problem]. Tokyo, Japan: The University of Tokyo.
Belgrad, E. & Nachmias, N. (Eds.). (1997). *The politics of international humanitarian aid operations,* London: Praeger.
Berry, J. W. (1989). Acculturation experiences, appraisal, coping and adaptation. *Canadian Journal of Behavioral Science, 21,* 259-309.

Berry, J. W. (1990). Psychology of acculturation. In J. Berman (Ed.), *Nebraska symposium on motivation, 1989: Cross cultural perspectives. Current theory and research in motivation, Vol. 37* (pp. 201-234). NE: University of Nebraska Press.

Betts, A. (2004). *International cooperation and the targeting of development assistance for refugee solutions: Lessons from the 1980s*, (Working Paper 107). UNHCR.

Betts, T. F. (1984). Evolution and promotion of the integrated rural development approach to refugee policy in Africa. In R. F. Gorman (Ed.), (1993), *Refugee aid and development: Theory and practice* (pp. 15-18). CT: Greenwood Press.

Bradbury, M. (1998). Normalising the crisis in Africa. *Disasters, 22(4)*, 328-338.

Bulcha, M. (1987). Sociological and economic factors in refugee integration: The case of Ethiopian exiles in the Sudan. In P. Nobel (Ed.), *Refugee aid and development in Africa* (pp. 73-90). Uddevalla: Bohunslaningens Boktrychkeri.

Bulcha, M., Kibreab, G. & Nobel, P. (1987). Sociology, economy and law: Views in common. In P. Nobel (Ed.), *Refugee aid and development in Africa* (pp. 93-103). Uddevalla: Bohunslaningens Boktrychkeri.

Burnham, G. M., Rowley, E.A. & Ovberedjo, M.O. (2003). Quality design: A planning methodology for the integration of refugee and local health services, West Nile, Uganda. *Disasters, 27(1)*, 54-71.

Callamard, A. (1991). Refugee assistance and development: But what sort of development? In R. F. Gorman (Ed.) (1993), *Refugee aid and development: Theory and practice* (pp. 129-146). CT: Greenwood Press.

Callamard, A. (1994). Refugees and local hosts: A study of the trading interactions between Mozambican refugees and Malawian villagers in the district of Mwanza. *Journal of Refugee Studies, 7(1)*, 39-62.

Caspersz, P. (2004). *The new international economic order [NIEO]*. Retrieved 11 December 2004 from http://www.satyodaya.org/Articles/NIEO.htm.

Cassen, R. & Associates. (1994). *Does aid work?* Oxford: Clarendon Press.

Chambers, R. (1979). Rural refugees in Africa. *Disasters, 3(4)*, 381-392.
Chambers, R. (1982). Rural refugees in Africa: Past experience, future pointers. *Disasters, 6(1)*, 21-30.
Chambers, R. (1983). *Rural development: Putting the last first*. Essex: Longman.
Chambers, R. (1986). Hidden losers? The impact of rural refugees and refugee programs on poorer hosts. In R. F. Gorman (Ed.), (1993), *Refugee aid and development: Theory and practice* (pp. 29-43). CT: Greenwood Press.
Cleaver, F. (2001). Institutions, agency and the limitations of participatory approaches to development. In B. Cooke & U. Kothari (Eds.), *Participation: The new tyranny?* (pp. 36-55). London: Zed Books Ltd.
Cliffe, L. & Luckham, R. (1999). Complex political emergencies and the state: failure and the fate of the state. *Third World Quarterly, 20(1)*, 27-50.
Collier, P. (2000). *Policy for Post-conflict Societies: Reducing the risks of renewed conflict*, Prepared for the Economics of Political Violence Conference, March 18-19, 2000, Princeton University.
Commission on Human Security. (2003). *Human security now*. NY.
Cooke, B. & Kothari, U. (2001a). The case for participation as tyranny. In B. Cooke & U. Kothari (Eds.), *Participation: The new tyranny?* (pp. 1-15). London: Zed Books Ltd.
Cooke, B. & Kothari, U. (Eds.). (2001b). *Participation: The new tyranny?* London: Zed Books Ltd.
Cooley, A. & Ron, J. (2002). The NGO scramble: Organizational insecurity and the political economy of translational action. *International Security, 27(1)*, 5-39.
Crisp, J. (2001). *Mind the gap! UNHCR, humanitarian assistance and the development process*, (Working Paper No. 43). UNHCR.
Crisp, J. (2003). *No solutions in sight: the problem of protracted refugee situations in Africa*, (Working Paper No. 75). UNHCR.
Crisp, J. (2004). *The local integration and local settlement of refugees: a conceptual and historical analysis*, (Working Paper No. 102).

UNHCR.

Curtis, D. (2001). *Politics and humanitarian aid: Debates, dilemmas and dissension*, (HPG Report No. 10). London: Overseas Development Institute.

Damme, v. W. (1999). How Liberian and Sierra Leonean refugees settled in the forest regions of Guinea (1990-96). *Journal of Refugee Studies, 12(1)*, 36-53.

Danish Ministry of Foreign Affairs. (2000). *The multilateral aid response to violent conflict: More than linking relief and development*, draft report. Centre for Development Research.

De Montclos, P. M. A. (2000). Refugee camps or cities? The socio-economic dynamics of the Dadaab and Kakuma camps in northern Kenya. *Journal of Refugee Studies, 13(2)*, 205-222.

Desbarats, J. (1992). Refugee policies and labour flows. In M. M. Kritz, L. L. Lim & H. Zlotnik (Eds.), *International migration systems: A global approach* (pp. 278-299). New York: Oxford University Press.

Dieng, A. (1987). Background to and growth of the right to development: The role of law and lawyers in development. In P. Nobel (Ed.), *Refugee and development in Africa* (pp. 55-60). Uddevalla: Nohuslaningens.

Duffield, M. (1997) NGO relief in war zones: Towards an analysis of the new aid paradigm. *Third World Quarterly, 18(3)*, 527-545.

Esho, H. (1998). Keizai kaihatsu ron no tenkai to kokusai kikan [Evolution of theories of development economy and international organisations]. In Institute of Social Science of (Ed.), *20 seiki shisutemu 4 kaihatsu shugi* (pp. 47-75). Tokyo, Japan: The University of Tokyo.

Farr, G. (1991). Refugee aid and development in Pakistan: Afghan aid after ten years. In R. F. Gorman (Ed.), (1993), *Refugee aid and development: Theory and practice* (pp. 111-126). CT: Greenwood.

Fukada, F. (1999, June). Nanmin mondai to kaihatsu enjo: Jindo enjo to kaihatsu enjo kan no gyappu wo ikani umeru ka [Refugee issues and development aid: How to fill a gap between humanitarian assistance and development aid]. *International Development Journal*, 60-62.

Gasarasi, C. (1990). The mass naturalization and further integration of Rwandese refugees in Tanzania: Process, problems and prospects. *Journal of Refugee Studies, 3(2)*, 88-109.

Gingyera-Pinycwa, A.G.G. (1998). *Sharing with the refugees in our midst: The experience of Uganda.* Retrieved 30/11/2002 from http://www.afrst.uiuc.edu/Makerere/Vol_2/chapter_one.html.
Goldsmith, A. A. (2001). Foreign aid and statehood in Africa. *International Organization, 55(1),* 123-148.
Gorman, R. F. (1986). Beyond ICARA II: Implementing refugee-related development assistance. *International Migration Review, 20(2),* 283-298.
Gorman, R. F. (1990). Linking refugee aid and development in Africa. In R. F. Gorman (Ed.) (1993), *Refugee aid and development: Theory and practice* (pp. 61-82). CT: Greenwood Press.
Gorman, R. F. (1991a). The quest for a theory of refugee aid and development: Empirical limits to a theory of obligation. In R. F. Gorman (Ed.), (1993), *Refugee aid and development: Theory and practice* (pp. 147-155). CT: Greenwood Press.
Gorman, R. F. (1991b). Prospects for refugee aid and development. In R. F. Gorman (Ed.), (1993), *Refugee aid and development: Theory and practice* (pp. 157-169). CT: Greenwood Press.
Gorman, R. F. (Ed.). (1993). *Refugee aid and development: Theory and practice.* CT: Greenwood Press.
Grare, F. (2003). The geopolitics of Afghan refugees in Pakistan. In S. Stedman & F. Tanner (Eds.), *Refugee manipulation: War, politics, and the abuse of human suffering* (pp. 57-94). DC: Brooking Institute Press.
Hall, E. (2003). *With an eye to the future: ILO refugee programmes in Africa.* In Focus Programme on Crisis Response and Reconstruction. Working Paper 12, ILO.
Hardin, G. (1968). The tragedy of the commons. *Science, 162,* 1243-1248, Retrieved 13/7/2004 from http://www.sciencemag.org.
Hardin, G. (1974). Living on a lifeboat. *Bioscience, 24(10),* 561-568. Retrieved 13/7/2004 from http://www.garretthardinsociety.org/articles/art_living_on_a_lifeboat.html.
Harrell-Bond, B. E. (1986). *Imposing aid.* Oxford: Oxford University Press.
Hendrickson, D. (1998). *Humanitarian action in protracted crisis: An*

overview of the debates and dilemmas. Disasters, 22(4), 283-287.

Hickey, S. & Mohan, G. (2005). Towards participation as transformation: Critical themes and challenges. In S. Hickey & G. Mohan (Eds.), *Participation: From Tyranny to transformation?* (pp. 3-24). London: Zed Books.

Higashino, M. (2003). *Ogata Sadako: Nanmin shien no genba kara* [Sadako Ogata: From the field of refugee assistance]. Tokyo, Japan: Shuei.

Hoeing, W. (2004). *Self-image and the well-being of refugees in Rhino Camp, Uganda.* (Working Paper No.103). UNHCR.

Holmgren, T., Kasekende, L., Atingi-Ego, M. & Ddamulira, D. (1999). *Aid and reform in Uganda: Country case study.* World Bank/Bank of Uganda.

Homma, H. (1986). Nanmin mondai no kaiketsu wo motomete [In search for solutions of refugee problems]. In UNU & Soka University (Eds.), *Nanmin mondai no gakusai teki kenkyu* (pp. 149-173). Tokyo, Japan: Ochanomizu.

Homma, H. (1990). *Nanmin mondai toha nanika* [What are refugee issues?]. Tokyo, Japan: Iwanami.

Homma, H. (2000). Nanmin to jinken [Refugees and human rights]. In M. Ueda (Ed.), *Kokusaika no naka no jinken mondai dai 2 han* (pp. 36-55). Tokyo, Japan: Akashi.

Homma, H. (2001). Nihon no nanmin seido: Kokusai ho no tachiba kara [Japan's system of refugee assistance: From the perspectives of international laws]. In Nanmin-mondai Kenkyu Foramu (Ed.), *Nanmin to jinken: Shinseiki no shiza* (pp. 9-27). Tokyo, Japan: Gendai-jinbun.

Hovil, L. (2003). *Local integration as a durable solution: Refugees, host populations and education in Uganda,* (Working Paper. 93). UNHCR.

Independent Commission on International Humanitarian Issues. (1986). *Refugees: The dynamics of displacement —a report for the independent commission on international humanitarian issues.* London: Zed Books.

Institute for the Study of Social Justice, (2002). *Nanmin to NGO: Sekai no taio: Nihon no taio* [Refugees and NGOs: World response and Japan's response]. Tokyo, Japan: San Pauro.

Iyotani, T. (2001). *Gurobarizeshon to imin* [Globalization and immigrants]. Tokyo, Japan: Yushindo-kobun.

Jackson, R. H. (1990). *'Quasi-states!: Sovereignty, international relations and the Third World*. Cambridge: Cambridge University Press.

Jacobsen, K. (2001). *The forgotten solution: local integration for refugees in developing countries*, (Working Paper No. 45). UNHCR.

Jacobsen, K. & Landau, L. B. (2003). The dual imperative in refugee research: Some methodological and ethical considerations in social science research on forced migration. *Disasters, 27(3)*, 95-116.

Jones, R. A. (2002). *Participatory poverty assessment of Nakivale and Oruchinga refugee camps in southern Uganda: Livelihood characteristics, economic constraints and recommendations for change*. Postwar Reconstruction and Development Unit, University of York.

Kagohashi, H. (1998). NGO, dona, kokka: Kaihatsu wo meguru aratana dainamikusu [NGOs, donors and states: New dynamics surrounding development]. In J. Kawata et al. (Eds.), *Kaihatsu to bunka 6: Kaihatsu to seiji* (pp. 171-199). Tokyo, Japan: Iwanami.

Kaiser, T. (2000). *UNHCR's withdrawal from Kiryandongo: Anatomy of a handover*, (Working Paper No. 32). UNHCR.

Kajita, T. (Ed.). (1996). Kokusai shakai gaku dai 2 han [Transnational sociology]. Aichi, Japan: The University of Nagoya.

Kato, S. (1994). Kokumin kokka to nanmin mondai [Nation-states and refugees issues]. In S. Kato & T. Miyajima (Eds.), *Nanmin* (pp. 1-20). Tokyo, Japan: The University of Tokyo.

Kato, S. & Miyajima, T. (Eds.). (1994). *Nanmin* [Refugees]. Tokyo, Japan: University of Tokyo.

Kawamura, M. (2003). *Nanmin no kokusai teki hogo* [International protection of refugees]. Tokyo, Japan: Gendai-jinbun.

Khulman, T. (1991). The economic integration of refugees in developing countries. *Journal of Refugee Studies, 2(1)*, 1-20.

Khulman, T. (1994). Organized versus spontaneous settlement of refugees in Africa. In H. Adelman & J. Sorenson (Eds.), *African refugees: Development aid and repatriation* (pp. 117-142). CO: Westview Press.

Kibreab, G. (1987). Rural refugee land settlement in eastern Sudan: On the road to self-sufficiency? In P. Nobel (Ed.), *Refugee aid and development in Africa* (pp. 63-72). Skandinavian Institute of African Studies, Uppsala.

Kibreab, G. (1989). Local settlement in Africa: A misconceived option? *Journal of Refugee Studies, 2(4)*, 468-490.

Kim, D. (2003). *Kokusai jinken ho to mainoriti no chii* [International human rights laws and status of minorities]. Tokyo, Japan: Toshin.

Koizumi, K. (1994). Nanmin to kaihatsu: Rinen no suii to ryosha no tsunagari [Refugees and development: Ideas and its interrelationships]. *Journal of International Development Studies, 3*, 155-162.

Koizumi, K. (1995). Funso-ka no nanmin kikan to kaihatsu enjo: Ryosha no nozomashii rinku toha nanika [Voluntary repatriation of refugees during conflicts and development assistance: In search of a desirable link between the two]. *Journal of International Development Studies, 4*, 69-76.

Koizumi, K. (2000). Nanmin kikan to kokusai kaihatsu enjo [Refugee repatriation and international development assistance]. *International Relations, 137*, 83-102.

Koizumi, K. (2001). Nanmin kenkyu: Mondai no shozai to shorai no kenkyu hoko [Refugee studies: Its challenges and future direction]. In Nanmin-mondai Kenkyu Foramu (Ed.), *Nanmin to jinken: Shinseiki no shiza* (pp. 195-222). Tokyo, Japan: Gendai-jinbun.

Koizumi, K. (2005). *Kokusai kyosei ido no seiji shakai gaku* [The study of forced migration]. Tokyo, Japan: Keiso.

Koizumi, K. (1998). *Nanmin mondai toha nani ka* [What are the problems of refugees?]. Tokyo, Japan: San-itsu.

Kok, W. (1989). Self-settled refugees and the socio-economic impact of their presence on Kassala, eastern Sudan. *Journal of Refugee Studies, 2(4)*, 419-440.

Kothari, U. (2001). Power, knowledge and social control in participatory development. In B. Cooke & U. Kothari (Eds.), *Participation: The new tyranny?* (pp. 139-153). London: Zed Books Ltd.

Kumar, S. (2002). *Methods for community participation: A complete guide for practitioners*. London: ITDG.

Kurimoto, E. (1994). Civil war & regional conflicts: The Pari & their neighbours in south-eastern Sudan. In K. Fukui & J. Markakis (Eds.), *Ethnicity & conflict in the horn of Africa* (pp. 95-111). OH: Ohio University Press.

Kurimoto, E. (1996). *Minzoku funso wo ikiru hitobito: Gendai afurika no kokka to mainoriti* [People living in ethnic conflicts: Modern African states and minorities]. Kyoto, Japan: Sekai-shiso.

Kurino, O. (1986). Nanmin no tairyo ryusyutsu no gen-in ni tsuite no ichikosatsu: Indoshina nanmin no tokusyusei [Study on the causes of a large scale refugee outflow: Characteristics of Indochinese refugees]. In UNU & Soka University (Eds.), *Nanmin mondai no gakusai teki kenkyu* (pp. 47-62). Tokyo, Japan: Ochanomizu.

Kurosawa, S. (2003). UNHCR no heiwa kochiku ni hatasu yakuwari [Roles of UNHCR in peacebuilding]. *Ritsumeikan International Affairs, 21*, 165-179.

Landau, B. L. (2000). Crisis and authority: A research agenda for exploring political transformation in refugee-affected Tanzania. *The Journal of Humanitarian Affairs.* Retrieved 1/5/02 from http://www.jha.ac/greatlakes/b005.htm.

Landau, B. L. (2001). *The humanitarian hangover: Transnationalization of governmental practice in Tanzania's refugee-populated areas*, (Working Paper No. 40). UNHCR.

Lauterpacht, E. & Bethlehem, D. (2001). *The scope and content of the principle of non-refoulement: Opinion.* UNHCR.

Leeuwis, G. (2000). Reconceptualizing participation for sustainable rural development: Towards a negotiation approach. *Development and Change, 31*, 931-959.

Loescher, G. (2001). *The UNHCR and world politics: A perilous path.* Oxford: Oxford Press.

Loescher, G. (2003). UNHCR at fifty: Refugee protection and world politics. In N. Steiner, M. Gibney & G. Loeshcer (Eds.), *Problems of protection: The UNHCR, refugees and human rights* (pp. 3-18). NY: Routledge.

Looney, R. (1999). *New international economic order.* Retrieved 11/12/04, from http://web.nps.navy.mil~relooney/routledge_15b.htm.

Macchiavello, M. (2003). *Forced migrants as an under-utilized asset:*

Refugee skills, livelihoods, and achievements in Kampala, Uganda, (Working Paper No. 95). UNHCR.

Mackintosh, K. (2000). *Principles of humanitarian action in international humanitarian law: Study 4 in the politics of principle: the principles of humanitarian action in practice*, (HPG Report No. 15). Overseas Development Institute.

Macrae, J. (1997). Dilemmas of legitimacy, sustainability, and coherence: Rehabilitating the health sector. In K. Kumar (Ed.), *Rebuilding societies after civil war: Critical roles for international assistance* (pp. 183-201). CO:Lynne Rienner Publishers.

Macrae, J. (1999). *Aiding peace and war....: UNHCR, returnee, reintegration, and the relief-development debate*, (Working Paper No. 14). UNHCR.

Macrae, J. (2001). *Aiding recovery? The crisis of aid in chronic political emergencies*. London:Zed Books.

Macrae, J. (Ed.). (2002). *The new humanitarianisms: a review of trends in global humanitarian action*, (HPG Report No.11). Overseas Development Institute.

Macrae, J. & Bradbury, M. (1998). *Aid in the twilight zone: A critical analysis of humanitarian-development aid linkages in situations of chronic instability.* Report for UNICEF.

Macrae, J. & Leader, N. (2000). *Shifting sands: The search for 'coherence' between political and humanitarian responses to complex emergencies*, (HPG Report No. 8). Overseas Development Institute.

Macrae, J., Collinson, S., Buchanan-Smith, M., Reindorp, N., Schmidt, A., Mowjee, T. et al. (2002). *Uncertain power: The changing role of official donors in humanitarian action*, (HPG Report No.12). Overseas Development Institute.

Mansuri, G. & Rao, V. (2004). *Community-based and -driven development: A critical review*, (Policy Research Working Paper No. 3209). World Bank.

Marx, E. (1990). The social world of refugees: A conceptual framework. *Journal of Refugee Studies, 3(3)*, 189-203.

Matsusumi, J. (1999). Nanmin joyaku [Refugee laws]. In H. Hata & C. Mizukami (Eds.), *Kokusai jinken ho gairon dai 3 han* (pp. 52-65).

Tokyo, Japan: Yu-shin.
Mc.Ginness, M. E. (2003). Legal and normative dimensions of the manipulation of refugees. In S. Stedman & F. Tanner (Eds.), *Refugee manipulation: War, politics, and the abuse of human suffering*, (pp. 135-166). DC: Brooking Institute Press.
Meadows, H. D., Meadows, L. D., Randers, J. & Behrens III, W. W. (1972). S. Okita (Trans.). *Seicho no genkai: Roma kurabu "Jinrui no kiki"* [The limits to growth]. Tokyo, Japan: Diamond.
Meeren, v. d. R. (1996). Three decades in exile: Rwandan refuges 1960-1990. *Journal of Refugee Studies, 9(3)*, 252-267.
Merks, J. (2000). *Refugee identities and relief in an African borderland: a study of northern Uganda and southern Sudan*, (Working paper No. 19). UNHCR.
Mochizuki, K. (2006). *Ningen no anzen hosho no shatei: Afurika ni okeru kadai* [The scope of human security: Agendas in Africa]. Chiba, Japan: Institute of Developing Economies.
Mohan, G. (2001). Beyond participation: Strategies for deeper empowerment. In B. Cooke & U. Kothari (Eds.), *Participation: The new tyranny?* (pp. 153-167). London: Zed Books.
Moro, L. N. (n.d.). *Refugee camps in northern Uganda: Sanctuaries or battlegrounds?* Retrieved 6/12/04 from http://www.sudanstudies.org/leben03.pdf.
Mosse, D. (1994). Authority, gender and knowledge: Theoretical reflections on the practice of participatory rural appraisal. *Development and Change, 25*, 497-526.
Mosse, D. (2001). 'People's knowledge', participation and patronage: Operations and representations in rural development. In B. Cooke & U. Kothari (Eds.), *Participation: The new tyranny?* (pp. 16-35). London: Zed Books.
Mugumya, G. (2000). *"Not a continuum of relief to development: But development-oriented relief" with a case-study of lessons learnt from the United Nations High Commissioner for Refugees's assistance programmes in Uganda*. MA dissertation.
Mugwara, R. (1994). Linking relief with development in southern Africa: A SADC perspective on the 1991/92 drought emergency. *IDS Bulletin,*

25(4), 92-95.

Museveni, Y. K. (1997). *Sowing the mustard seed: The struggle for freedom and democracy in Uganda.* London: Macmillan.

Nilsson, D. (2000). *Internally displaced, refugees and returnees from and in the Sudan: A review, Studies on emergencies and disaster relief,* (Report No 8). Department of peace and conflict research, Uppsala university, Sweden.

Nobel, P. (1987a). Notes on the right to development. In P. Nobel (Ed.), *Refugee and development in Africa* (pp. 47-52). Uddevalla: Nohuslaningens.

Nobel, P. (Ed). (1987b). *Refugees and development in Africa.* Uddevalla: Nohuslaningens.

Noda, N. (2003). "Sankagata kaihatsu" wo meguru shuho to rinen [Methods and ideas surrounding "participatory development"]. In H. Sato (Ed.), *Sankagata kaihatsu no saikento* (pp. 61-86). Chiba, Japan: Institute of Developing Economies.

Nzita, R. & Niwampa, M. (1993). *People and cultures of Uganda.* Kampala: Fountain Publishers Ltd.

Obi, N. (2004). *Nanmin mondai heno atarashii apurochi? Ajia no nanmin hongoku ni okeru kokuren nanmin koto benmukan jimusho no katsudo* [New approaches to refugee issues? UNHCR involvement in countries of origin in Asia]. Tokyo, Japan: Kokusai Shoin.

Ogata, S. (1995). *From humanitarian relief to rehabilitation: A comprehensive response.* Keynote address at the fourth advanced development management program, Sophia University, Tokyo.

Ogata, S. (2002). *Watashi no shigoto* [My job]. Tokyo, Japan: Soshi.

Ogata, S. (2005). *The turbulent decade: Confronting the refugee crises of the 1990s.* NY: Norton & Company.

Oman, P. C. & Wignaraja, G. (1991). *The postwar evolution of development thinking.* NY: St. Martin's Press, Inc.

Onda, M. (2001). *Kaihatsu shakai gaku: Riron to jissen* [International sociology: Theory and practice]. Kyoto, Japan: Minerva.

Parnwell, M. (1993). *Population movements and the third world.* London: Routledge.

Payne, L. (1998). *Rebuilding communities in a refugee settlement: A*

casebook from Uganda. OXFAM: Oxfam Publicaion.
Pearce, J. (1999). Peace-building in the periphery: Lessons from Central America. *Third World Quarterly, 20(1),* 51-68.
Petrin, S. (2002). *Refugee return and state reconstruction: A comparative analysis,* (Working Paper No. 66). UNHCR.
Phillips, M. (2003). *The role and impact of humanitarian assets in refugee-hosting countries,* (Working Paper No. 84). UNHCR.
Pirouet, L. (1988). Refugees in and from Uganda in the post-colonial period. In H. B. Hansen & M. Twadda (Eds.), *Uganda now: Between decay and development* (pp. 239-253). London: James Currey Ltd.
Pretty, N. J. (1994). Alternative systems of inquiry for a sustainable agriculture. *IDS Bulletin, 25(2),* 37-48.
Rutinwa B. (1996) The Tanzanian government's response to the Rwandan emergency. *Journal of refugee Studies, 9(3),* 291-302.
Rutinwa, B. (1999). *The end of asylum? The changing nature of refugee policies in Africa,* (Working Paper No. 5). UNHCR.
Saito, F. (2000). Uganda ni okeru chiho bunkenka seisaku no genjo to tenbo [Present and future of Uganda's decentralisation policy]. *Africa Report, 30,* 24-28.
Saito, K. (1985). Aga Kan hokokusho wo megutte: Jinken to hitobito no tairyo ryushutsu [Some thoughts on Aga Khan Report: Human rights and massive displacement of people]. In Institute of Foreign Affairs (Ed.), *Jinteki ido ni tomonau shakai hendo to bunka masatsu* (pp. 77-91). Tokyo, Japan: Tokyo University of Foreign Studies.
Saito, M. (1995). *Kokusai kaihatsu ron: Kaihatsu, heiwa, kankyo* [International development: Development, peace and environment]. Tokyo, Japan: Yuhikaku.
Sakata, S. (2003). Sankagata kaihatsu gainen saiko [Revisit to participatory development]. In H. Sato (Ed.), *Sankagata kaihatsu no saikento* (pp. 37-59). Chiba, Japan: Institute of Developing Economies.
Saleebey, D. (1997). Introduction: Power in people. In D. Saleebey (Ed.), *The strength perspective in social work practice, third edition* (pp. 1-22). MA: Allyn and Bacon.
Santel, B. (1996). European union and asylum seekers. In D. Thranhardt (Ed.), *Europe - A new immigration continent: Policies and politics in*

comparative perspective, second edition (pp. 117-133). Munster: LIT.
Sato, H. (1994). Enjo no shakai teki eikyo no sain toshite no masatsu, atsureki [Frictions and conflicts as signs of social impacts of assistance]. In H. Sato (Ed.), *Enjo no shakai teki eikyo* (pp. 117-139). Chiba, Japan: Institute of Developing Economies.
Sato, H. (Ed.). (1995). *Enjo to shakai no koyu yoin* [Factors of assistance and aid], Keizai kyoryoku shiriizu 177. Chiba, Japan: Institute of Developing Economies.
Sato, H. (Ed.). (2001). *Enjo to shakai kankei shihon: Sosharu kyapitaru ron no kanosei* [Assistance and social capital: Possibility of social capital theory]. Chiba, Japan: Institute of Developing Economies.
Sato, H. (2003a). Sankagata kaihatsu no "saikento" [Revisit to participatory development]. In H. Sato (Ed.), *Sankagata kaihatsu no saikento* (pp. 3-36). Chiba, Japan: Institute of Developing Economies.
Sato, H. (Ed.). (2003b). *Sankagata kaihatsu no saikento* [Revisit to participatory development]. Chiba, Japan: Institute of Developing Economies.
Sato, H. (Ed.). (2004). *Enjo to jumin soshiki ka* [Assistance and community mobilization]. Chiba, Japan: Institute of Developing Economies.
Shepherd, A. (1998). *Sustainable rural development.* London: Macmillan Press Ltd.
Shigematsu, S. (Ed.). (1986). *Gendai ajia imin: Sono kyosei genri wo motomete* [Present-day migrants toward coexistence]. Aichi, Japan: The University of Nagoya.
Shimada, Y. (2002). Sekai no nanmin mondai to kokuren no torikumi [World refugee issues and UN responses]. *International Affairs, 513,* 2-14.
Shimamura, Y. (2001). *Uganda kyowakoku ni okeru kokka yosan, yosan seido no gaiyo* [National budget and budget system in Uganda]. Ugandan Ministry of Finance, Planning, Economic Development.
Shimizu, Y. (1997). Funso no naka no nanmin enjo [Refugee assistance in a conflict situation]. *Econo forum, 2,* 116-123. Nishinomiya, Japan: School of Economics, Kwansei Gakuin University.
Shimizu, Y. (2000). Uganda ni okeru nanmin seisaku to UNHCR: Jimoto

teiju seisaku kara "jiritsu heno senryaku" he [UNHCR and Uganda's policy on refugee assistance: From local settlement to self-reliance strategy]. *Africa Report, 31*,15-18.

Shimizu, Y. (2000). *Uganda nyusu 2000 nen aki* [Uganda news, fall 2000].

Shimizu, Y. (2002). The linkage between refugee aid and development: Do we need a new aid model? *KGU Review*, 1, 19-34.

Shimizu, Y. (2005). Nanmin shien to chiiki kaihatsu [Refugee assistance and development]. In N. Anbo et al. (Eds.), *Kurosuboda kara miru kyosei to fukushi: Seikatsu kukan ni miru ekkyo sei* (pp. 10-43). Kyoto, Japan: Minerva.

Siddiqui, F. (2000). *Evaluation of the UNDP/UNHCR joint reintegration programming unit in Rwanda*. Report of the Mission, September 22 - October 25.

Smyke, J. R. & Smyke, P. (1988). Refugee and development in Africa. *Associations Transnationales, 2*, 72-79 & 85.

Stake, R. E. (1995). *The art of case study research*. CA: Sage Publication.

Stedman, S. & Tanner, F. (2003a). Refugees as resources of war. In S. Stedman & F. Tanner (Eds.), *Refugee manipulation: War, politics, and the abuse of human suffering* (pp. 1-16). DC: Brooking Institute Press.

Stedman, S. & Tanner, F. (Eds.). (2003b). *Refugee manipulation: War, politics, and the abuse of human suffering*. DC: Brooking Institute Press.

Stein, B. N. (1997). Reintegrating returning refugees in Central America. In K. Kumar (Ed.), *Rebuilding societies after civil war: Critical roles for international assistance* (pp. 155-182). CO: Reiner.

Stein, B. N. & Clark, L. (1990). *Refugee integration and older refugee settlements in Africa*. Paper presented at the 1990 meeting of the American Anthropolical Association. New Orleans. Retrieved 14/6/04 from http://www.msu.edu.

Suhrke, A. (1994). Towards a comprehensive refugee policy: Conflict and refugees in the post-Cold War world. In B.R. Bohning and M.L. Scholeter-Paredes (Eds.), *Aid in place of migration* (pp. 13-38). ILO.

Suhrke, A., Barutcski, M., Sandison, P. & Garlock, R. (2000). *The Kosovo crisis: An independent evaluation of UNHCR's emergency preparedness and response*. PAU/2000/001. UNHCR.

Sustainable Development Policy Institute. (2003). *Assessment and recommendations for the rehabilitation of refugee hosting areas in Balochistan and the NWFP*. unpublished paper.

Takeda, I. (1991). *Imin, nanmin, enjo no seijigaku: Osutoraria to kokusai shakai* [Politics of aid for migrants and refugees: Australia and international community]. Tokyo, Japan: Keiso

Tardif-Douglin, D. (1997). Rehabilitating household food production after war: The Rwanda experience. In K. Kumar (Ed.), *Rebuilding societies after civil war: Critical roles for international assistance* (pp. 265-285). CO: Reiner.

Thranhardt, D. (Ed). (1992). *Europe: A new immigration continent*. Humburg: Lit Verlag.

Tsunekawa, K. (1998). Kaihatsu keizai gaku kara kaihatsu seiji gaku he [From development economics to development politics]. In J. Kawata et al. (Eds.), *Kaihatsu to bunka 6: Kaihatsu to seiji* (pp. 1-28). Tokyo, Japan: Iwanami.

Tsurumi, K. & Kawada, T. (Eds.). (1989). *Naihatsu teki hatten ron* [Endogenous development]. Tokyo, Japan: University of Tokyo.

Van Evera, S. (1997). *Guide to methods for students of political science*. Ithaca:Cornell University Press.

Weiner, M. (1995=1999). Y. Naito (Trans.). *Imin to nanmin no kokusai seiji gaku* [The global migration crisis: Challenge to states and to human rights]. Tokyo, Japan: Akashi.

Westermeyer, J. (1985). Mental health of Southeast Asian refugees: Observations over two decades from Laos and the United States. In T.C. Owan (Ed.), *Southeast Asian mental health: Treatment, prevention, services, training, and research* (pp. 65-89). DC: U.S. Department of Health and Human Services.

Westermeyer, J. (1988). DSM-III psychiatric disorders among Hmong refugees in the USL a point prevalence study. *American Journal of Psychiatry, 145*, 197-202.

Wijk, van, C. (1998). *Gender in water resource management, water sup-

ply and sanitation: Roles and realities revisited. IRC Technical Paper 33.

Woodward, P. (1988). Uganda and southern Sudan: Peripheral politics and neighbour relations. In H. B. Hansen & M. Twadda (Eds.), *Uganda now: Between decay and development* (pp. 224-238). London: James Currey Ltd.

Yamate, O. & Kasai, S. (Eds.). (2003). *21 seiki kokusai shakai ni okeru jinken to heiwa: Kokusai ho no atarashii hatten wo mezashite, gekan, gendai kokusai ho ni okeru jinken to heiwa no hosho* [Human rights and peace in the international community of the 21st century: For the development of international laws - to secure human rights and peace in the present-day international laws]. Tokyo, Japan: Toshin.

Zastrow, C. (1992). *The practice of social work, 4th edition*. CA:Wadswoth Publishing Company.

Zolberg, A. & Callamard, A. (1994). Displacement-generating conflicts and international assistance in the Horn of Africa. In W.R. Böhning & M.-L. Scholeter-Paredes (Eds.), *Aid in place of migration* (pp. 101-118). ILO.

Index

4Rs *See* Repatriation, Reintegration, Rehabilitation and Reconstruction.

A

Academics 7, 22, 25, 33, 37, 42
Actor(-s) 19, 25, 30, 37, 42, 57, 60, 61, 64, 65, 69, 80, 92, 96, 98, 105-108, 113, 115, 117, 132, 159, 161, 162, 165, 176, 179, 180, 181, 183, 186, 187, 189, 245, 246, 249
African countries 19, 55, 82, 83, 86-90, 96-98, 122, 195
Agriculture 8, 17, 62, 91, 95, 99, 106, 111, 120, 125-127, 137, 148-151, 161, 164, 166, 169, 170, 172, 188, 193, 195, 200, 202, 209, 217, 224, 229, 231, 233-235, 239, 249
Animal husbandry 125, 126, 234
Asylum
  Asylum country(-ies) 18, 42, 49, 70, 76, 173, 250
  Asylum seekers 14, 50, 51, 69-72, 74, 75

B

Brookings Process 100
Burden(-s) 45, 54, 69, 72, 73, 75, 76, 78, 80, 81, 86, 90, 93, 103, 113, 116, 117, 180, 220, 222, 239, 243
Burden-sharing 86, 90-93, 103, 109, 116, 117, 247
Burden of proof 74

C

Capacity Development 129, 131, 137, 139, 229
Care and Maintenance 54, 91, 93, 108, 122, 123, 181
Charter of Economic Rights and Duties of States 87, 88
Coexistence 45, 78, 79, 80, 81, 116, 117, 130, 137, 143, 155, 157, 161
Cold War 48, 56, 83, 85, 99
Construction 18, 91, 97, 120, 121, 123, 129-131, 137, 173, 174, 201, 205, 228, 229, 236, 244, 249
Convention Plus Initiative 101-106
Coordination 24, 28, 64-66, 68, 69, 80, 94, 108, 140, 161, 181, 183, 204, 216, 225, 246
Crop production 123, 125-127, 137, 149, 170, 233

D

DAC *See* Development Assistance Committee.
DAR *See* Development Assistance for Refugees.
Declaration and Program of Action of the New International Economic Order 87
Denmark 53, 63, 102, 104, 105, 251
Developing country(-ies) 14, 18, 21, 72, 75, 77, 82, 86-88, 134, 140, 142, 248
Development
  Advantages and Constraints of Development 137
  Development actors 19, 95, 99, 100, 107, 108, 110, 113, 133, 140, 141, 143, 160, 161, 185, 192, 203, 229,

Index

243, 245, 248, 249, 250
Development agency(-ies) 9, 19, 96, 98, 100, 105-108, 133, 140, 141, 192, 203, 220, 229, 244, 246, 249, 250
Development assistance 37, 97, 104, 129, 140, 250
Development programme(-s) 8, 9, 15-17, 62, 79, 90, 96, 101, 106, 110, 115, 116, 128, 133-135, 138-140, 161, 171, 204, 229, 230, 244, 246, 247
Development projects 63, 90, 97, 106, 168, 250
Need for development 112
Development-oriented 94, 98, 106, 108, 116, 135, 143, 145, 146, 162, 189
Development-oriented assistance 111
Developmental activities 92, 98, 99, 110, 115, 116, 125, 132-135, 138, 142, 143, 246, 249
Development Assistance Committee (DAC) 67, 105, 133
Development Assistance for Refugees (DAR) 93, 96, 102-104, 106, 107, 176, 180, 188, 251
Development through Local Integration (DLI) 93, 101, 103, 106, 107
DLI *See* Development through Local Integration.
Do-no-Harm 100
Donor(-s) 11, 18, 19, 24, 30, 37, 38, 54, 62, 63, 65, 67, 68, 93, 95-97, 99, 100, 103-108, 113, 130, 136, 137, 140, 141, 165, 167, 168, 170, 171, 192, 203, 206, 216, 219, 223, 229, 243, 245, 246, 248, 249, 251
Downward accountability 176
Durable solution(-s) 46, 47, 49, 51, 52, 55, 56, 59, 85, 92, 93, 102, 103, 108, 118, 119, 153, 158

E

Education 31, 32, 40, 51, 62, 91, 101, 102, 104, 111, 117, 123, 125, 127, 128, 136, 139, 148-150, 158, 164, 172, 195, 196, 198, 201, 202, 205, 221-224, 228, 232-235, 237, 239, 240
Emergency(-ies) 27, 63, 67-69, 100, 111, 170, 209, 226, 241
Environment(-s) 11, 22, 25, 29-33, 73, 79, 82, 86
EU *See* European Union.
European Union (EU) 67

F

FAO *See* Food and Agriculture Organisation.
Food-For-Work 62
Food and Agriculture Organisation (FAO) 62
Fridtjof Nansen 14, 46

G

Gap(-s) 9, 11, 13, 33, 43, 63, 68, 87, 96, 100, 140, 196, 242
Funding gap 100
Gaps related to programme management 100
Relief-development gap 100
Gender 28, 29, 30, 131, 137, 178
Government(-s) 10-12, 20, 30, 32-39, 41, 42, 48, 49, 54, 57, 58, 60-62, 64, 65, 67, 68, 70-72, 74-76, 80, 81, 86, 89, 95, 97, 98, 100, 104, 105, 107, 108, 112, 117, 120, 129, 131-133, 137, 141, 142, 148, 151, 152, 154, 156, 158- 163, 170, 171, 175, 176, 181, 183, 185, 188, 190, 192, 193, 195, 196, 200-205, 207, 209, 210,

212, 213, 216, 218-220, 222-225, 228, 230, 234, 237-247, 249

H

Hardin, Garrett James 73
Host community(-ies) 8, 9, 17, 18, 23, 30, 31, 33, 45, 69, 77, 78, 80, 81, 98, 99, 106, 109, 116, 118, 125, 129, 132, 134, 135, 138, 156, 157, 160, 189, 190, 215, 221, 227, 229, 244, 247, 249
  Activities for Development of Host Communities 129
Host country(-ies) 14, 27, 31, 38, 46, 54, 64, 75, 77-79, 86, 90, 92, 94, 96, 97, 99, 101, 103, 105, 106, 108, 112, 116, 117, 120, 129, 132, 133, 138, 140, 143, 152, 155, 159, 160, 162, 163, 171, 181, 185, 187, 190, 215, 245, 247, 251
  Activities for the development of host countries 132
  Burden of the host countries 92
  Responsibilities of host countries 86, 103, 104, 108
Human security 107, 113, 251
Humanitarian(-s) 9-11, 50, 53, 57-59, 64, 67, 69, 70, 80, 81, 100, 107-110, 140, 141, 143, 224, 233, 250
Humanitarian agencies 12, 106, 110, 134, 138, 192, 250
Humanitarian assistance 27, 57, 64, 65, 67, 100, 109, 116, 135, 136, 140, 142, 159, 160, 223, 240
Humanitarian principle(-s) 18, 20, 45, 57, 59, 80, 109, 247
Hungarian Crisis 48

I

ICARA *See* International Conferences on Assistance to Refugees in Africa.
ICARA I 86, 90, 92
ICARA II 86, 89-92, 94, 97, 98, 132-134
ICARA process 82, 86, 89, 94-96, 98-100, 103, 105-107, 113, 132, 134
ICRC *See* International Committee of the Red Cross.
IDPs *See* Internally displaced persons.
ILO *See* International Labour Organisation.
Immigrant(-s) 50, 71, 73-76, 85, 177, 211
Implementing agency(-ies) 61, 62, 64, 65, 162, 163, 201, 202, 204, 216, 234, 235, 238-240
Income-Generating Activities 125
Indochinese refugees 52, 70, 85
Infrastructure projects 9, 91, 98, 99, 110, 129, 134, 137, 229, 230
Integration
  Integration of refugees 83, 131, 133, 142, 154, 157, 160, 203, 221
  Integration of refugee services 131, 159, 203-204, 221-226
Internally displaced persons (IDPs) 7, 14, 97, 173, 241
International Committee of the Red Cross (ICRC) 14, 46, 62
International Conferences on Assistance to Refugees in Africa (ICARA) 86, 133
International Labour Organisation (ILO) 46
International Organisation for Migration (IOM) 62
IOM *See* International Organisation for Migration.

J

Japan 26, 53, 70, 72, 79, 102, 104, 105, 138, 250
Japan International Cooperation Agency (JICA) 12, 99, 138, 250
JICA *See* Japan International Cooperation Agency.

K

Kosovo refugees 67

L

Leadership training 125, 128, 149
League of Nation(-s) 14, 46, 48
Local community(-ies) 15, 16, 19, 45, 81, 94, 117, 129, 132, 139, 148, 155, 161, 163, 181, 205, 215, 221, 225, 229, 238, 247
Local Council(-s) 203, 204, 206, 211, 216, 218
Local integration 51, 52, 92, 93, 100, 102, 118-120, 145, 153, 158
Local settlement(-s) 8, 9, 11, 17, 51, 54, 79, 91, 92, 94, 95, 115, 116, 118-124, 132-135, 140-143, 145-147, 150-153, 155, 160, 162, 169, 179, 182, 185-190, 192, 199, 200, 209, 210, 215, 216, 219, 220, 224, 233, 242-248
Local settlement policy(-ies) 8, 11, 111-113, 116, 133, 134, 142, 162, 188, 189, 192, 215
Local settlement programme(-s) 64, 106, 115, 116, 120-123, 132, 140, 147, 151-153, 185, 187, 188, 200, 207, 209, 210, 215, 229, 230, 244, 248
Local settlement projects 94

M

Malawi 55, 95, 120
Micro-credit schemes 125
Militarisation of refugee camps 76
Multidisciplinary Approach 20
Multidisciplinary aspect(-s) 13, 27, 28, 33, 42

N

Nansen Passports 14, 46
Naturalisation 158, 159, 211
New International Economic Order (NIEO) 82, 87-89, 95
NGOs *See* Non-governmental organisations.
NIEO *See* New International Economic Order.
Non-governmental organisations (NGOs) 24, 60-62, 65, 67, 68, 134, 137, 162, 174, 201, 203
Non-refoulement principle 35, 50, 51

O

ODA *See* Official Development Aid.
Official Development Aid (ODA) 63, 138, 250
Ogata, Sadako 12, 27, 58, 59
Operationalisation 19, 20, 112, 115
OPM *See* Office of the Prime Minister.

P

Pakistan 55, 70, 75-77, 95, 120, 158, 175
Participation 22, 29, 61, 69, 93, 94, 104, 113, 152, 162, 164-169, 171-173, 176-178, 182, 183, 189, 190, 192, 212,

216, 218, 219, 244, 246, 249, 250
Hierarchy of participation 166, 249
Level(-s) of participation 165, 169, 171, 173, 175, 183
Limitation of participation 164, 167, 169, 170, 173, 175
Participation process 171, 215
Participatory
   Participatory approach 146, 162-164, 167-169, 175, 176, 178, 179, 183, 185, 215, 216, 245, 248, 249
   Participatory development 164, 167-169, 171, 179
   Participatory process 152, 171, 179, 180-182, 215, 245
   Participatory refugee assistance 171, 181
Partnership(-s) 38, 65, 202
Person-in-Environment model 25, 42, 186, 248
Post-conflict situations 99, 110, 141, 250
Poverty Reduction Strategy Papers (PRSPs) 105, 141, 142, 250
Practitioner(-s) 7, 8, 10, 22, 24-26, 33, 36, 37, 42, 95, 98, 107, 162, 164, 165, 169, 177, 182, 183, 191, 251
Protection 14, 15, 21, 26-28, 34-40, 45-51, 60, 61, 69, 71, 74, 75, 78-80, 93, 102, 104, 105, 112, 118-120, 143, 147, 150, 157, 159, 161, 180, 202, 205, 218, 226
Protocol Relating to the Status of Refugees 48
Protracted refugee situation(-s) 68, 98, 101, 102, 141, 188
Proxy wars 55, 56, 83, 99
PRSPs *See* Poverty Reduction Strategy Papers.

Q

QIPs *See* Quick Impact Projects.

Quick Impact Projects (QIPs) 229

R

RAD *See* Refugee Aid and Development.
Refugee(-s)
   Definition of refugees 50, 73
   Naturalisation of refugees 158
   Refugee-as-threat 73, 75, 78, 80
   Refugees-as-assets 73
   Refugee aid 8, 9, 11, 18, 27, 29, 30, 35, 37, 42, 95, 96, 107, 108, 115, 139, 145, 162, 164, 165, 168, 177, 179, 183, 189, 221, 232, 249, 251
   Refugee camps 40, 58, 60, 61, 68, 75, 76, 86, 108, 122, 123, 150, 205, 209
   Refugee participation 61, 100, 117, 142, 145, 152, 177, 180
   Refugee presence 72, 75, 76, 83, 134, 180, 230
   Refugee problems 45, 46, 48, 55, 85, 90, 91, 97, 153
   Refugee self-reliance 8, 93, 102, 116, 125, 126, 132, 142, 145, 146, 147, 162, 172, 210, 212, 219, 224, 231
   Refugee self-sufficiency 120, 200, 201
   Refugee settlement(-s) 20, 64, 121, 125, 130, 132, 133, 150, 157, 170, 171, 191, 195-197, 200, 201, 205, 207, 213, 221-223, 225, 226, 228, 230, 231, 233, 236
   Refugee situations 9, 11, 14, 15, 19, 20, 25, 31, 40-43, 48, 61, 62, 68, 69, 79-83, 85, 86, 89, 95, 98, 101-103, 111, 127, 134, 139, 140, 141, 143, 145, 146, 153, 160, 168, 169, 180, 181, 185, 187, 191, 216, 221, 248-250
   Refugee status 71, 72, 75, 79

Index

Vulnerable refugees 29, 36, 42, 59, 112, 123, 126-128, 137, 148, 149, 151, 167, 219, 225, 238, 239
Refugee(-s) assistance 8, 9, 15-23, 26, 27, 29, 30, 37, 39, 43, 45, 60, 64, 65, 69, 82, 89, 90, 93, 96-98, 101, 109, 113, 115-117, 120, 122, 127, 128, 131-133, 137-139, 142, 143, 145, 146, 149, 152, 156-159, 161-165, 167, 169-172, 175, 176, 180, 181, 183, 189, 191-193, 195, 205, 217-222, 227, 229, 230, 242-245, 247, 248, 251
Development-oriented refugee assistance 91, 219
Developmental refugee assistance 115, 116, 125, 133, 135, 141, 145, 162, 163, 229, 244, 249
Refugee assistance and international communities 59
Refugee-hosting communities 91, 94, 97, 105, 108-110, 112, 117, 133, 140, 141, 213, 249-251
Refugee-in-environment model 20, 45, 120
Refugees from Germany 47, 48
Refugee Aid and Development (RAD) 8-10, 15, 17, 18, 22, 27, 42, 82, 86, 87, 89-91, 93-96, 98, 99, 101, 103, 106, 108-113, 116, 132-134, 140, 143, 180, 185, 203, 247
Criticism of 81, 109-110
Refugee Aid and Development debate 30, 81, 87, 88, 97, 195
Refugee Aid and Development discourse 82
Refugee Aid and Development Doctrine 8, 9, 11, 17-19, 30, 81, 82, 94, 97, 101, 106-109, 111-113, 115, 116, 133, 134, 139, 141, 142, 145, 185, 189, 249, 250
Refugee community(-ies) 28, 29, 31, 32, 40, 42, 123, 149, 164, 171, 181, 190, 211, 215, 237, 239
Refugee influx 27, 60, 96, 110, 116, 135, 193, 200, 226, 247
Impact of refugee influx 36
Refugee protection 8, 11, 17, 18, 20, 26-28, 30, 33, 35-39, 41, 45, 46, 50, 59-61, 69, 80, 81, 99, 101, 103, 108, 109, 112, 115, 117, 129, 137, 139, 141, 143, 177, 185, 189, 247, 248
Refugee studies 11, 13, 20, 22, 24, 26, 27, 33, 42, 45, 192
Refugee women 29, 30, 34, 58, 59, 129-131, 157, 227, 236, 237, 243
Rehabilitation 18, 38, 47, 63, 91-93, 103, 129, 228
Relief-oriented refugee assistance 54, 162, 181
Repatriation, Reintegration, Rehabilitation and Reconstruction (4Rs) 93, 103
Resettlement 22, 46, 47, 51-55, 62, 83, 85, 86, 103
Rights to Development 88
Rural development 22, 135, 136, 138, 164, 168, 171, 183, 250
Rural settlement(-s) 95, 120, 128, 188, 199, 201, 203
Russian refugees 14, 46, 47
Rwandan refugees 40, 69, 75, 158, 211

S

Self-help 29, 31, 212
Self-image 153, 240
Self-reliance
Indicators of self-reliance 147, 187
Level of self-reliance 112, 147, 151, 187, 189, 244
Self-reliant 17, 28, 54, 93, 102, 104, 108, 111-113, 117, 118, 128, 129, 137, 142, 145-152, 155, 156, 160-162, 168, 182, 185, 186, 188, 189, 199-204, 206, 207,

Index 293

212, 218-220, 222, 224, 228, 230-233, 235, 237-239, 243, 244, 247-249
Self-sufficient 52, 76, 94, 102, 117, 118, 120, 123, 147, 150, 151, 188, 193, 201, 231
Skills training 121, 125, 128, 139, 149, 229, 235
Solution-oriented 54, 91, 92
Somalia 55, 95, 120
Southern Sudan 21, 193, 198-200, 208, 209, 226, 242, 250
SPLA *See* Sudanese People's Liberation Army.
Stakeholders 9, 25, 29, 60, 64, 65, 69, 80, 105, 146, 164, 176, 177, 179, 180, 182, 183, 190, 203, 215-218, 220, 222, 245, 246, 249
State(-s) 7, 16, 24, 30-32, 35, 37-39, 46, 50-52, 55, 56, 58-61, 70-73, 77, 80, 82, 83, 89, 95-97, 99, 101, 103, 104, 106, 120, 122, 133-135, 155, 165, 177-179, 211, 213, 224, 226, 232
Statute of the Office of the United Nations High Commissioner for Refugees 38, 49
Sudan 55, 89, 120, 126, 150, 157, 188, 193, 198, 199, 201, 208, 209, 226, 241, 242, 244, 250
Sudanese People's Liberation Army (SPLA) 193, 200, 208, 209
Sudanese refugees 11, 122, 126, 138, 153, 187, 188, 190, 192, 193, 198-200, 209, 211, 212, 217, 226, 227, 231, 241, 242

T

Tanzania 120, 122, 125, 126
Targeting Development Assistance for Refugee Solutions (TDA) 103-105
TDA *See* Targeting Development Assistance for Refugee Solutions.

Theory of the commons 73

U

Uganda 11, 21, 55, 56, 95, 120, 122-124, 126, 130, 132, 147, 150, 153, 170, 175, 179, 185, 187, 188, 190-202, 204-213, 215-220, 222-226, 228, 230-234, 237, 238, 240-245, 249, 251
Control of Alien Refugee Act 211, 212
Decentralisation 202, 205-207
District Directorate of Health Services (DDHS) 204, 222-226
Ministry of Local Government (MoLG) 201, 206, 213
Office of the Prime Minister (OPM) 201, 203-207, 213, 214, 216, 222, 224, 233
Refugee Desk 216
Refugee Welfare Councils (RWCs) 212, 237, 239
Self-Reliance Strategy (SRS) 188, 199-207, 212, 216-222, 224, 228, 232, 241
Uganda's Control of Alien Refugees Act 210
Uganda's Local Council 237
Uganda's rural settlement 201
West Nile 188, 198, 200, 207, 241
West Nile Bank Front (WNBF) 207
UNCTAD *See* United Nations Conference on Trade and Development.
UNDP *See* United Nations Development Programme.
UNHCR *See* United Nations High Commissioner for Refugees.
UNICEF *See* United Nations Children's Funds.
United Nations Children's Funds (UNICEF) 62, 63, 92

United Nations Conference on Trade and Development (UNCTAD) 63, 67, 88
United Nations Development Programme (UNDP) 62, 68, 92, 94, 97, 98, 131, 134, 140, 195, 196, 197
United Nations High Commissioner for Refugees (UNHCR) 10, 14, 18-20, 26, 29, 31, 35, 37, 38, 45-51, 53-65, 67, 68, 70, 72, 75-77, 80-85, 89, 91-108, 115, 116, 118, 120-124, 126, 129, 133-135, 140-143, 147, 153, 158, 161-163, 170, 171, 173, 174, 176, 179-181, 183, 193, 194, 200-209, 212, 213, 216-220, 222, 223-226, 228, 229, 232-234, 237-240, 245, 246, 249, 250
UN Convention Relating to the Status of Refugees 21, 31, 47, 60, 103

V

Vocational training 83, 125, 139, 234, 235
Voluntary repatriation 47, 49, 51, 52, 58, 85, 91, 92, 98, 108, 133, 152

W

Water 62, 64, 77, 91, 110, 111, 123, 129, 131, 136-138, 148, 150, 163, 196, 197, 202, 232, 233, 235, 237
Well-being of refugees 116, 143, 145, 189
WFP *See* World Food Programme.
World Bank 99, 100, 105, 120, 121, 141, 178
World Food Programme (WFP) 62, 63, 92, 123, 134, 162, 163, 170, 171, 175, 201, 216, 232, 233

X

Xenophobia 71, 72

Z

Zaire 40, 56, 58, 69, 75, 76, 198
Zambia 55, 76, 95, 120, 122
Zonal development 90

清水康子（Yasuko Shimizu）

　国連難民高等弁務官事務所の上級職員。ジュネーブ本部、ウガンダ、ロシア、コソボ、アルバニア、アフガニスタンに勤務。独立行政法人国際協力機構においてシニア・アドバイザーを務める。2006年に関西学院大学から博士（総合政策）を取得。

Linking Refugee Aid with Development :
Development for Refugees, or Refugees for Development?

2008年5月15日　初版第一刷発行

著　者	清水康子
発行者	宮原浩二郎
発行所	関西学院大学出版会
所在地	〒662-0891 兵庫県西宮市上ケ原一番町1-155
電　話	0798-53-7002
印　刷	大和出版印刷株式会社

©Yasuko Shimizu 2008
Printed in Japan by Kwansei Gakuin University Press
ISBN 978-4-86283-032-6
乱丁・落丁本はお取り替えいたします。
本書の全部または一部を無断で複写・複製することを禁じます。
http://www.kwansei.ac.jp/press